COLLEGE OF ALAMEDA LIBRARY

WITHDRAWN

D0401696

PS
1541   Shurr, William
Z5   THe marriage of Emily
S55   Dickinson

DATE DUE

DEC 4 '89			
OCT 5 '88			
JUN 12			
JUL 15 '92			
MAR 08 '95			
MAR 29 '99			

LENDING POLICY

IF YOU DAMAGE OR LOSE LIBRARY
MATERIALS, THEN YOU WILL BE
CHARGED FOR REPLACEMENT. FAIL
URE TO PAY AFFECTS LIBRARY
PRIVILEGES GRADES, TRANSCRIPTS,
DIPLOMAS, AND REGISTRATION
PRIVILEGES OR ANY COMBINATION
THEREOF.

DEMCO

WITHDRAWN

The Marriage of
EMILY DICKINSON

The Marriage of
EMILY DICKINSON

A Study of the Fascicles

WILLIAM H. SHURR

THE UNIVERSITY PRESS OF KENTUCKY

Emily Dickinson's poetry is reprinted by permission of the publishers and the Trustees of Amherst College from *The Poems of Emily Dickinson,* edited by Thomas H. Johnson, Cambridge, Mass.: The Belknap Press of Harvard University Press, Copyright © 1951, © 1955, 1979 by the President and Fellows of Harvard College.

Additional poems are reprinted from *The Single Hound,* copyright © 1914, 1942 by Martha Dickinson Bianchi; *Further Poems,* copyright © 1929, 1957 by Mary L. Hampson; and *Unpublished Poems,* copyright © 1935, 1963 by Mary L. Hampson, by permission of Little, Brown and Company.

"Great Caesar! Condescend" quoted from *Emily Dickinson Face to Face* by Martha Dickinson Bianchi, copyright 1932 by Martha Dickinson Bianchi, copyright © renewed 1960 by Alfred Leete Hampson, by permission of Houghton Mifflin Company.

Publication of this book was assisted by a grant from the National Endowment for the Humanities.

Copyright © 1983 by The University Press of Kentucky

Scholarly publisher for the Commonwealth,
serving Bellarmine College, Berea College, Centre
College of Kentucky, Eastern Kentucky University,
The Filson Club, Georgetown College, Kentucky
Historical Society, Kentucky State University,
Morehead State University, Murray State University,
Northern Kentucky University, Transylvania University,
University of Kentucky, University of Louisville,
and Western Kentucky University.

Editorial and Sales Offices: Lexington, Kentucky 40506-0024

Library of Congress Cataloging in Publication Data

Shurr, William.
    The marriage of Emily Dickinson.

    Includes indexes.
    1. Dickinson, Emily, 1830–1886—Criticism and interpretation.   2. Dickinson, Emily, 1830–1886—Chronology.
I. Title.
PS1541.Z5S55   1983   811'.4   83-6862
ISBN: 0-8131-1499-3

for Georgia Grey
and for another Emily

Other books by William H. Shurr

The Mystery of Iniquity: Melville as Poet, 1857-1891
Rappaccini's Children: American Writers in a Calvinist World

Contents

Acknowledgments

I am greatly indebted to the work of my predecessors, writers whose respect for Emily Dickinson has provided a wealth of fact and interpretation. Visible on every page, I believe, will be my debts to Charles Anderson, Millicent Todd Bingham, Sharon Cameron, Richard Chase, John Cody, Albert Gelpi, Inder Nath Kher, Karl Keller, Jay Leyda, Brita Lindberg-Seyersted, Ruth Miller, Rebecca Patterson, David Porter, William Sherwood, Mabel Loomis Todd, Robert Weisbuch, and George Frisbie Whicher. The name of Richard B. Sewall should stand apart from this list for special mention, for his incomparable biography of Dickinson, as should the name of Thomas H. Johnson, for his historic editions of Dickinson's poems and letters. Professor Sewall read an earlier draft of this work and I have benefited greatly from his comments.

It will be recognized immediately that behind this book stands the editorial work of Ralph W. Franklin. Since the death of Emily Dickinson no one has been able to study her poems exactly as Dickinson left them, until the reconstruction of the original booklets was published by Franklin. I have profited immensely from his prompt and generous answers to my every inquiry, from his published works on Dickinson, and—not at all the least of his generosities—from his careful and critical reading of an early draft of my first chapter.

My wife, Professor Georgia Hooks Shurr, has also read the manuscript at various stages, suggesting new insights, pointing out obscurities, and issuing sharp warnings where I seemed to be overstating my case or indulging in peculiarly "male" readings. I am also indebted to John Lancaster, Special Collections Librarian at the Amherst College Library, for technical assistance; to Daniel Lombardo, archivist of the Jones Library, Amherst; and to Mrs. Elizabeth Elder, historian of the Dickinson family's church in Amherst and custodian of its records. All of these have given me generous access to their expertise and to the materials in their keeping. The staffs of the Houghton Library at Harvard and the Presbyterian Historical Society in Philadelphia have also been helpful with their quick responses to my inquiries. Professors Donald Ringe, Barton St. Armand, and George Monteiro also read the manuscript; I am as grateful for their generous encouragement as for their suggestions.

The "other Emily" to whom this book is dedicated constantly refreshed my study of Dickinson by her delighted response to the humor which pervades the poetry.

Introduction

Once an area of knowledge has been reduced to a
self-regulating system or 'structure,' the feeling that one has
at last come upon its innermost source of movement is
hardly avoidable.—Piaget[1]

The story of the discovery of Emily Dickinson's poems and how they barely escaped destruction is now a familiar one. After she died on May 15, 1886, her sister Lavinia went through her personal papers. Believing that she was acting in accord with Emily's wishes, Lavinia burned many manuscripts and letters, some of which, according to Lavinia, were from well-known persons. Fortunately for posterity, when she came upon the unsuspected trove of Dickinson's poems, her zeal was checked, was actually turned in another direction. For now she looked first to her sister-in-law, Susan Dickinson, then to Mabel Loomis Todd, insisting on help in publishing "Emily's volumes."

Dickinson's poetry was preserved in forty small "fascicles," which she herself had bound with string, in fifteen other "sets," which she had copied and gathered but did not bind, and in several hundred other poems which were found on loose sheets and in various stages of completion. The fair copies of still other poems were later retrieved from friends and acquaintances to whom she had sent them. The total came to 1775 poems in Thomas H. Johnson's variorum edition of 1955.

Mabel Loomis Todd indexed and transcribed many of the poems and, in consultation with Thomas Wentworth Higginson, selected what she considered to be the best, for three volumes of Dickinson's poems which were published in the 1890s. Unfortunately, the booklets and collections into which Dickinson had gathered nearly half of her total poetic output were dismantled in the process.

These "fascicles," which provide the main materials for the present study, are manuscript booklets which Dickinson herself put together. When Dickinson purchased her paper from the stationer each sheet was already folded once, giving her four sides to write on. For each of her fascicles she used from four to seven of these folded sheets. When the copying was completed she stacked the sheets one on top of another, stabbed holes through them at the edge, and secured the booklets with string. There are forty of these fascicles, with an average of twenty poems in each.

The fascicles contain almost all of the poetry we have from Dickinson's first six years as a practicing poet, arranged as she wanted it to be, and tied into booklets for some purpose. These were the years 1858 to 1863, when the poet was in her late twenties and early thirties. By all biographical accounts, they seem to have been years of some turmoil for the poet. After 1863 the force that created the fascicles seemed to break down somewhat: she continued to write out fair or nearly finished copies and to gather some of them into "sets" during the next decade or so, but without going through the final process of binding them.

And her practice as a poet may have become intermittent in later years. After 1863, according to the preserved record, she occasionally returned to themes and subjects started in the fascicles, stimulated as we shall see by events that recalled interests of the fascicle years; she wrote occasional verse, lines to greet a friend or accompany a gift; and she continued to write nature poems. But the quantity of her poetry never again reached that of the fascicle years.

The accidents of preservation and publication have in most cases obscured Dickinson's intended settings and sequences. The original dismantling of the fascicles and sets, subsequent publication of the poems under artificial headings or subjects, even chronological printing of the poems by Johnson, where the chronology is determined by the latest version of each poem—all of these conditions have removed or obscured signs of any connections Dickinson may have established when she gathered the poems into collections. In some cases poems which appear sequentially in the fascicles are found separated by as many as several hundred other poems in Johnson's critical edition.

It is obvious from the care in selection, transcription, and binding which she lavished on them that the fascicles were of some significance to Dickinson. But because of their dispersed state for almost a hundred years there has been relatively little interest in them. Where that interest has occurred, however, it has been intense. Ruth Miller was the first to give the problem of the fascicles extended attention, and she published her considerations on the subject in *The Poetry of Emily Dickinson* (1968). But Miller was working under a severe handicap because of the imperfect reconstruction of the fascicles which was possible at that time.

Nevertheless, Miller believed that she had found the key to the construction of each individual fascicle, in a dramatic pattern of abstractions similar in each fascicle. Each fascicle, according to Miller, moves from a stated quest or desire, through suffering, to resolution. The quest may be for friendship, for acceptance, or for knowledge; the suffering always takes the form of rejection, deprivation, or limitation; and the resolution may be in Jesus, or in the self, or in religious faith.[2] Such patterning has seemed overly abstract, if not mechanical, and Miller's readers have generally been unable to verify her perceptions in their own studies of Dickinson's poems.

Another, and briefer, attempt has recently been made to find the key to the fascicles. In an ingenious essay Martha O'Keefe has defined what she calls "primal words," words whose various meanings are opposed. Thus "rock" can signify either steady motion or utter stability; "fast" means exactly the opposite in the phrases "hold fast" and "run fast"; "cleave" can join man and woman together or chop things apart. Working with one of the fascicles, O'Keefe shows convincingly that Dickinson has indeed paired poems according to opposed meanings of such primal words. Apparently she has uncovered one of Dickinson's structural patternings or verbal strategies.[3] Whether the pattern will fit all of the fascicles and whether Dickinson consciously employed this technique remain to be determined.

With the appearance of R.W. Franklin's reconstruction of the originals, published in facsimile by Harvard in 1981,[4] more progress can now be made in understanding Dickinson's fascicles. Some pursuits can first of all be ruled out as unprofitable. Ruth Miller provided a list some years ago with which one can still concur: "It was not recipients: there is no Higginson fascicle, no Helen Hunt Jackson grouping, no Bowles, no Holland booklet. There are no gatherings according to single events or subjects, for there are no flower or sky gatherings, no death or nature booklets, no romantic attachment fascicles. Neither are they organized according to emotions or feelings, for ironic poems, happy, sad, wistful and gay poems all mingle in a single fascicle."[5]

R.W. Franklin accepted and extended this list, warning against the attempt to read the fascicles as "careful constructs governed by theme, imagery, narrative and dramatic movement, or similar pursuit."[6] Franklin argued that Dickinson's fascicles were merely gatherings of her best poems—indeed that they are nearly the only poems of hers we have from the years she was constructing the fascicles—and that the poems were actually copied into the fascicles with major consideration given to the nonesthetic question of available space: she frequently began a fascicle with her longer poems, as if to insure that she would have enough space for them, and frequently her shorter poems were reserved for filling in spaces left over when longer poems had been completed. It is quite unlikely, Franklin believed, that the fascicles are anything more than loose anthologies, in fairly chronological order, of the poems Dickinson most wanted to preserve during these years.

Though one is tightly hedged about by the restrictions of both Miller and Franklin, there still remains to be satisfied one's sense of some unimpeachable unities deriving from the voice of the speaker in the poems, the continuity of experiences recorded in them, and, underlying both, the sense of intense presence of the writer in the poems. One still feels the force of David Porter's questions some years ago: "What, then, holds the poetry together? In what pattern of obsessions sits its generating core?"[7]

In answering these questions for myself, one primary consideration has stood out. There are in Dickinson's fascicle poems frequent small snatches of narrative, raids on the concrete, patches of realism that connect to establish a "program" which is carried on throughout the fascicles and beyond, into the later poetry. The poems are full of remembered scenes, though there is no "plot" in the technical sense of the word, as narrative shaped in one work with a preconceived beginning, middle, and end. The poems, rather, suggest meditations on events as they happened, meditations shared with a specific addressee. These elements can be isolated and studied to see what they contain, to see how they relate to one another, and to see how they relate even to some of the known events of Dickinson's life.

Many mysteries have attached themselves to Dickinson and her works. The following questions have been asked, and answered in one way or another, by Dickinson's critics and biographers: Did she fall in love with someone or not? If she did, was the love reciprocated? Was she heterosexual or homosexual? Was she religious or anti-religious, a mystic or a sceptic? Did she write erotic poetry or not? Did she write great love poems or are the love poems her only descent into bathos and conventionality? Was the father (or the mother) a warm and nurturing presence or a monster of indifference? Did she have spells of painful insanity or was she, in Ruth Miller's words, "a tough-minded, independent woman whose self-doubt and timidities were a mask"? Added to these are questions about why she first bound her poems into booklets, why she then continued to gather collections without binding them, and why she finally abandoned the gathering process altogether. Most of these questions have a profound bearing on the nature of her poetry and how it is to be understood.

At least some of these questions can now begin to answer themselves, if a study is undertaken of the poems as Dickinson herself arranged them. There is a wealth of "incident" in her fascicle poems. Investigation of this narrative material and of the people it involved as the story progresses in the fascicles, then in the sets, and finally beyond, in the poems of Dickinson's later years, in some ways alters and in some ways enlarges the portrait of Emily Dickinson that we have had heretofore.

The present study begins from an analysis of the fascicles as they have been restored by R.W. Franklin. Chapter 1 isolates significant characteristics of the forty fascicles, the major distinguishing characteristics they present. Chapter 2 then follows the fascicles chronologically, determining the phases or stages of the events as they developed. Finally, chapter 3 moves beyond the fascicle years to follow, in Dickinson's later writings, lines started in the fascicle years. Though it has been impossible to avoid following out biographical implications where they have naturally suggested themselves, especially in chapter 2, it is in chapter 3 that the problems are discussed most fully.

There is now the possibility of some confusion in the numbering of the fascicles. When Mabel Loomis Todd received the collections of poems from Lavinia Dickinson she numbered them 1-38, 40, and 80-112. These numbers have stood until just recently, but will now have to be abandoned. Franklin was able to put the fascicles into chronological order and renumber them from 1 to 40; he renumbered the "sets" (the later collections which Dickinson did not bind with string) from 1 to 15. It is Franklin's new numbering system that I use in this study. The complete list of the fascicles and their contents is given in Appendix B.

Since 1955 it has been standard practice to number the poems themselves according to the three-volume variorum edition of Thomas H. Johnson, and I follow that practice here.

Chapter One

Characteristics of the Fascicles

I cannot make sense of a part without placing it in relation to a whole.—Frank Kermode[1]

The reader of Emily Dickinson's poems has hitherto had a collection of no fewer than 1775 poems to deal with. Each poem is a complex mechanism requiring the most concentrated effort. All readers may experience some relief, then, some sign of help from the poet herself, upon finding that Dickinson has cut that number approximately in half in the especially selected and arranged collections that form the main subject of this book.

But it is quite likely that readers will now face a new set of problems, or perhaps a new set of opportunities. They must now confront, in the fascicles, not only concentrated new groupings of poems, but the possibilities of larger organizational principles. It is likely that there are continuities and connections which are visible only now that the poems are available as Dickinson intended them to be. The work of this first chapter will be to isolate and describe some of the main features which characterize the fascicles as a unified series of collections.

The Addressee of the Fascicles

The first puzzle that the reader of Dickinson's fascicle poetry encounters is the identity of the "you" to whom many of the poems are addressed.

It is true that the general reader can comfortably situate himself in the universe of some of the poems. We find ourselves delighted to be addressed by a poem which begins "I'll tell you how the Sun rose" (318). We may be uneasy with the subject but we readily accept identification of ourselves as reader when Dickinson writes about "When simple You and I,/Present our meek escutcheon/And claim the rank to die" (98). We can even puzzle our way through to some wider applicability of her insight that "For each extatic instant/We must an anguish pay" (125).

But in more than 125 of the fascicle poems this "general reader" is excluded. There is no way in which he can understand himself as the "you" to whom these thoughts and recollections are addressed, or situate himself in the universe of "we" established by the poems. When Dickinson writes directly "You constituted Time" for me (765), or "You left me–Sire–two Legacies" (644), or "You taught me Waiting with Myself" (740), the general reader becomes a third party, rhetorically excluded from this "I-You" communication. The exclusion is even more intense when he reads " 'Why do I love' You, Sir?" (480). These are private poems, which the later reader feels he has stumbled on as a privileged witness, as an intruder unforeseen by the poet. It must be someone other than the general reader to whom these 125 fascicle poems are addressed.[2]

To whom, then, are they addressed? Dickinson provides us with some identification of her addressee in fifty of the fascicle poems, most of which are also addressed to this exclusive "You." He is "Sir" or "Sire" in fourteen poems, and "Signor" in two poems. He is addressed as "Sweet" in ten poems; he is "Master" in six poems, "Sovreign" in three poems, "Lover" in three poems, and "King" in two poems. Four poems call him "Dear" and three other poems address him as her "Lord," in a sense other than that used for God or Jesus. And three poems indentify him as "Beloved."[3]

Thus it is clear that about 150 of the 814 fascicle poems are love poems addressed to a specific individual. (The qualification "about" is added because some of the poems in the previous paragraph are also addressed to the exclusive "You." The two categories overlap.) There are enough of these exclusive poems–and they appear in every fascicle–to allow us at least to suspect, at this point, since Dickinson herself bound the fascicles into unified groups, that we have here the addressee of the fascicles themselves.

There are, in addition, many other poems which refer to events or conversations which the poet and her addressee have shared, about which the general reader has no knowledge. We have, for example, no knowledge of the events to which Dickinson refers in 616 when she writes about some occasion when "I rose–because He sank," when "I cheered my fainting Prince" and encouraged him to persevere in some path they both had chosen. There are many poems in the fascicles which assume that her reader can recall an experience they have had together, but of which the general reader stands in ignorance. In other poems Dickinson recalls snatches of conversations with her addressee in which the later reader was surely no participant: " 'Would I be whole' He sudden broached" in 643; "You said that I 'was Great'–one Day" in 738; "It was a quiet way–/He asked if I was his" in 1053; and of course the greatest of the conversation poems, "I cannot live with You" (640).

Jay Leyda noticed this phenomenon in many poems, where the

reader feels that some essential information is missing, and called it her device of the "omitted center";[4] and many critics have since offered their own analyses of Dickinson's lack of "referentiality." But if the "center" seems to us later readers to have been omitted, that does not warrant our assuming that the events and conversations alluded to by Dickinson were unknown as well to her primary intended reader, the male "You" defined by the poems themselves.

The fascicles present another kind of physical evidence which must be inserted into this puzzle of Dickinson's addressee. Three of the surviving fascicle sheets have been folded as if for mailing; one of these sheets actually had an addressee written on the back of it, but the name was subsequently heavily erased.

The first of these poems was number 7, in Fascicle 14, beginning "The feet of people walking home." It is a religious meditation on death as the experience which turns our attention to the subject of immortality. The handwriting is noticeably clearer than that of the poems around it in the same fascicle. It may be that Dickinson had finished the fair copy for mailing but then felt she could not send it when she noticed the misspelling of "Bargemen" in line 7. She had to squeeze the first "e" in later. The copy was then kept as her own record copy and a more respectable fair copy was made for the addressee.

The second of these folded sheets contains poem 433, in Fascicle 19. The poem is a plea for the ability to "forget" the "You" to whom the poem is addressed. This "You" is emphasized by underlining. Her need to forget him, according to the poem, is an expression of her love. Sometime after finishing this copy Dickinson must have turned it over on some other freshly written page. There are noticeable ink blots marring the bottom third of this page, rendering it unsuitable for sending. Again, this copy may then have been kept for her record and a fresh copy made for the correspondent.

The third folded sheet contains poem 336, also in Fascicle 19. It is addressed to "You" and "Sir"; the correspondent is also identified as "Master," and Dickinson anticipates their ecstatic reunion in heaven. It begins, "The face I carry with me—last—/When I go out of Time—/To take my Rank—by—in the West—/That face—will just be thine." The addressee may be a clergyman, since he has in some way communicated with "the Raised," with Jesus, regarding the nature of the afterlife. Dickinson's reason for not sending this copy may have been the spacing; the writing becomes quite crowded and compressed at the bottom of the sheet.

On the back of this sheet the addressee's name was actually written. Later it was thoroughly erased, by Dickinson or by someone close to her. No trace of the original writing remains. The erasure has removed more than half the thickness of the paper, and with it all the latent ink or graphite that might be recovered under ultraviolet light or by other photographic means. The identity of Dickinson's correspondent does not seem to be discernible here. If the erasure prevents our solving the mystery of her addressee at this point, at least it serves the purpose of confirming the fact there is a valid mystery. Other hints toward its solution will have to be explored.

Actually, one of those hints suggests itself with regard to this erasure. It is not likely that Dickinson herself did the erasing. It would have been the matter of a few minutes for her to recopy the text if she had wanted to remove all traces of the addressee's name from among her papers. Rather it must have been another party, someone who was caught in the dilemma of wanting to preserve Dickinson's *ipsissima verba* out of high respect for her art, and wanting to preserve the secret out of high respect for the family.

Attention can here fall on Mabel Loomis Todd and her own lover, Dickinson's brother Austin. Mrs. Todd asked Austin and Lavinia whether Dickinson had fallen in love with the Reverend Charles Wadsworth. There must have been something like this kind of address in the papers Todd was editing to stimulate such a sharply focused question. The answer from Dickinson's brother and sister seems to have been framed as if to contain a mental reservation. There was such a "notion" abroad, they said, "kept alive" for some time, but based on "hearsay." There is no really definite assertion in their repeated answer, "They both *thought* not."[5]

The case for Wadsworth will probably always rest on "Acres of Supposition," but it will be interesting to notice in the course of this study that wherever there is evidence for identifying the lover, Wadsworth alone is always among those who fit the identification. The claim cannot be made for any other contender. An expert in statistics and probability would appreciate this configuration.

Another kind of evidence in the fascicles also suggests that Dickinson actually sent copies of her fascicle poems to this same "You." Poem 224 in Fascicle 10 begins "I've nothing else—to bring, You know—/So I keep bringing These." In a poem that concludes a bound fascicle of twenty-two poems, "These" can hardly refer to anything but the poems themselves.

In several poems Dickinson refers to the "Flowers" she is sending to her correspondent. In 32, for example, she begs "Sir. . . . take my flowers." To her absent friend, in 905, "Flowers—negotiate between us—/As Ministry." It has been recognized for many years that Dickinson was referring to her poems as flowers. She also records having had an actual response to them from her addressee: in the first of the letters addressed to

"Master" she wrote, "You asked me what my flowers said—then they were disobedient—I gave them messages."[6] The plural "flowers" seems to indicate that more than one poem was sent at a time.

Another physical characteristic of the fascicles is more tentative. As Franklin observed, one of Dickinson's primary concerns in compiling the fascicles was spacing. Most frequently, though not always, Dickinson begins with her longer poems, as if to make sure she will have room for them. Shorter poems then appear to fill out the fascicles to an average of about twenty poems each. One notes as well that, as the fascicles progress, more and more alternatives are left in the poems, as if these are semifinal drafts, kept as her record of poems whose fair copies were sent to someone else. The questions have never been asked—whether the poems were sent in a steady stream to the beloved, whether the fascicles as we have them, with some roughness quite visible, might not be mock-ups, drafts of more finished versions actually sent.

The physical evidence of the fascicles thus suggests a high degree of probability that these poems were written not as public works of art but as private communications to a specific lover. Evidence also exists that some of them were sent as individual poems. Whether fair copies of whole fascicles were sent as well can be asserted only in the case of Fascicle 10. But it should perhaps be observed that if these intensely personal love poems were not sent, then we are set light-years back to some earlier version of "poor Emily," talking only to herself.

Such a situation throws entirely new light on the fascicles of Emily Dickinson, demands a new way of reading her poems. The canons of esthetics still apply, but now as secondary to the canons of correspondence and autobiography. We shall return in a later chapter to this characteristic of the fascicles; for now it is worth noting that Dickinson built into them many signs that they were sent as private communications to one beloved person. The poems, for us, thus become "overheard"; the modern reader is a third and accidental presence. Dickinson's poetry is impoverished if this passionately defined addressee is not retained as a dominant figure in her poetic world.

The Marriage Day

One reads the fascicles of Emily Dickinson with the growing sense that there came to be one day in her life which she considered to be unique. Many poems in the fascicles celebrate that day and analyze its importance.

One would expect "day" to occur frequently in lyric poetry, and Dickinson confirms that expectation. S.P. Rosenbaum, in the concordance to her poems, records 268 uses of the word "day" in the entire canon of her poetry.[7] She celebrates sunrise at "break of day" and sunset as "the ebbing day," as well as the days which demonstrate the beauty of a particular season. She universally delights her readers with descriptions of "Nature's—Summer Day" and "The far Theatricals of Day." "Day" also functions as a simple time reference in phrases such as "Many a day," "all day long," and "every day."

But in a large number of poems, especially later in the fascicles, in poems dating from "early 1860," the word "day" comes to isolate itself frequently as a reference to a particular day, one of immense personal importance. It is a day of unique difference, unlike any other day in her life. She begins poem 322 with the statement, "There came a Day—at Summer's full—/Entirely for me." A love poem begins "You said that I 'was Great'—one Day" (738). In a letter-poem, which she says is "Going to Him," she seems to relive that Day for a moment, pushing away the Night which now surrounds her (494). The "Day" is celebrated again, in 638, as one "without the News of Night." In another poem of the same year, 1862, she mentions that same day, "That first Day, when you praised Me, Sweet"; and she insists "That Day—the Days among—/Glows Central—like a Jewel" (659). The Day is, according to poem 356, "The Day that I was crowned"; because of "coronation" that day now stands in her mind as "Otherwise."

But a note of tragedy was also struck that day; it was "the Day/That Night—begun" (400). This is later expanded to "a Day/We thought the Mighty Funeral—/Of All Conceived Joy" (660). In a poem addressed to "Sir," she states "I lost a World—the other day!" (181). The tragic dimension of that day is explored further in a poem which begins "The first Day's Night had come," and which contains the lines "a Day as huge/As Yesterdays in pairs,/Unrolled it's horror in my face" (410). Such a blow was given to the mind's stability that day that the poem ends with the inquiry, "Could it be Madness—this?" The absolute pastness of that unique day is recorded in another poem from the same year, 1862, "So—Goodnight—Day!" (425). It is, in poem 878, "an expended Day/[which the sun] helped to make too bright." A sense emerges, in another poem of the same era, that the Day will somehow be repeated, but only after a long intervening Night (471).

The day is further described as the Day "I hoped. . . . I feared. . . . And the Day that I despaired" in poem 768. In a love poem that begins "Always Mine!" Dickinson writes of "Term of Light this Day begun!" (839). But another poem reconsiders the matter: it was the Day that life both began and ended (902). It is "The Day the Heaven died . . ./The spoiler of Our Home" (965). The speaker in Emily Dickinson's fascicles, then, quite obviously feels that there is a unique day in her life, central to the experience she has to relate as a poet. Poem 473 ends with the addition of a striking detail: "Baptized—this Day—A Bride."

Dickinson's unique experience that day, as recorded within the narrative world of her fascicles, was her marriage. The experience permeates her subsequent poetry never to be forgotten or set aside. It is, as well, the experience from which much of her poetry flows as from a center. In the scenario of the fascicles, the central poem is the following:

There came a Day—at Summer's full—
Entirely for me—
I thought that such—were for the Saints—
Where Resurrections—be—   Resurrections] Revelations

The Sun—as Common—went abroad
The Flowers—accustomed—blew—
~~While our two souls that~~ Solstice passed—   As if no Soul the
~~Which~~ maketh all things new.   That

The time was scarce profaned—by speech—
The ~~falling~~ of a word   ~~figure~~ / *symbol*
Was needless—as at Sacrament—
The wardrobe—of Our Lord—

Each was to each—the sealed church—
Permitted to commune—this time—
Lest we too awkward—show—
At "Supper of the Lamb."

The hours slid fast—as hours will—
Clutched tight—by greedy hands—
So—faces on two Decks—look back—
Bound to opposing Lands—

And so—when all the time had ~~leaked~~   failed
Without external sound—
Each—bound the other's Crucifix—
We gave no other bond—

Sufficient troth—that we shall rise—
Deposed—at length—the Grave—
To *that* New Marriage—
Justified—through Calvaries of Love! [322]

There is much to be noticed in this poem; it is a detailed narrative in itself, and many of the later fascicle poems will develop segments of the narrative outlined here. First of all, the poem isolates and records a unique Day in the speaker's life, the fullest and most explicit record of that day we have from her pen. It is dated "at Summer's full," made more precise by the later line "As if no Soul the Solstice passed." In the first version of this line she has made it more personal: "While our two Souls that Solstice passed." For its sense of time the poem is set on June 21-22, in the month of brides. She shares the sense of every bride that it was a day "Entirely for me."

The ceremony is recorded in a thoroughly religious ambience, as would be proper for a marriage in the Dickinson family. She joins the ranks of "the Saints" in a sacrament similar to that of the hushed celebration of the Lord's Supper. The two sacraments are joined in the poem: the marriage parallels the "Sacrament" of the Lord's Supper; and as a sacrament it prefigures the "Resurrection" at the end of time.

The word "troth" stands out in the poem for its formal rarity. It appears in nearly every marriage service, in the ceremony of the exchange of rings: "With this ring I thee wed, I plight unto thee my troth." But instead of rings, other objects are exchanged as more appropriate symbols in this particular marriage: "Each—bound the other's Crucifix—/We gave no other bond." The appropriateness of this symbol does not emerge entirely from this poem, though at the end we find that this particular marriage will be finally fulfilled beyond the grave in *"that* New Marriage" and that the new marriage will be "Justified—through Calvaries of Love."

Although it is a marriage poem, Death appears in the scenario, as a royal figure well within the narrative pattern; but he appears in the firmly Christian context of belief that the tyrant will be "Deposed." St. Paul's taunt appears to be in the background here: "Death, where is thy victory!" (I Corinthians 15.55). In fact, the poem slants sharply in the direction of immortality and the afterlife, especially by the selection of biblical allusions. In Revelations 7, the "sealing" of the Church is described, with twelve thousand from each of the twelve tribes, to indicate that a sense of completeness enhances the perfection of Paradise. The great multitude who "stood before the throne, and before the Lamb" are of course "clothed in white robes," a practice Dickinson herself would undertake and maintain until her death.

Dickinson's allusion to this chapter in the line "Each was to each—the sealed church" does double duty: each was utter completion to the other in the present moment; and their union confirmed and foreshadowed the union of the Saints in heaven. In line 8 Dickinson refers to the words spoken in the Heavenly City of Jerusalem from her favorite "Gem Chapter": "Behold, I make all things new" (Revelations 21.5); and the expectations of the Christian couple are clearly asserted, that their marriage is a sign and anticipation of the heavenly marriage after death. The sacraments are unique in that they are celebrated in earthly time and space, but in anticipation of fulfillment beyond time and space. The major movement of the poem is from marriage here on earth to the New

Marriage in heaven. There is also a minor parallel movement from celebration of the Lord's Supper here, where the Lord must be clothed in visible symbols ("wardrobe") to fulfillment of both sacraments in the Marriage Feast of the Lamb, alluded to in line 16 of the poem.

But Christian marriage that this is, it is nevertheless a marriage with a crippling and anomalous element. This is to be the only time they are "Permitted to commune." For reasons not fully expressed in the poem, but fully discernible in other poems, the couple must part after the brief exchange. There is to be no earthly career to their marriage; they are left with their faith, which will alternately support and torment them, that their marriage union will be finally consummated in the greater rapture of Eternity after their deaths. The intervening time, as the poem ends, will be occupied by a love which is also a Calvary.

Thus, two of Dickinson's most striking themes, found throughout the later fascicles, are started here: that the lovers will meet beyond the grave, and that the intervening years of separation will be suffered as their Calvary.

St. Paul's central religious concept of "justification" also appears in the final line of this poem. The way to "repair" the sin of Adam as well as the personal sins of the self is through the process of justification detailed by Paul in the seventh and eighth chapters of his Letter to the Romans. Dickinson's marriage is an anomalous one, "justified" in this case only by a lifetime of separation, of suffering, and of keeping her love alive. As Hester says to Dimmesdale, in another anomalous marriage whose fulfillment was expected in heaven: "What we did had a consecration of its own."

Was Emily Dickinson actually married? If we restrict this question to the world of her fascicles, there is no doubt in the mind of the speaker that she was. A poem addressed apparently to a woman friend begins "Ourselves were wed one summer—dear" (631). She exclaims in poem 199 "I'm 'wife'—I've finished that—/That other state." The poem ends with the firm assertion "I'm 'Wife'! Stop there!" The poem explores her old and new states through a series of vivid contrasts: Czar (*versus* peasant?), Woman *versus* Girl, Heaven *versus* Earth, comfort *versus* pain. The burden of the poem is to assert that a qualitative change has been made in her life, by marriage. And still another aspect of the marriage, its "contractual" or legal aspect, binding for life, is expressed in the first stanza of 580: "I gave myself to Him—/—And took Himself, for Pay,/The solemn contract of a Life/Was ratified, this way—." Those who wish to see this poem as a mystical one, in which God and the soul are married, must account for the following two items in the poem: that she might the "poorer prove" for this transaction, and that the contract is "Mutual—Risk."

The fact of marriage is confirmed in a significant number of other poems, as actuality and not as trope for some other experience. In humble celebration of the event she begins a poem, "I am ashamed—I hide—/What right have I—to be a Bride—/So late a Dowerless Girl" (473). Another poem, which looks back upon the day of marriage and reflects on the experience in a calm and ordered way, begins, "The World—stands—solemner—to me—/Since I was wed—to Him" (493). The poem merits a high place in any collection of marriage poetry.

One of the most excited of all the marriage poems is 1737, which begins "Rearrange a 'Wife's' affection"; it addresses the "Thee" of the fascicles and anticipates joyful reunion with him after death. The poem immediately attracts attention. It was in its fascicle when Mabel Loomis Todd received the poems from Lavinia Dickinson, indexed them in her notebook, and transcribed them all for possible publication. It was not among those poems which she and Colonel Higginson chose to publish in the 1890s and it did not appear in print until 1945, when Todd and her daughter published the Todd transcription of it in *Bolts of Melody*. The original hand-written versions of the poems had all been sent back to Lavinia, at whose death they went to her heirs, her sister-in-law Susan Dickinson and her family. When the manuscripts were finally deposited at the Harvard and Amherst libraries this was one of the poems which had disappeared. The fascicle had been "mutilated," in Franklin's word, presumably by Susan Dickinson or her daughter.[8] It owes its present existence to Todd's transcription. The poem is quite frank about Dickinson's "secret," and it may be a secret which the family wanted kept for their own sake as well as hers.

> Rearrange a "Wife's" affection!
> When they dislocate my Brain!
> Amputate my freckled Bosom!
> Make me bearded like a man!
>
> Blush, my spirit, in thy Fastness—
> Blush, my unacknowledged clay—
> Seven years of troth have taught thee
> More than Wifehood ever may!
>
> Love that never leaped its socket—
> Trust entrenched in narrow pain—
> Constancy thro' fire—awarded—
> Anguish—bare of anodyne!
>
> Burden—borne so far triumphant—
> None suspect me of the crown,
> For I wear the "Thorns" till *Sunset*—
> Then—my Diadem put on.

> Big my Secret but it's *bandaged*—
> It will never get away
> Till the Day its Weary Keeper
> Leads it through the Grave to thee.   [1737]

The poem is an exercise in definition of the unique experience Dickinson had undergone. "Wife" is the closest word from ordinary language, but it must be put in quotation marks in the first line, and distinguished from conventional "Wifehood" in line 8. Since the other poems in the fascicle are dated, from their handwriting, at "around 1861," one can assume that this poem was written about the same time. Line 7 of the poem then establishes a point of chronology within the narrative of the fascicles: "Seven years of troth have taught thee." "Troth," as noted earlier, seems to be reserved in Dickinson's vocabulary to the marriage relationship. It may be that she alludes to a conventional time of fidelity, as in Jacob's proving his fidelity to Rachel by agreeing to work for her father Laban for seven years in order to gain her hand (Genesis 29.18). But in the Dickinson chronology the poem could also look to a time some seven or so years previous, when she first sensed her commitment to the man she came to call her husband. Seven years from "around 1861" would bring us near to the time when she is assumed to have first met the Reverend Charles Wadsworth, 1855, though the dating also coincides with the departure of Henry Vaughan Emmons from Amherst (an early candidate for the beloved) and the arrival in Amherst of one of her favorite clergymen, Reverend E.S. Dwight, who served her family's church from 1854 to 1860. Dickinson's relationship to Dwight will be studied at more length in chapter 2.

The first stanza has been gravely misread, it seems to me, as an expression of Dickinson's horror of everything male.[9] The poem as a whole surely renders this interpretation impossible. It is a lover's extravaganza addressed to "Thee," recounting in hyperbole the tortures she would be willing to undergo to preserve her "affection."

The second stanza contains concepts and phrasings which we would not willingly have lost. Both spirit and flesh can "Blush" and the deprivation of sensual fulfillment is combined with the body's need for completion by another in the invention of the phrase "my unacknowledged clay." As in many of Dickinson's best poems the voice that is heard here is carefully controlled to a pitch just this side of emotional explosion.[10]

In the middle stanza of this poem Dickinson continues to protest her fidelity, but now with more emphasis on the pain it causes her. And the emphasis on pain tips the poem toward its multifaceted ending, where the crown of Royalty ("Diadem") merges with the crown of Calvary ("Thorns"), the thought of death immediately suggests links to immortality and reunion with the beloved, and the "Secret" of her commitment is at once her grandeur and her pain. As a marriage poem it is surely continuous with the great marriage poem 322.

The Erotic Poetry of the Fascicles

Was Dickinson the marrying kind? We have been hindered from seeing erotic sensuality in Dickinson's poetry by words like "nun" and "spinster" from an earlier generation of critics. Her friend and literary mentor, Thomas Wentworth Higginson, referred to her as "that virgin recluse."[11]

A later generation of critics proved to be similarly resistant to Dickinson as a writer of enormous sexual force. In 1964 Clark Griffith surveyed Dickinson's love poems and judged them few and bad. He suggested that "from time to time she ground out a set of love lyrics, for no better reason than her belief that this was the accepted thing—the conventional thing—for poets of the age to do." Griffith declared that there was a "complete lack of erotic detail in her love poems," and felt that she became a poet only after she left this phase and "fell fervently in love with God."[12]

In 1968 William R. Sherwood found the same love poems of 1860 and 1861 "smug. . . . at once effusive and insipid." He felt that in poems 211, 213, 212, and 246, three of which I shall consider shortly, Dickinson "slaps together a few stock symbols"; Sherwood also felt that Dickinson became a poet only after "a conversion. . . . an experience of grace." By 1968 this pattern seemed to have been firmly set. Ruth Miller felt that some of these love poems just mentioned are about Dickinson's desire for publication of her poems and that she became a mature poet, and a mystical poet as well, only after she had rejected Samuel Bowles both as lover and as potential publisher. By 1974 a new line of criticism was opened by Inder Nath Kher, who read Dickinson's poetry against the background of Existentialist thought; but he also found that "she is not interested in merely physical love" and denied any "sexual urge" in the poem "Wild Nights" (249).[13]

While the substantial contributions of each of these critics must be appreciated, it seems that now, in the light of the placement of the poems in their fascicles, an opposing case can more readily be made.

Dickinson knew, for example, the erotic function of clothes, to hide and highlight at the same time, long before modern anthropologists had begun to study the subject: "as laces just reveal the surge" is the simile she creates to suggest that the reader of poetry is more stimulated to find its meaning when that meaning is decoratively hidden (210). In using such a simile Dickinson shows that she knows how a man looks at a woman in whom he is sexually interested. The same point is made, no longer as a

le, in poem 485. There she laments that it is harder to dress attrac-
ely when one's lover is forbidden than when he is dead. It is "difficult,"
e writes, to "make the Boddice gay—/When eyes that fondled it are
wrenched/By Decalogues—away."

Much of Dickinson's erotic poetry is carried either by images from the
sea or by the convention of the bee's ways with his flower. Central to the
first category, and one of the great erotic poems in any language, is the
following, addressed to the "Thee" of the fascicles:

> Wild Nights—Wild Nights!
> Were I with thee
> Wild Nights should be
> Our luxury!
>
> Futile—the Winds—
> To a Heart in port—
> Done with the Compass—
> Done with the Chart!
>
> Rowing in Eden—
> Ah, the Sea!
> Might I but moor—Tonight—
> In Thee! [249]

In breathless exclamation, with barely two unstressed syllables in the
whole first stanza, Dickinson here introduces her frequently used theme
of "Eden" as the paradise of sexual security and enjoyment. Once again,
those who would see this as a divine poem have much to contend with:
"Night" in mystical poetry is the dark night of the soul, where the soul
senses itself to be utterly separated from God; and the lover in Eden is the
human male, with God as the judgmental third party standing by. The
poet whose companion for several years was her lexicon could not have
been insensitive to the overtones of sensual excess in the long history of
the word "luxuria."

Eden is prominent in one of the major bee poems as well, a poem
whose lush physicality contains no hint of the divine:

> Come slowly—Eden!
> Lips unused to Thee—
> Bashful—sip thy Jessamines—
> As the fainting Bee—
>
> Reaching late his flower,
> Round her chamber hums—
> Counts his nectars—
> Enters—and is lost in Balms. [211]

Other sea poems explore the union of lovers in various ways. Poem 162 begins "My River runs to Thee" and ends with the intense line"*Say Sea—take me.*" In a two-line poem from the same year, 1860, the point is made with less emotional overflow, more compression:

> Least Rivers—docile to some sea.
> My Caspian—thee. [212]

In a society that studied the Bible as closely as did Dickinson's, she would have known that one of the rivers that runs into the Caspian sea is the Gihon, mentioned in the second chapter of Genesis as one of the rivers of "Eden."

The imagery of the sea plays a different role in defining the relationship between the lovers in poem 368. Someone else has tried to console the speaker when she seemed tired or in pain; she rejects the comfort abruptly:

> *That* right—was thine—
> *One port*—suffices—for a Brig—like *mine*—
>
> Our's be the tossing—wild though the sea—
> Rather than a Mooring—unshared by thee.

But the continuity of imagery between this poem and 249—in both poems the ship has found a quiet haven from the dangerous sea—suggests a continuity between the two aspects of the relationship explored in the two poems: as wife she expects ecstasy, as well as solace and understanding, only from the beloved. It seems, in the repetition of this imagery, as if she is reminding him of a poem he already knows, and is building on it. The present poem, 368, continues to explore the possibilities of the same erotic trope; and Dickinson underlines words to prod his recollection: "Our's be the Cargo—*unladen—here*—/Rather than the *'spicy isles—'*/ And thou—not there—." And the imagery again proves useful in a poem (506) where she begins to explore her sense of loss and loneliness after the ecstasy of her marriage day; the lines center on one of the most famous wives of the Bible: "Into this Port, if I might come,/Rebecca, to Jerusalem,/Would not so ravished turn—."

Another facet of the erotic sea imagery involves the moon as a character, and the moon and sea are linked even though a great distance separates them. One of these poems (429) achieves the success of shifting the gender tags in the last stanza so that each of the lovers, male and female, can be seen as "obedient" to the magnetic command of the other.

Finally, the trope of the male as sea may provide the clue to interpreting a poem whose dreamlike quality has stimulated much discussion and disagreement:

I started Early—Took my Dog—
And visited the Sea—
The Mermaids in the Basement
Came out to look at me—

And Frigates—in the Upper Floor
Extended Hempen Hands—
Presuming Me to be a Mouse—
Aground—upon the Sands—

But no Man moved Me—till the Tide
Went past my simple Shoe—
And past my Apron—and my Belt
And past my Boddice—too—

And made as He would eat me up—
As wholly as a Dew
Upon a Dandelion's Sleeve—
And then—I started—too—

And He—He followed—close behind—
I felt His Silver Heel
Upon my Ancle—Then my Shoes
Would overflow with Pearl—

Until We met the Solid Town—
No One He seemed to know—
And bowing—with a Mighty look—
At me—The Sea withdrew—   [520]

Granted the poem is cast as a fantasy; it becomes a fairly clear allegory if the passionate male "sea" pursues the not entirely unwilling damsel all the way up to "the Solid Town"—and then withdraws his pursuit when ethical bounds and social *mores* impede. The third stanza indicates a shift, a rapid development of physical responses that the speaker has never experienced before. One finds in the middle of the poem the quite natural sense of fear, that the imperious demands of the other, the beloved, begin to threaten the self. The progression of details—from shoe to apron to belt to "boddice"—make it plain that the experience was felt as sensuous and that her role was flirtatious.

The other major set of imagery in the erotic poetry, as noted above, is the bee/flower imagery. This imagery had some currency in American poetry of the time; Melville can be found using it with good effect in his poem "After the Pleasure Party," where the frustrated female speaker laments, "How glad with all my starry lore,/I'd buy the veriest wanton's rose/Would but my bee therein repose." The bee is the aggressive (and frequently promiscuous) male, in the genre; the flower he "enters" is the passive female. Erotic details of the sting, the opening of the petals, the vibrations of rapture, are part of the genre. There is precedence for this convention in English poetry, for example in Thomas Carew's poem "A Rapture":

> Then, as the empty bee, that lately bore
> Into the common treasure all her store,
> Flies 'bout the painted field with nimble wing
> Deflow'ring the fresh virgins of the Spring,
> So will I rifle all the sweets that dwell
> In my delicious paradise. . . .

Closer in time to Dickinson is the 1856 passage from Walt Whitman's "Spontaneous Me, Nature": "The hairy wild-bee that murmurs and hankers up and down, that gripes the full-grown lady-flower, curves upon her with amorous firm legs, takes his will of her, and holds himself tremulous and tight till he is satisfied."

Dickinson uses the convention as substance for some two dozen poems, and shows acquaintance with it even in the first of her poems represented in the Johnson edition. The Eden and balms found in the sea poems are merged with the bee/flower convention in 211, where the lady is the sensuous bee, sipping nectar, and "lost in Balms." Poem 213 is one of her most charmingly coquettish bits of erotica, based on the lady's coy question, But will you still respect me in the morning?:

> Did the Harebell loose her girdle
> To the lover Bee
> Would the Bee the Harebell *hallow*
> Much as formerly?
>
> Did the "Paradise"—persuaded—
> Yield her moat of pearl—
> Would the Eden *be* an Eden,
> Or the Earl—an *Earl?*

The details are as much a seduction of the lover as a protestation of the lady's honor. A frank and mature humor characterizes the sensuality here. Though this 1860 poem does not appear in the fascicles, still it furnishes another example of Dickinson's interest in sexually explicit situations at the time when she was putting these fascicles together.

The erotic details of the bee-flower convention are explored with even more surprising frankness in 339, which did find its way into a fascicle. This is the poem where the lady details her floral treasures for the absent lover: "My Fuschzia's Coral Seams/Rip—while the Sower—dreams" and "My Cactus—splits her Beard/To show her throat,"

> Carnations—tip their spice—
> And Bees—pick up—
> A Hyacinth—I hid—
> Puts out a Ruffled Head—
> And odors fall
> From flasks—so small—
> You marvel how they held—

It seems excessively naive to read these lines as a simple report on how her flowers are growing, with no erotic overtones, especially in a poem in which the speaker offers herself as "Daisy" to "thee—/Bright Absentee . . . Her Lord—away."

In 869 she would be either bee or flower, just so she could "worship Thee." The fascicle version of 903 (written in 1859) reads, "I hide myself within my flower/That wearing on your breast,/You—unsuspecting, wear me too—/And angels know the rest!" Further astonishing details from this supposedly "cloistered" lady appear in 334. A hummingbird here substitutes for the bee in a poem which a lover could not but take as erotic:

> All the letters I can write
> Are not fair as this—
> Syllables of Velvet—
> Sentences of Plush,
> Depths of Ruby, undrained,
> Hid, Lip, for Thee—
> Play it were a Humming Bird—
> And just sipped—me—

If poem 321 develops in some detail, as it seems to, a comparison between the way the wind moves across the landscape and the way the hand of a lover moves across a woman's body, then the critics' description of Dickinson as a "nun" somewhat misses its mark. Dickinson's more complete phrase for herself, in fact, was "The Wayward Nun" (722).

The biographical and critical tradition surrounding Dickinson has at times attempted to persuade us otherwise, but there can be found within the world of her fascicles a body of love poetry to rival any in the tradition, including those of her favorite poet, Elizabeth Barrett Browning. One agrees with John Crowe Ransom who, in 1956, recognized "an erotic tone which is unmistakable" in the poems of Dickinson and declared it "decisive" in assessing her literary personality.[14]

Over the years the love poems, like truthful witnesses whose stories all agree, consistently deal with the same narrative—the awakening of love, a moment of commitment and bliss in an anomalous marriage, a lifetime of separation and terrible emptiness conceived of as their "Calvary," and the hope for ecstatic reunion beyond the grave. The narrative is most succinctly presented in the central marriage poem, "There came a Day—at Summer's full" (322). But multitudes of fascicle poems support that narrative and lead out from it.

The Effects of Marriage

As Dickinson analyzed her marriage, one of its effects was to raise her to a new state of being, a new status in life: "I'm 'wife'—I've finished that—/That other state" (199). She explores this transition further in 461, from "Maid" and "Child" to "Wife" and "Bride." The transition happened on "such a day" and now it is "As if I breathed superior air—/Or brushed a Royal Gown" (506). "She rose to His Requirement" to assume the rank "Of Woman, and of Wife" (732). She is Royalty now, a Queen in many of the marriage poems. She owns a "Diadem" and is pelted with rubies by "the Emperor" in 466. She now possesses an unimpeachable "Crown" (608). As early as 1860 she finished a poem celebrating this crown: "Death . . . cannot touch" it; the crown is proof against "Wilderness," against "Desert," against "frost," and it symbolizes the only human experience fit to be compared with that of the "Saints" in glory (195).

Dickinson calls this new state "degree," as in 586, "When Girls to Women, softly raised/We—occupy—Degree." The transition to wife is great enough to be called a new form of being, a new form of life celebrated by a second baptism. So different is the new state that it might be mistaken for death; but she literally checks for vital signs and finds herself "Alive—two-fold—The Birth I had—/And this—besides, in—Thee!" (470). The most elaborate poem of transition to wife must be quoted in full:

> I'm ceded—I've stopped being Their's—
> The name They dropped upon my face
> With water, in the country church
> Is finished using, now,
> And They can put it with my Dolls,
> My childhood, and the string of spools,
> I've finished threading—too—
>
> Baptized, before, without the choice,
> But this time, consciously, of Grace—
> Unto supremest name—
> Called to my Full—The Crescent dropped—
> Existence's whole Arc, filled up,
> With one small Diadem.

> My second Rank–too small the first–
> Crowned–Crowing–on my Father's breast–
> A half unconscious Queen–
> But this time–Adequate–Erect,
> With Will to choose, or to reject,
> And I choose, just a Crown–   [508]

The first stanza records the dropping of the maiden name and assumption of the husband's, dropping as well the toys of childhood. The second stanza opposes two transitions, marked by two baptisms: where the first was presumably decided on by her family, the second is conscious and willed. The new state is one of fulfillment and completion, the state in which she receives her crown. The themes of both stanzas are restated in the third, with the insistence on her new "Rank" as "Queen."

But if she had moved through her marriage to a higher state of Royalty and Queenship, her ideal of marriage remained close to the "domesticity" of nineteenth-century women portrayed in such manuals as Catherine Beecher's *A Treastise on Domestic Economy* (1841), and recently studied by Nancy F. Cott and Barbara J. Berg.[15] The word "home," for example, appears prominently in her poems about marriage, as her own "sphere." "Home," the "fire," and "Extasy" are linked in a poem she wrote when she was about thirty (207). In 366 she acknowledges that she has denied herself the public role of wife, and imagines the kinds of functions she would have performed for "Sir": "This might have been the Hand" that planted his favorite flowers, soothed his pain, played his favorite song; she would have been servant to his command, would have carried sticks for his fire, made his cottage gay. Poem 589 ends with the reflection that bad weather with a husband in the house is better than good weather without him. The day of her marriage also inspired the poem beginning "To my small Hearth His fire came–/And all my House aglow/Did fan and rock, with sudden light" (638).

It is clear that, from her side, she offers the lover total devotion as a wife, whether he be ill, or homeless, or accused, or poor–as she lists her offerings in 961: "No Service has Thou, I would not achieve it–/To die–or live–/The first–Sweet, proved I, ere I saw thee–/For Life–be Love–." But she is prevented from all of this. She glimpses what marriage would be for her, and the vision increases the misery:

> A Door just opened on a street–
> I–lost–was passing by–
> An instant's Width of Warmth disclosed–
> And Wealth–and Company.
>
> The Door as instant shut–And I–
> I–lost–was passing by–

Lost doubly—but by contrast—most—
Informing—misery— [953]

Dickinson offered herself as a woman of nearly incredible warmth and intelligence, of passion and generosity. It is difficult to realize that someone received these poems and declined the gift.

All marriages, however anomalous, have anniversaries, and Dickinson celebrates hers in at least one of the fascicle poems:

One Year ago—jots what?
God—spell the word! I—cant—
Was't Grace? Not that—
Was't Glory? That—will do—
Spell slower—Glory—

Such Anniversary shall be—
Sometimes—not often—in Eternity—
When farther Parted, than the Common Wo—
Look—feed upon each other's faces—so—
In doubtful meal, if it be possible
Their Banquet's real—

I tasted—careless—then—
I did not know the Wine
Came once a World—Did you?
Oh, had you told me so—
This Thirst would blister—easier—now—
You said it hurt you—most—
Mine—was an Acorn's Breast—
And could not know how fondness grew
In Shaggier Vest—
Perhaps—I could'nt—
But, had you looked in—
A Giant—eye to eye with you, had been—
No Acorn—then—

So—Twelve months ago—
We breathed—
Then dropped the Air—
Which bore it best?
Was this—the patientest—
Because it was a Child, you know—
And could not value—Air?

If to be "Elder"—mean most pain—
I'm old enough, today, I'm certain—then—
As old as thee—how soon?
One—Birthday more—or Ten?

> Let me—choose!
> Ah, Sir, None! [296]

The experience is analyzed at some length for Dickinson: the first five lines are occupied with deciding the name of the experience of a year ago; the word "Glory" is finally selected as the most appropriate. The second stanza introduces the actual word "anniversary," along with the information tht the lovers have now separated permanently: "farther Parted, than the Common Wo" must mean separated more definitively than if one of the lovers had died. The central stanza expresses two observations with remarkable immediacy and intensity: she had not realized that the intoxication of a year ago would happen only once; and there had been some lovers' debate about who had suffered more from the experience. The last two stanzas add the information that he was the elder of the two, though the conceit is then developed that, if pain ages, they are now equal in years. A possible reading of the final lines is that there was actually something like a decade between their ages, but that she has caught up with him because of the greatness of her suffering. The poem is twice specific that this is their *first* anniversary, and its addess to "Sir" adds still another reason for categorizing it among the marriage poems. The poem is dated by handwriting at "around 1861," suggesting the time of the actual marriage as around 1860.

One other poem seems also to record an anniversary. Poem 445 begins " 'Twas just this time, last year, I died." The narrative sequence in the poem begins in late summer. The expression of the first line may seem odd for a marriage poem, but in a very real sense, as will be seen, the marriage was a death to earthly enjoyment, with the only hope of fulfillment in heaven. As she expressed it in a poem of 1862, not found in the fascicles, she was "Born—Bridalled—Shrouded—/In a Day" (1072).

The Marriage Wager

Dickinson's fascicle poetry presents us with a unified persona throughout; there seems to be one voice speaking in all of the poems. The voice is that of a woman of great passion. About a third of the way through the fascicles, she announces that she has already lived the main day of her life. It was a day of reckless daring when she committed herself to a man with the promise of fidelity until death. The man was already married and apparently did not feel it possible to divorce his wife—almost everything in the social, legal, and religious atmosphere of the day would have prevented it. But his love is felt to match hers and, as she saw it, he is equal party to the anomalous marriage they celebrated. The fascicles are

in great part an exploration of the many facets of this "pathetic history,"
to borrow an apt phrase from outside the fascicles, from poem 955.

The action involved a considerable risk, a wager like Pascal's in which
all was staked on the Christian doctrine of the immortality of the soul. If it
turned out that there was no such thing as personal immortality and
union of lovers after death, then she would have wasted the unique thing
she had, her life. But to win the wager was to come into the greatest bliss
she could imagine, her dream of Eden come true.

This risk begins as early as the poems of 1860 and permeates the
fascicles from that time on. She claims in one poem that she has "ventured all upon a throw" and continues recklessly: "Life is but Life! And
Death, but Death!/Bliss is but Bliss, and Breath but Breath!/And if indeed
I fail,/At least, to know the worst, is sweet!" (172).

Several poems contain explicit links between this sense of risk and the
day of her unique marriage. An important poem about risk, 270, was
written very close to the time of the major marriage poems (it is dated
"about 1861") and contains many of the images from those poems: the
"Pearl," the *"Sea,"* the *"Gem"* and *"Diadem,"* and the sense of the two
lovers as now *"Monarchs"*:

> *One Life* of so much Consequence!
> Yet I—for it—would pay—
> My Soul's *entire income*—
> In ceaseless—salary—
>
> *One Pearl*—to me—so signal—
> That I would instant dive—
> Although—I *knew*—to *take* it—
> Would *cost* me— *just a life*!
>
> The Sea is full—I know it!
> That—does not blur *my Gem*!
> It burns—distinct from all the row—
> *Intact—in Diadem*!
>
> The life is thick—I know it!
> Yet—not so dense a crowd—
> But *Monarchs*—are *perceptible*—
> Far down the dustiest Road! [270]

This is, in fact, a much more complex and surprising poem than it initially
appears to be. Dickinson would risk her "life" in the second stanza, and
this seems conventional enough in a love poem. But she would risk also
"My Soul's *entire income*" in the first stanza. In a Christian ambience this
can only suggest her willingness to risk the eternal loss of her soul. But for
what would she risk hell and damnation? The beginning of the third

stanza suggests the conventional adage to solace a lover's loss: there are many fish in the sea. It may be suggested that "Pearl" is the image from the New Testament, comparing the Kingdom of Heaven to a pearl of great price. Yet one does not agree to go to hell in order to get to heaven.

The risk inherent in her situation is great indeed, and Dickinson announces herself ready to take it. More evidence for the extent of this risk will have to be investigated toward the end of Chapter 3.

Other poems of risk and wager contain similar links to that Day: "Bliss" is risked in 359, and there is as well the sense of transition from "Beggar" in an instant of "Grace"; poem 971 mentions what she "endured" for "the Brave Beloved" in the context of "Staking our entire Possession/On a Hair's result." Another poem of risk begins "When I hoped—I feared—/Since—I hoped—I dared." In this poem the enigmatic lines then appear: "Everywhere—alone—/As a Church—remain" (1181). The phrase is surely related to the line "Each was to each—the sealed Church" in Dickinson's main marriage poem (322).

Religious literature contains many subjects on which faith has been assaulted by doubt: doubt of the existence of God, of the inspiration of the Bible, of the divinity of Christ, of the inerrancy of the Church, of the efficacy of the sacraments and ordinances. The writings of mystics and theologians can be cited on each of these subjects.

Dickinson shares the great faith/doubt problem of nineteenth-century thinkers in many of her fascicle poems. But it is worthy of note that all of her poems of faith and doubt are concerned uniquely with the subject of immortality. Such a concentration makes sense, in view of the risk she had taken that all would be fulfilled in heaven.

In some of the fascicle poems Dickinson projects a serene and untroubled faith, a confidence in her own immortality. These are few, but one of her strongest assertions of faith is in a poem about "Paradise" and "Saints" which begins in wonder that she will be accepted there: "Me—come! My dazzled face/In such a shining place!/Me—hear! My foreign Ear/The sounds of Welcome—there!" (431, lines 1-4). In one of the earliest fascicle poems she writes that "Death [is] but our rapt attention/To Immortality" (7). Another early poem (24), presents a detailed imaginary picture of heaven and expresses the desire to be there; nowhere in the poem is there anything but confidence in the reality of this heaven and a serene hope that she will eventually take up residence there.

The most confident of all faith poems is 673 where she begins "The Love a Life can show Below/Is but a filament, I know,/Of that diviner thing/That faints upon the face of Noon"; ecstatic fulfillment is confidently anticipated. The poem proceeds through two analogues that suggest such a fulfillment—music and the beauty of sunset and sunrise—and ends with twelve verbs for the heaven beyond: " 'Tis this—invites—appalls—endows—/Flits—glimmers—proves—dissolves—/Returns—suggests—convicts—enchants—/Then—flings in Paradise—". Another joyful poem proclaims, "My Faith is larger than the Hills"; after inventorying nature she calls her faith "The Rivet in the Bands" that hold her world together (766).

Dickinson again asserts her belief in heaven in 463: "I stand alive—Today—/To witness to the Certainty/Of Immortality." But some new experience has occurred, in this poem of about 1862, to introduce an element of uncertainty; she still has the "Conviction—Every day—/That Life like This—is stopless," but "Judgment" enters at the end of the poem to throw her own status there into question.

So the poems of faith are a preliminary stage in the progression of the fascicle poems to uncertainty and doubt. In 696 heaven has become "The House of Supposition—/ . . . Acres of Perhaps." And heaven may be purely subjective, merely a state of mind, in another poem: "Heaven is so far of the Mind/That were the Mind dissolved—/The Site—of it—by Architect/Could not again be proved—" (370, line 1-4). Poem 350 ends, "Eternity is ample,/And quick enough, if true." Poem 408 imagines a dialogue between the living and the dead, in which conversation reduces to "a Syllable" from the living and silence from "The Coy Dead"; this poem ends with "A tremor just, that All's not sure." Poem 501 describes the "Evidence" that solicits our belief in what "stands beyond," but this poem too ends with a doubt: "Narcotics cannot still the Tooth/That nibbles at the soul."

Several poems tie this need for immortality directly to the marriage experience and its suspended fulfillment. The last two stanzas of 511, for example, conclude a series of statements about her need to be sure that the lovers will be together sometime:

> If certain, when this life was out—
> That your's and mine, should be—
> I'd toss it yonder, like a Rind,
> And take Eternity—
>
> But, now, uncertain of the length
> Of this, that is between,
> It goads me, like the Goblin Bee—
> That will not state—it's sting.

One of the most pronounced liabilities of transition to maturity through marriage is the loss of her "Child's faith" (637). A fascicle poem bases its argument on "compensation" or justice: life is too short to compensate for the absoluteness of anguish; some "Equation" must then exist in heaven; however, the futility of such reasoning is indicated by the line which ends each stanza, "But, what of that?" (301).

Clearly, then, Dickinson shares the faith/doubt problem of her contemporaries. Just as clearly she limits the subject of faith or doubt to one specific and highly personal concern, the risk she has undertaken of placing all of her hopes for marital fulfillment in the Christian afterlife.

The Guilty Marriage

The narrative core of Emily Dickinson's fascicle poetry is the classic love triangle involving the married couple and the outsider. The complications of this basic narrative are visible throughout the fascicles.

One of her poems clearly recognizes the presence of the lover's legal wife. This version of the guilty triangle and the wronged wife appears in a poem from about 1861, where Dickinson again uses the imagery, from the love poems, of the lover as sea and herself as either moon, stream, or drop—all inexorably united to the sea. The legal wife appears at the end of this poem:

> The Drop, that wrestles in the Sea—
> Forgets her own locality
> As I, in Thee—
>
> She knows herself an Offering small—
> Yet small she sighs, if All, is All,
> How larger—be?
>
> The Ocean, smiles at her conceit—
> But she, forgetting Amphitrite—
> Pleads—"Me"?   [284]

The poem clearly begins as a love poem, with the assertion of the possibility that the speaker can merge her individuality entirely in the beloved Sea. She senses her smallness, but hopes that the fact that she is giving "All" will be enough to content the beloved. But in the final stanza the facts of classical mythology dissolve the lovely scene: "Ocean" is already married; "Amphitrite" has claims on him that will have to be acknowledged.

But if Dickinson can only once bring herself to face the actuality that her beloved has a legal wife, she frequently reflects on the legal and religious fact that her sexual feelings and impulses are adulterous and therefore forbidden. Perhaps they were only impulses that were never carried into action, if we take the meaning of the following line correctly: "We did'nt do it—tho!" (190). The poem recalls a meeting with the lover during which each had the right strengths to counter the other's weaknesses. Poem 286 recalls a dangerous moment when escape was just "by a Hair"; it may be that the poem reflects on a sudden and serious illness that ended happily, but there are two people involved and much in the poem suggests rather a moral danger luckily overcome. Poem 455 describes three kinds of "Triumph": the Triumph of Faith over the fear of Death, the Triumph of Truth, and the Triumph over some strongly felt Temptation. The ramifications of this final Triumph occupy half of the poem: it is "Severer Triumph" because one remains alive to see the joy that has been forgone and the life "upon the Rack" that has been accepted. One must keep the reward in view: that one will be "Acquitted" before "Jehovah's Countenance" at the bar of final judgment. Similarly, poem 801 recalls an occasion on which "With Want, and Opportunity—/I could have done a Sin."

There is a strong sense, throughout the fascicles, that the speaker and her lover have found a paradise that is forbidden. In 239 "Paradise" is "The interdicted Land—/Behind the Hill." In another poem the "Strawberries" grow over the fence; she could attempt to get them, "But—if I stained my Apron—/God would surely scold," though it is likely that God himself would go after the strawberries were He in a similar situation (251). In 398 she protests that no physical obstacles could keep her from union with the beloved:

> But 'tis a single Hair—
> A filament—a law—
> A Cobweb—wove in Adamant—
> A Battlement—of Straw—
>
> A limit like the Vail
> Unto the Lady's face—
> But every Mesh—a Citadel—
> And Dragons—in the Crease—
> [398, lines 9-16]

This forbidden paradise is also called "the interdicted Way." Poem 498 is a love poem in which the speaker envies the sea and hills on which the beloved travels, the sparrows that surround his house, even the fly on the window pane, the light that awakens him, and the bells which tell him it is noon. But this heaven "is forbidden utterly." The poem ends with the religious sanction opposing their union: "Yet interdict—my Blossom—/And abrogate—my Bee—/Lest Noon in Everlasting Night—/Drop Gabriel—and Me—."

But for all of her abstinence there is still the sense that the law has been disobeyed: "Did we disobey Him?/Just one time!" (267). And thus a

sense of guilt runs throughout the fascicles. Dickinson's speaker antici-
pates the need to be "forgiven" at the judgment after death (237). She
entertains the possibility "If I'm lost" in 256. In 394 her "Love" and her
"Guilt" are so inextricably intermeshed that she cannot tell them apart.
Conscience figures in several poems. It is "the most agonizing Spy—/An
Enemy—could send" (683). "Remorse" is the subject of a lengthy de-
scription in 744; it is "cureless," the "institution" of God, and "The
Adequate of Hell."

A major image for Dickinson's guilty situation is presented in 1712,
the manuscript of which was apparently destroyed by Dickinson's heirs;
it survives only in transcriptions made by Mrs. Todd: "A Pit—but Heaven
over it—/And Heaven beside, and Heaven abroad;/And yet a Pit—/With
Heaven over it" (1712, lines 1-4).

Related to Dickinson's sense of guilt is the subject of the "Secret"
which she feels she must keep, a subject that runs throughout the fascicles. Her face must be arranged as a mask, "Fresh gilded—to elude the
eyes/Unqualified, to scan" (353). It is a secret that would "appal" others;
to share it with someone would give you reason to fear him as well as the
secret (381). The secret is a grief that cannot be told; it is "Tongueless,"
the "Vast Dark," "before He'll tell—/Burn Him in the Public Square"
(793). Her sorrow is so secret that it must be known only to God (626).
"Big my Secret, but it's *bandaged*—/It will never get away/Till the day its
Weary Keeper/Leads it through the Grave to thee" (1737).

The guilty secret of Dickinson's adulterous situation brings her into
direct conflict with the religious code she inherited. She was not particularly disturbed by the conventional religiosity of people around her. She
frequently satirized their smug superficiality. One famous poem outside
the fascicles condemns the "Dimity Convictions" of the "Soft—Cherubic
. . . Gentlewomen." They do not understand the spiritual meaning of
Christianity and are hardly alive physically, surely are not alive to any
sexual stimulus: "One would as soon assault a Plush—/Or violate a Star."
They need to fear that "Redemption" will be ashamed even to notice
them (401). Similarly, those "Safe in their Alabaster Chambers," in both
fascicle versions of another famous poem, seem to have led lives so
remote from true spirituality that they have no souls to be summoned
forth in an afterlife (216). Dickinson's speaker can pray for the conven-
tionally religious, even if their code shut off her route to the very kind of
happiness they enjoyed (538).

But the religion she inherited must be looked at on two levels. If she
parodies a smug religious complacency in her society, there still remain
the inherited doctrines and the code of behavior of traditional Christianity
to make enormous demands on her. Twentieth-century critics have

applauded what they take to be her free-spirited rejection of ready-made religiosity, but many have overlooked her involvement with its doctrines at a deeper and more personal level. Her religion engaged her at the same level and with the same energy as her love. The two are in conflict from the beginning, and some of the major work of the fascicles is to turn the situation around, to make her love and her religion mutually supportive.

If Dickinson rejects meretricious religion, she is deeply engaged in the search for authentic belief. The only authentication of a life, as she pares it down toward the end of the fascicles, is "Jehovah's Estimate" (982). In her preceptions human life has meaning and purpose only from religious faith: "Annihilate a single clause [of 'faith']—/And Being's—Beggary" (377). Two of her most concise and memorable apothegms from outside the fascicles state this unequivocally: "The Abdication of Belief/Makes the Behavior small" (1551); and "He has obligation/Who has Paradise" (1348).

In her search for an authentic religious response to her anomalous marriage relationship, the death of Christ furnishes the most significant model from scriptures. The main marriage poem begins the theme, that their marriage will be "Justified—through Calvaries of Love" (322). Crucifixion is the common Christian experience: "One Crucifixion is recorded—only," but "As many be/As Persons"; "Gethsemane—/Is but a Province—in the Being's Centre" (553). In 313, "Heaven," "the Joy," "The Palm" cannot be had "without the Calvary." Dickinson in the fascicles affirmed a great amount of the traditional Christianity of her era and surroundings, though in a highly personal way. The following poem seems as cold and rigorous in its diction as the doctrine it espouses:

> Through the Strait Pass of Suffering
> The Martyrs even trod—
> Their feet upon Temptation—
> Their foreheads—upon God—
>
> A Stately—Shriven Company—
> Convulsion playing round—
> Harmless as Streaks of Meteor—
> Upon a Planet's Bond—
>
> Their faith the Everlasting Troth—
> Their Expectation—sure—
> The Needle to the North Degree
> Wades so—through Polar Air— [792]

But is the story Dickinson has to tell one of temptation successfully overcome? The following poem records a moment of spiritual danger, a request or demand from the lover which put her in an immediate moral dilemma, according to lines 7 and 8. The outcome suggests further developments in her fascicle story:

> I could suffice for Him, I knew—
> He—could suffice for Me—
> Yet Hesitating Fractions—Both
> Surveyed Infinity—
>
> "Would I be Whole" He sudden broached—
> My syllable rebelled—
> 'Twas face to face with Nature—forced—
> 'Twas face to face with God—
>
> Withdrew the Sun—to Other Wests—
> Withdrew the furthest Star
> Before Decision—stooped to speech—
> And then—be audibler
>
> The Answer of the Sea unto
> The Motion of the Moon—
> Herself adjust Her Tides—unto—
> Could I—do else—with Mine? [643]

The poem is a very private one; the occasion is recalled for her addressee by a fragment of their conversation and a hint of what followed. The trope in the last stanza is identical with the Moon/Sea relationship in the marriage poems. The word "Fractions" of line 3 recalls the Platonic myth of the Androgyne, that the individual has only half a soul and can be completed by finding the other half; the question then in line 5, "Would I be Whole," is his proposal in recognition of their role of fulfilling one another. The "Syllable" of line 6 must be her Yes which she cannot bring herself to speak. "Infinity" is on the scene, and the two contending ethical forces of Nature and God. The strength of a "natural" attraction comes into conflict with divine imperatives. The last eight lines are compressed and elided, but it seems that the only answer possible was the inevitable response of the sea to the pull of the moon; if nature could not go against herself, then neither could she.

The plot, then, which Dickinson recorded in her fascicles, involves the attraction of two linked souls, standard in literature since Tristan and Iseult and before. Dickinson's speakers admit that they are powerfully attracted to each other and respond accordingly. Whether "adjustment" progressed any farther will be left to some conjectures in chapter 3.

The Scarlet Experiment

At the center of the Protestant tradition was the consideration that the individual's conscience was sacred; the Bible would reveal its truth to the individual seeker, unmediated by priest or church. But there might come a time when the individual's perceptions would take him beyond the doctrines sanctioned by that same tradition, when devout meditation or the press of circumstances might produce what the institution could not accommodate. The phenomenon, a classic example of the double bind for the person caught between the imperatives of the private conscience and the public institution, was then called "heresy." In American Christianity the phenomenon crystalized early in the famous case of Anne Hutchinson, who was declared "Antinomian" (against the Law) by the church in Massachusetts for asserting her protestant right to follow her own sense of divine counsel rather than that sanctioned by the reigning orthodoxy.

Dickinson was in her own way a daughter of Anne Hutchinson. She continued the antinomian strain that has characterized some of our best writers. In the famous poem "Some—Keep the Sabbath—going to church" she does not sense herself a part of that community; but her isolation by no means alienates her from God: "instead of getting to Heaven—at last—/I'm—going—all along" (324).

At the center of Dickinson's antinomianism is her heterodox marriage, which she once called "The Sweetest Heresy" (387). And, as in the case of Anne Hutchinson, it is precisely by means of fidelity to this heresy that salvation is to be achieved, as the antinomian has always felt about his own private revelations. At least the following poem seems to have such reasoning behind it:

> The face I carry with me—last—
> When I go out of Time—
> To take my Rank—by—in the West—
> That face—will just be thine—
>
> I'll hand it to the Angel—
> That—Sir—was my Degree—
> In Kingdoms—you have heard the Raised—
> Refer to—possibly.
>
> He'll take it—scan it—step aside—
> Return—with such a crown
> As Gabriel—never capered at—
> And beg me put it on—
>
> And then—he'll turn me round and round—
> To an admiring sky—
> As one that bore her Master's name—
> Sufficient Royalty! [336]

Their love, and the unique way they managed it, will lead not only to salvation but to the brightest crown in heaven. The thought that the individual can be right against the convictions of the majority may have been something Dickinson learned from Emerson. Her own version of self-reliance is stated in 789: "On a Columnar Self—/How ample to rely." The poem ends,

> Though None be on our Side—
>
> Suffice Us—for a Crowd—
> Ourself—and Rectitude—
> And that Assembly—not far off
> From furthest Spirit—God—

The major classic of antinomian literature in America is Hawthorne's *The Scarlet Letter*. Hester's sexual passion for the clergyman Dimmesdale is adulterous. She keeps their relationship a secret, but the love is kept alive with the romantic hope that the separated lovers will be united in a permanent marriage in heaven. Dickinson's fascicles present a similar story. In Hester's thought, Dimmesdale is someone "with whom she deemed herself connected in a union that, unrecognized on earth, would bring them together before the bar of final judgment."[16] At Dimmesdale's death Hester asks, "shall we at least hope to share eternity together?"

Hester is ennobled through her suffering, so much so as to achieve the unusual bestowal of "an engraved escutcheon," a coat of arms, on her tombstone. Dickinson uses the same word. It is her desire (in poem 98) that, when she and the "You" to whom the poems are addressed have lived through their ordeal, they may "Present our meek escutcheon/And claim the rank to die."

In Dickinson's poetry one encounters the word "Scarlet," always capitalized, in some interesting contexts. In 861, a love poem, the speaker protests her enduring fidelity, and refers to the course of their unusual love as the "Scarlet Experiment." In 527 "renunciation" is "the Scarlet way." In 528, from the same fascicle, Dickinson feels herself caught in a "Scarlet prison," introducing another prominent image from Hawthorne's story.

Hester says to her clergyman lover, in one of her most memorable speeches, "What we did had a consecration of its own"; Dickinson's anomalous marriage, according to the central marriage poem, will be "Justified—through Calvaries of Love" (322). The one who died for Beauty and the one who died for Truth were buried in adjacent but not touching tombs (449), as were Hester and Dimmesdale. There is a curious similarity in Dickinson's "The Lands we thought that we should seek/ When large enough to run" (1293), and Hester's suggestion in the forest that she and Dimmesdale escape New England to live anonymously, as man and wife, in a foreign land. In 961 Dickinson's speaker wants to attend her lover when he is ill and share if necessary his ignominy—as does Hester. A memorable scene from *The Scarlet Letter* has the child Pearl playing across the brook from her parents, the scarlet letter reflecting in the brook; Dickinson's poetry is full of lost "pearls," and the scene itself seems like a shadowy dimension behind a late poem of Dickinson's, not found in the fascicles:

> I do remember when a Child
> With bolder Playmates straying
> To where a Brook that seemed a Sea
> Withheld us by its roaring
> From just a Purple Flower beyond
> [1558, lines 9-13]

It would be more than the evidence warrants to claim that Dickinson consciously repeats the plot of *The Scarlet Letter* in her fascicles, but it seems to do less than justice to the evidence to deny that Dickinson takes some clues from Hawthorne's story to shape her own perceptions, to express her own situation.

The White Sustenance, Despair

The critical tradition has identified and traced a theme of tragedy in Dickinson's poetry. Clark Griffith's 1964 study was entitled *The Long Shadow: Emily Dickinson's Tragic Poetry.* The subtitle of Inder Nath Kher's *Emily Dickinson's Poetry* ten years later was *The Landscape of Absence.* Though it would be an oversimplification to identify this tragic strain as the main thread running through her poetry, the fact remains that Dickinson's chosen narrative involved nearly intolerable suffering, as the fascicles clearly show.

In Dickinson's world, as in Hester Prynne's, the modern ideal of a guilt-free divorce was simply not a feasible answer to her problem. Dickinson had seen at first hand how her society dealt with the permanence of the marriage bond, no matter how reasonably dissolution might be argued. In 1853, when Dickinson was in her early twenties, her father defended the Reverend John Eastman of nearby Hawley. Mrs. Eastman had sued for divorce, charging that her husband, according to the newspaper account, "treated his wife with coldness and harshness, and on several occasions with violence, that he abused and neglected her in sickness, intercepted her letters and restrained her liberty, and that last December he carried her to the Brattleboro Hospital on a pretence of insanity." The case was decided in favor of Edward Dickinson's client, furnishing little hope for his daughter that she might find a solution to her star-crossed love affair through legal means.[17]

Hawthorne had ended *The Scarlet Letter* by describing Hester's mission to wronged and wounded women: "She assured them, too, of her firm belief, that, at some brighter period, when the world should have grown ripe for it, in Heaven's own time, a new truth would be revealed, in order to establish the whole relation between man and woman on a surer ground of mutual happiness." Dickinson may have had the same hopes—her lifelong curiosity about George Eliot's story suggests as much—but there was no way they could be realized in a conservative New England family.

Dickinson's voluntary separation from the beloved may have settled her sense of ethical and religious obligation, but it left her facing decades of loneliness that would at times become excruciating. Much in her poetry feeds upon "that White Sustenance—/Despair" (640).

Tragedy is built into the narrative line we have been examining. Even the poems of 1859 and 1860 show that her life situation, as she had identified and accepted it, was already in place early in the fascicles, that the situation would necessarily include separation and consequent loneliness and pain, and that the pain of separation would be in direct "ratio" (125) to the "Transport" (167) experienced in love. "Anguish" is one of the most frequently used words of 1859-61.

In view of the detailed studies of tragic themes in her poetry which I have already mentioned, I would like to concentrate my own efforts on the following question: Do the fascicles contain any concrete evidence concerning the cause of her pain and suffering? The answer is an unqualified affirmative. Though the connections have not been noticed, there is a direct link between her love, her anomalous marriage, the subsequent separation, and the painful loneliness that would presumably fill the rest of her earthly life until reunion after death.

The theme is present in the central marriage poem itself, 322. In that poem the theme of separation begins to gain momentum only in the last three stanzas, rising to a mighty climax in the last stanza:

> The hours slid fast—as hours will,
> Clutched tight—by greedy hands—
> So—faces on two Decks—look back—
> Bound to opposing Lands—
>
> And so—when all the time had failed—
> Without external sound—
> Each—bound the other's Crucifix—
> We gave no other bond—
>
> Sufficient troth—that we shall rise—
> Deposed—at length—the Grave—
> To *that* New Marriage—
> Justified—through Calvaries of Love!

The separation is definitive, included in the marriage contract as one of its conditions. The connection between pain and love, and the assertion that they are redemptive, are explicit in the final line. Only "at length," beyond the experience of death, will the reunion take place of the two who are utterly necessary to each other.

Other poems also link this sense of suffering unequivocally to the beloved. These are love poems, addressed to "You," in which the suffering is linked directly to separation from him. Poem 181 is addressed to "Sir" and laments the loss of "a World" on his account. In a poem that rises to a definition of "Despair" and "Misery" Dickinson itemizes details concerning the absent lover that make up her sadness: "his name," the "Angle in the floor" where he stood, "the Box—/In which his letters grew"; so powerful is he still in her mental horizon that he blocks out the greater figure of God (293). In 504 she associates the face in the moon with the face of her beloved: both are equally distant and inaccessible. In 660 she relives one summer "Day" in her life, as "the Mighty Funeral/Of All Conceived Joy." Poem 725 is addressed also to "Sir" and declares "Where Thou art—that—is Home—/ . . . Where Thou art not—is Wo." Poem 786 speaks of "the awful Vacuum/Your life had left behind." The link is quite clear then: her suffering is caused by loneliness, the loss of the beloved to whom she wrote so many love poems.

This line of consideration leads into the heart of Dickinson's fascicles, to one of the techniques most characteristic of her poetry. Nearly all of her readers have recognized the large number of poems generated by the paradox that one knows or fully values only what one is deprived of. The poem "Success is counted sweetest/By those who ne'er succeed" (67) appears in virtually all anthologies of Dickinson's poetry. And the paradox is continued in many poems, so frequently that it must be considered one of her major poetic themes. "Delight—becomes pictorial—" she writes in 572, "When viewed through Pain." Similarly in 771 she says, "None can experience stint/Who Bounty—have not known." The perception is firmy rooted in her own life and experience:

> It would have starved a Gnat—
> To live so small as I—
> And yet I was a living Child—
> With Food's necessity
>
> Upon me—like a Claw—
> [612, lines 1-5]

Vivian R. Pollak has isolated a large number of these poems under the heading "Thirst and Starvation" poems,[18] where the sufferer knows the exquisite refreshment of particular metaphoric foods and beverages precisely because she is denied them: "It was the Distance—/ Was Savory"

(439). It becomes obvious to the reader of the fascicles that these metaphors stand for the loss of the beloved.

Some students of Dickinson have assumed that her suffering drove her into suicidal moods and even into mental breakdown. Whatever may be so in the case of the writer of these poems, the fascicles themselves must be analyzed for their exact statements on such matters.

The earliest poem that has been suggested as a "suicide" poem is from 1861 and, like the love poems with which it might better be categorized, it is addressed to "thee":

> What if I say I shall not wait!
> What if I burst the fleshly Gate—
> And pass escaped—to thee!
>
> What if I file this Mortal—off—
> See where it hurt me—That's enough—
> And step in Liberty!
>
> They cannot take me—any more!
> Dungeons can call—and Guns implore—
> Unmeaning—now—to me—
>
> As laughter—was—an hour ago—
> Or Laces—or a Traveling Show—
> Or who died—yesterday! [277]

It takes a rather unimaginative seriousness to read this poem, so full of wit and hyperbole, as a suicidal threat. It is a lover's mock protest, rather, addressed to her beloved "thee." "Dungeons" and "Guns" are in exactly the same category as climbing highest mountains and swimming deepest seas. The critic bent on finding a straightforward suicidal threat here will surely have missed the flirtatious scenario played in the second stanza. In order to "step in Liberty" one would have to "file this Mortal off" as if it were a leg iron. In another poem, 512, the lady imagines herself similarly fettered, with "shackles on the plumed feet." In the present poem the lady lifts her long skirt briefly to show her ankle, "See where it hurt me," then coquettishly scolds her lover's interest: "That's enough." An antisuicidal buoyancy is surely more in evidence here.

Nor do other poems that have been called suicidal really seem to qualify.[19] Poem 279 imagines both the lovers in a carriage, riding willingly together toward Judgment. The poem really mirrors not a death wish but another (and more joyful) version of their acknowledged oneness, their certain union in heaven, and their secure feelings toward Judgment because of their sacrifice.

Poem 296 has also been called suicidal because it ends with a desire for no more birthdays. But this is a poem we have already seen, commemorating the lovers' first anniversary, and ending with a plea for no more years of pain like the one she has just experienced. In poem 670 "The Prudent—carries a Revolver," but it turns out to be an ineffective defense against the frightening presences within one's own soul, not an instrument for self-destruction. Poem 786 does propose the "alternative to die" to counter the pain of "Being's Malady," but not, it seems, in any stronger or more active sense than a willingness to die to be relieved of present pain. A passive willingness to die does not equal an active suicidal mood. This poem comes late among the fascicles and explicitly ties her sorrow to loss of the beloved: she worries how "To fill the awful Vacuum / Your life had left behind."

We must conclude that, suffering as much as she undoubtedly did, there is nowhere recorded in the fascicles the kind of denial of life implied in suicide. In fact, suicide itself is denied and renounced in at least two poems. In 565 the speaker asserts from her experience that the human is "that Repealless thing—/ A Being—impotent to end—/ When once it has begun." And 612 denies to the human the privilege of the gnat, "To gad my little Being out" by flying against a window in search of the food it needs. In her mind as in Hamlet's the Everlasting has fixed his canon against self-slaughter. Whether on moral and religious grounds or on the grounds of psychic health and wholeness, the route of suicide was never what William James would call a "live option" in Dickinson's fascicles.

Another aspect of suffering, mental breakdown, has been argued persuasively by a professional therapist, John Cody, in *After Great Pain: The Inner Life of Emily Dickinson*. The layman falters before such a subject and some have echoed Richard B. Sewall's reservation that, whatever happened to their author, the poems themselves show remarkable mental clarity and control. Cody had already answered this objection to some extent by informing us that it is not unusual for the victim of mental breakdown to give a thoroughly lucid account of himself and of his terrifying experiences. Moreover, Cody argues, it would be difficult to account for the details, the clinical staging of the descent into mental breakdown found in Dickinson's poems, if she had had no personal encounters with the experience herself.[20]

Without feeling either the need or the professional competence to adjudicate the matter finally in the case of Emily Dickinson the person, I believe one can be led deeper into the fascicles by considering some of the poems of exquisite mental suffering to which Cody has drawn our attention. Cody himself generously acknowledges that the "level of meaning" which he explicates "is generally one that was beneath the poet's level of awareness. It is assumed that the reader will not conclude that the psychoanalytic meaning is the only one."[21]

The fascicles contain several of the poems in which Cody has found signs of severe mental suffering and breakdown, and generally they add still another dimension to the experience of the marriage day and its anguished separation. In at least two of them one finds explicit links between separation from the lover and the breakdown. Poem 512 describes the "Bandaged moments" of the Soul:

> She feels some ghastly Fright come up
> And stop to look at her—
>
> Salute her—with long fingers—
> Caress her freezing hair—
> Sip, Goblin, from the very lips
> The Lover—hovered—o'er—

Her mental "Goblin" comes to frighten her after separation from the "Lover." And in 410 the Soul finds "her Strings were snapt—/ Her Bow—to Atoms blown," and ends "Could it be Madness—this?" The experience is sensed as new, and it is dated from the Day of her anomalous marriage: "The first Day's Night had come." These poems of extreme mental anguish and breakdown, if it is such, are a fully integrated part of the total fascicle narrative.

The Art of Poetry

Many of the biographically interesting events in the life of Emily Dickinson occurred within a few years around her thirtieth birthday. It was during this relatively short period that she probably began wearing white, began her extended withdrawal from the world, considered herself to be living more for heavenly fulfillment than for earthly, began to consider herself a serious poet, wrote a greater quantity of poems than during any comparable period of years, and sought professional advice about her poetry from Thomas Wentworth Higginson. During the same period Wadsworth visited Amherst for the first time (in the spring of 1860), she wrote the great marriage poems, and she created the forty fascicles we are studying.

According to the speaker in Dickinson's fascicles she began writing poetry seriously as a direct result of her marriage and the events that led up to and away from it; she derives her vocation as a poet at least partly from these experiences. No fewer than fifteen poems on the art of poetry itself date from the year of the central marriage poem, 1862, and nearly a hundred others on the nature of poetry and the problems of the artist appear elsewhere in her work. The groups of poems I want to look at explore the following themes, some of them quite traditional for poets but in each case brought down to the personal condition by Dickinson's speaker: poetry as divine art, immortal fame as a poet, the immortalization of the beloved in the poet's works, the discovery of a role model in another great wife-poet, and the sense of the Beloved as the primary audience for her poems.

Just as her marriage was attended by religious symbols and elevated her to a higher or more "regal" state of being through its sacramental grace, so at the same time she came to see her poetry as a divine activity, as work now carried out at a higher level of seriousness. In 1862 Dickinson stated the newly elevated direction of her art, the sacredness of her vocation:

> Myself was formed—a Carpenter—
> An unpretending time
> My Plane—and I, together wrought
> Before a Builder came—
>
> To measure our attainments—
> Had we the Art of Boards
> Sufficiently developed—He'd hire us
> At Halves—
>
> My Tools took Human—Faces—
> The Bench, where we had toiled—
> Against the Man—persuaded—
> We—Temples build—I said— [488]

Also in 1862 she set down her highest estimate of the poet and his work; the poet here is the figure envisaged by Shelley, Poe, Emerson, and Whitman, occupying the highest rung of human genius, reconciling the whole of creation in a priestly, godlike action:

> I reckon—when I count at all—
> First—Poets—Then the Sun—
> Then Summer—Then the Heaven of God—
> And then—the List is done—
>
> But, looking back—the First so seems
> To Comprehend the Whole—
> The Others look a needless Show—
> So I write—Poets—All
>
> [569, lines 1-8]

As one element of this new and heightened vocation, Dickinson deprecated publication, as "the Auction/Of the Mind of Man." Poverty might justify "so foul a thing/Possibly." For her to sell her art, she reminds her addressee, would be like a clergyman to engage in simony, to "Be the Merchant/Of the Heavenly Grace" (709).

While money is out of the question, compensation is sought in a number of poems on the larger ground of immortal fame, where the tradition from Horace through Shakespeare had already asserted the poet's claim. Horace announced that he had, in words, executed a monument more lasting than bronze. For Shakespeare, "Not marble, nor the gilded monuments / Of princes, shall outlive this powerful rhyme." Dickinson anticipates similar literary immortality in nearly twenty poems. Her first declaration of the theme comes, once again, from the year of momentous change, 1862: "Some—Work for Immortality—/ The Chiefer part, for Time—/ He—Compensates—immediately—/ The former— Checks—on Fame—" (406, lines 1-4). At greater length, in the famous poem "This was a Poet," she emerges with the definition of the poet as her own "Fortune—Exterior—to Time" (448). She must have felt herself in possession of a great theme, to make such lofty claims in 1862 for the fascicles she was assembling.

At about the time of her marriage Dickinson also found and celebrated a great model for her role as poet. This was the "lyric Love" of Robert Browning, the partner in the most celebrated erotic and romantic marriage of the nineteenth century, Elizabeth Barrett Browning. When Mrs. Browning died in 1861 she was still better known than her husband and considered by far the better poet. Dickinson was one of her ardent readers[22] and commemorated the event of her death with a poem. The poem and Mrs. Browning's *Last Poems* both date from 1862.

> Her—last Poems—
> Poets ended—
> Silver—perished—with her Tongue—
> Not on Record—bubbled Other—
> Flute—or Woman—so divine—
>
> Not unto it's Summer Morning
> Robin—uttered half the Tune
> Gushed too full for the adoring—
> From the Anglo-Florentine—
>
> Late—the Praise—'Tis dull—Conferring
> On the Head too High—to Crown—
> Diadem—or Ducal symbol—
> Be it's Grave—sufficient Sign—
>
> Nought—that We—No Poet's Kinsman—
> Suffocate—with easy Wo—
> What—and if Ourself a Bridegroom—
> Put Her down—in Italy? [312]

There are several interesting features of this poem to be noted in the present context. In the first phase of the poem the death of the great poet ends an era and a tradition; the mold is broken. The connection of poets with "the divine" is noted, with the claim that Browning was the best of the divine poets. (The other fascicle poem of 1862 on Mrs. Browning, 593, likewise makes claims for the "divine" nature of Browning's poetry; it is "Conversion," "sanctifying in the Soul," and "Divine Insanity.") Lines 6-7 introduce, modestly and by indirection, a claim by Dickinson herself. She had, in 285, identified herself as poetic singer with the "Robin," and here the Robin is at least engaged in the same activity, even though with success in no way comparable to Browning's. Still the assertion is made that they work in the same area with the same ambitions. "Crown," "Diadem," and "Ducal Showing" then figure in the poem, items which Dickinson had begun to claim for herself in the new status conferred on her by marriage. Most notably the poem ends with great empathy for the loss a spouse might feel in the death of his poet-wife. The poem is distinctly *about* Elizabeth Barrett Browning, but spoken from the ground of Dickinson's developing diction and personal concerns. The signs of the teller and the personal circumstances currently transforming her life are very much in view in this poem, and for this reason it takes its rightful place in the fascicles.

Still another element of Dickinson's concern in her poems on the Art of Poetry is her sense of her audience: for whom does she write these fascicle poems? Surely this question is settled in the more than one hundred and fifty poems which are addressed to the exclusive "You" and in the many poems where she sends her meditations on the experiences they alone have shared. A famous poem adds interesting possibilities to this situation. Poem 441 claims "This was my letter to the World" and the subject is carefully defined: "The simple News that Nature told—/With tender Majesty." She continues with a statement about her audience: the "Message is committed/To Hands I cannot see." If Dickinson means that the Hands she cannot see belong to the now distant lover, then she must hope that her lover will do for her what Robert Browning did for his wife's *Sonnets from the Portuguese*, furnish these intensely private love poems to the world. Finally she would be a poet of at least national reputation, asking "Sweet—countrymen—/Judge tenderly—of Me." This justly famous poem, then, expands even more in the fascicle context.

In any physical description of the fascicles, the "nature poems" will be noticed both for their numbers and for their popularity with a wide audience. It must be noted, as well, that the nature poems form an enduring stratum of her poetry; she can be found writing them during almost any year of her poetic career. It is as if nature is the source to which she constantly returns both for renewal and for practice in her trade as a poet. Considerations of the art of her poetry must attend to this large segment of her writings.

If the fascicles are units (and Dickinson bound them as such), and if they were sent as frequent communications to the beloved "You," then these nature poems are also lover's communications by which Dickinson intends to share the full richness of her inner life: "By a flower—By a letter—/By a nimble love—/If I weld the Rivet faster—/Final fast—above" (109). These poems then serve to fill out each of the fascicles to roughly the same length; they serve as setting for the superb love poems and meditations on the marriage experience; but they function even more strongly as the gift of the self in a relationship that was carried on, except for a few meetings, totally by correspondence.

Within Dickinson's nature poetry I can determine four major categories. There are, first of all, poems of pure description—of sunsets, flowers, birds, insects, and other phenomena of her environment. A second category, closely allied, would add the poet's emotion, most frequently an exhilaration or a kind of nature-intoxication. In 122 there is "A something in a summer's Day . . . Transcending extasy." The Tippler of "a liquor never brewed" (214) is the one who writes these poems. A third category can be discerned where the primary interest is rather a subtle interior mood, and exterior nature is summoned as an analogue for that mood. Poem 258 is a clear example of this type:

> There's a certain Slant of light,
> Winter Afternoons—
> That oppresses, like the Heft
> Of Cathedral Tunes—
>
> Heavenly Hurt, it gives us—
> We can find no scar,
> But internal difference,
> Where the Meanings, are—

The "volcano" poems are interesting in this category, where the violent and repressed feelings of the poet can find adequate correlative only when she sees her face as "Vesuvius" (754), when she suspects "the stillness is Volcanic" on every human face. In this category Nature is consistently secondary to the personal focus of the poem.

But there is a fourth category of nature poems in which nature provides an analogue for fuller exploration of Dickinson's marriage situation itself. Poem 348 assumes major importance in this context:

> I dreaded that first Robin, so,
> But He is mastered, now,

I'm some accustomed to Him grown,
He hurts a little, though—

I thought if I could only live
Till that first Shout got by—
Not all Pianos in the Woods
Had power to mangle me—

I dared not meet the Daffodils—
For fear their Yellow Gown
Would pierce me with a fashion
So foreign to my own—

I wished the Grass would hurry—
So—when 'twas time to see—
He'd be too tall, the tallest one
Could stretch—to look at me—

I could not bear the Bees should come,
I wished they'd stay away
In those dim countries where they go,
What word had they, for me?

They're here, though; not a creature failed—
No Blossom stayed away
In gentle deference to me—
The Queen of Calvary—

Each one salutes me, as he goes,
And I, my childish Plumes,
Lift, in bereaved acknowledgement
Of their unthinking Drums—

The speaker of this poem senses a disjunction between herself and nature, surely a danger sign for the poet who at other times claims exhilaration and the ecstasy of perfect union with nature. One of the features of the poem is its control and rational strategy. It proceeds through a catalogue which includes Robin, Daffodils, Grass, Bees, and Blossom, testing each for the sympathy she had once enjoyed. Now she is an alien in their world: "What word had they, for me?" Worse, they cause dread, hurt, mangling. They function in the poem, though, to move toward a clarification of her interior state, baldly stated as "bereaved" in the final stanza. The poem thus far could appeal to any reader as generalized esthetic model for any wrenching pain that has served to isolate the sufferer from the nature he had once felt as his given environment. But at the climax of the poem a phrase occurs which Dickinson has come to use as one of the elements in the cluster of associations with her marriage. "Queen" is an example of the royalty imagery by which she expresses the sense of her transition to a higher state of being as one of the results of marriage. And

"Calvary," as we have seen in the central marriage poem (322) and extensively in the analysis of her loneliness poems, is the state of religious being she must endure if the heterodox marriage is to be "justified" at last. In this poem, then, Nature is secondary, used to clarify the interior emotions which are her primary focus.

The situation is nearly identical in 364, another poem from 1862:

> The Morning after Wo—
> 'Tis frequently the Way—
> Surpasses all that rose before—
> For utter Jubilee—
>
> As Nature did not care—
> And piled her Blossoms on—
> [364, lines 1-6]

Once again, nature's mood and the poet's situation are out of synchronization. The axis of vision does not coincide with the axis of things. The second half of the poem protests the joyful songs of the birds: if the birds knew that their joyful songs "fell/Like Litanies of Lead" on the suffering human, "They'd modify the Glee/To fit some Crucifixal Cleft—/Some Key of Calvary" (lines 14-16). The "musical key" of human suffering, which nature cannot provide, is once again the Calvary situation into which her marriage has put her.

As a final observation on Dickinson's *ars poetica*, I would like to comment on a critical opinion which seems in our time to have assumed the status of one of the certitudes concerning her poetry. This is the notion that her poems, in the main, are not *about* anything, are subjectless. According to this opinion, Dickinson has successfully removed from the poems all signs of a *sitz-im-leben*, a situation in real life, leaving them as detached esthetic forms.

The opinion has generated observations about the difficulties of her poems and has even defined critical approaches that are felt to be necessary in such a situation. Benefits have been felt to accrue to the general reader when he rushes in to fill this vacuum with his own experience, thus accounting for the wide popularity of the poems: they become immediately personal to each reader. It is as if each poem were a mere matrix, a form without content, which can give structure and meaning to the unformed experience of the reader. Benefits have also accrued to the critical theorist, who can approach the poems as abstract works of *poésie pure*.

Yvor Winters began this trend long ago when he wrote of Dickinson's "deliberate excursions into obscurity" and "the rendering of purely theoretic experience" in her poems. His opinion was that she "deliberately utilizes imagery irrelevant to the state with which she is concerned" and that the result, in his unfriendly view, is frequently "fraudulent." Richard Chase, in 1951, felt that many of her poems are "random gnomic observations" which do not seem to rise from any particular experience. R.P. Blackmur developed this opinion further: Dickinson's poetry, he says, is about "spontaneity" rather than about "experience"; "all her life was spent looking for a subject, and the looking *was* her subject . . . she looked only for a focus without having a target."[23]

For Eleanor Wilner in 1971 the words of Dickinson's poems were "Hieroglyphic," always pointing to "a higher and intangible meaning." The subject of the poem "can never be fully known, rationally phrased or directly stated." She took as example the simple poem beginning "A Bird came down the Walk" (328), a remarkably concrete observation of the bird's behavior, and concluded: "Behind this simple facade, a rich drama is being unfolded. For this can be read as a poem about God and his relation to man, the soul and its relation to the body, creatures and their relation to one another, the poet and his relation to his material."[24] The categories seem to go far beyond either the poem itself or Wilner's explication of it, demonstrating this "use" of Dickinson's poetry as matrix for stimulating the subjectivities of each reader.

Firmer theoretical speculation underlay Roland Hagenbüchle's article of 1974. Hagenbüchle wrote that he admired Dickinson's vagueness, what he called her "indeterminacy." He saw her images and metaphors as unimaginable and unvisualizable. He asserted that the subject matter in many of the poems "recedes into the background and becomes dispensible or even lost entirely." Her response to the mystery and terror of existence, he said, was precisely the flight to images that eluded precise formation in the reader's mind and imagination.[25]

The fullest defense of this method of reading Dickinson's poetry was undertaken in Robert Weisbuch's carefully meditated study of 1975. Weisbuch felt that "scenelessness . . . constitutes Dickinson's strategy." He wrote of the "self-containment of the language" and the "self-sufficient design" of the poems. As reader he found that the poems "point to no specific situation which occurs apart from the language." He described the reader as "adrift on a subjectless sea of thought." He described the critic's job as avoiding "referential" interpretation and reverting rather to "description of the poem's pattern in terms of nothing but itself."[26]

With this analysis the poems of Emily Dickinson seemed to escape into sheer abstract patterning. And Sharon Cameron, in a fascinating book on Dickinson and the nature of lyric poetry, went on to postulate that Dickinson wrote poems in which speech was displaced from any definite speech-context, motion was separated from any moving object, time was "unhinged" from any fixed points of reference, and the speaker herself had achieved utter namelessness and disassociation from any personal history.[27]

There is some danger here. If a critical theory would assert absolute scenelessness and subjectlessness, then this would be to remove all traces of plot, of narrative, of significant incident, indeed of significant statement, from the poems under consideration. The poetry is needlessly refined and, thus "to airy thinness beat," loses any relation to gruff life. A bloodless surrogate stands, with no relation to anything but Art, most narrowly conceived. In the rhetorical trinity of author, text, and audience—simultaneously one and three for the literary critic—these theorists misconceive audience, venturing to identify themselves as "Beloved," "Sweet," "Sire." Thus they misconstrue text, and by progression they misconceive the author herself. This is faulty employment of rhetorical method, severe blindness to the ways in which Dickinson's texts relate themselves to their one "intended reader"—to use a category described some years ago by Erwin Wolff.[28]

Dickinson's limitation of audience, the severe restriction to only one auditor, is built into many of the poems, is built into the fascicles themselves if they are the tightly unified packages they appear to be. To ignore an essential point of the artistic product is to solicit critical confusion.

It is this limitation of audience that makes the significant difference in determining the genre of Dickinson's lyrics. They escape the precise restrictions which standard theories of literary description would impose. As written to one private reader, and assuming experiences to which he alone is privy, Dickinson's love poems lack the public dimensions that would allow us to consider them as pure art. They are very much like personal correspondence.

Thus Dickinson eludes the theorists. Her reader is present as essential within many of the poems, addressed as they are to the singular beloved "You." A marriage is described with so many circumstantial details that scenelessness is hardly her endeavor. Instead of subjectlessness, a multitude of subjects develop and intersect, deriving their being quite clearly from the anomalous marriage. The central speaker of the poems clearly emerges, as her meditations work out into every conceivable facet of her marriage situation.

But the narrative and its meditations are recorded piecemeal and in a certain developing order in the fascicles and sets as they have been reconstructed. The precise sequence of Dickinson's narrative can now be followed in approaching the fascicles in their chronological order.

Chapter Two

The Fascicles
in Order

A Woman here descends into the most secret part of herself
and tells us about all she finds there with an unflinching
sincerity, as though there were only one listening.
—Simone de Beauvoir[1]

A chronological reading of the fascicles reveals that the story, displayed
synthetically in the previous chapter, has gradual unfoldings and developments. It does not appear all at once, nor does Dickinson seem to
know in advance the events she will describe. There are no fictional
techniques such as foreshadowing or deliberate irony which would demonstrate the art of the storyteller who has her tale fully in mind as she
begins.

These characteristics raise important questions regarding the relationship between Dickinson's art and her life, which will be considered
here and there in the present chapter, at length in the next chapter. Here it
may suffice to say that Dickinson could have chosen as the general title of
her fascicles "The Awakening," with as sure an instinct as Kate Chopin
was to follow in using that title for her novel of 1899.

In this chapter we shall be watching the narrative as it develops
through the forty fascicles, following R.W. Franklin's new order and
numbering. One seems to be able to discern "phases" in this narrative,
points at which a new event is recorded or a new set of subjects and
reflections is introduced.

Phase One: Fascicles 1-8

Thomas H. Johnson has dated the poems in these eight fascicles, by
their handwriting, from about 1858 to early 1860. Prominent in these
early fascicles are many "You" poems which address a specific individual
reader, and "we" poems which limit the sphere of communication to just
two people. In the first fascicle alone, five of the poems are addressed to
"Thee" or "You" in a way that the general reader or the casual friend
could hardly take to be himself (26, 31, 4, 34, and 35). One poem

addresses "Sir" (32) and another identifies him as her "Pilot" (4), as if some element of guidance is part of their relationship. He is not yet her "lover" in this first phase; but one poem in the first fascicle already identifies him as her "missing friend" (23), as if a relationship has already been well established.

This first fascicle is a rich trove. Nearly half of the poems sound as if they were written to a clergyman, suggesting topics that would interest him professionally. Poem 22 presents "chancel" and "chant" and her phrase "The Burglar cannot rob—then" surely expects him to recall "Lay up for yourselves treasures in heaven. . . . where thieves do not break through or steal" (Matthew 6.20). Poem 24 is her joyous version of those who dance and sing in heaven and her desire to be with them. Poem 7 is a small treatise on resurrection from the dead, and poem 27 argues that though death is "agony" for the bereaved, it should be viewed generously as "transport" for the deceased. Poem 28 argues that if the dead person is taken to heaven, so also should the beauties of the dying flower and the dying sunset. Poem 29 seeks to know the whereabouts of "those I loved," and asks the same question as "Philip" did at the Last Supper (John 14.8). Poem 30 is a plea for guidance of her "little boat", and Poem 4 asks her "Pilot" to guide her safely to eternity. The first poem of this first fascicle concludes with her own liturgy, paralleling his: "In the name of the Bee—/And of the Butterfly—/And of the Breeze—Amen!" (18). There are obvious parallels with the addressee's Trinitarian invocations here: the Bee is usually taken to be masculine; the Butterfly undergoes a glorious change after its apparent death; and "Breeze" is just as acceptable a translation for the biblical *ruah* as is "Spirit."

In this first poem of the first fascicle Dickinson also stakes her conscious claim as a poet in the American tradition. "The Gentian weaves her fringes," the first line of the poem, echoes one of the most famous poems of the era, William Cullen Bryant's "To the Fringed Gentian." Both Bryant and Dickinson stress the fact that the flower blooms late in the season, beautiful but the harbinger of death and winter, bearing in upon the human observer a strong sense of mortality and questions of the afterlife.

Critics have frequently lamented Dickinson's "mortuary theme," and it is one of the stronger themes characterizing this first fascicle, which is a romantic *liebestod* collection of flowers, death, love, and the maiden. But the mortuary theme was prominent in the American tradition, represented with unimpeachable credentials in Dickinson's time by Bryant. This poem, then, stands as an announcement that Dickinson was seriously undertaking the career of poet in mid-nineteenth-century America; but the exclusive "You" and "We" poems show that she had narrowed her intended audience to one person.

Flowers dominate this first fascicle also, specified as "Gentians" in two poems, as roses, the anemone, columbine, crocus, orchis and violets in one poem each. Three poems feature the "Daisy" prominently (22, 28, and 29), and Dickinson will come to identify herself as "Daisy" in later poems and in the last two Master letters, as if her addressee had noticed that she favored these flowers and gave her this nickname.

In some of these poems she identifies her poems themselves as "flowers": in 33 she sends them as signs that she misses and mourns the absence of her correspondent. And in a brilliant love poem she presents herself as "Anemone" with the charge, "Pray gather me/. . . . Thy flower—forevermore!" (31). The poem which follows is a charge for him to gather his rosebuds (herself) before they wilt and die.

There are two more messages in this first fascicle. One mentions "A brief, but patient illness" (18) that she has just experienced, and the other complains that an absent male friend has not communicated with her recently: he is a "traitor" who should show "repentance" by writing to her soon (23).

It appears that he must have responded, for the first fascicle fits tongue in groove with the first Master letter, dated by handwriting at about the same time. If this first fascicle drew a puzzled response from him, then this first Master letter is her answer to it:

Dear Master
    I am ill, but grieving more that you are ill, I make my stronger hand work long eno' to tell you. I thought perhaps you were in Heaven, and when you spoke again, it seemed quite sweet, and wonderful, and surprised me so—I wish that you were well.
    I would that all I love, should be weak no more. The Violets are by my side, the Robin very near, and "Spring"—they say, Who is she—going by the door—
    Indeed it is God's house—and these are gates of Heaven, and to and fro, the angels go, with their sweet postillions—I wish that I were great, like Mr. Michael Angelo, and could paint for you. You ask me what my flowers said—then they were disobedient—I gave them messages. They said what the lips in the West, say, when the sun goes down, and so says the Dawn.
    Listen again, Master. I did not tell you that today had been the Sabbath Day.
    Each Sabbath on the Sea, makes me count the Sabbaths, till we meet on shore—and (will the) whether the hills will look as blue as the sailors say. I cannot talk any more (stay any longer) tonight (now), for this pain denies me.
    How strong when weak to recollect, and easy, quite, to love. Will you tell me, please to tell me, soon as you are well.[2]

He apparently offered "illness" as his excuse for not writing; Dickinson replies sympathetically, citing her own illness as she had in Poem 18.

In the second paragraph she senses that "Violets" and "the Robins" are now close by her; in Poem 32 "Violets" are among the flowers she has sent him, representing herself, and in Poem 23 "Robin" is one of the names of her missing friend. In the third paragraph she responds to his query about what her "flowers" said. She has in her first fascicle identified her flowers as both her poems and her self, and her correspondent may well have been amazed at what seemed to be such lavish self-offerings. At this point, we may judge him a dull reader; these are clearly love-offerings, offerings of herself, definitions of their relationship as Dickinson sees it. Toward the end of the Master letter, Dickinson repeats in prose what she has already said in poems, that her desire for perfect union with others will only be fulfilled after death. The theme will grow.

Finally, another element of dialogue begins in this letter: "I wish that I were great." He must have responded later, and generously, to this sentiment, since a later poem begins, "You said that I 'was Great'—one Day" (738), and she will allude to this again in a letter to her pastor, the Reverend Dwight: "I have the friend who loves me—and thinks me larger than I am."[3]

As a final characteristic of this first fascicle, and of the poems of the first phase generally, we may note that Dickinson's poems express a complete harmony with nature, one that frequently moves on to ecstasy. The feeling will change dramatically in a later phase.

The remaining fascicles in this first phase, 2-8, expand and develop these subjects of the first fascicle. If Fascicle 1 is a bouquet of mixed flowers, then Fascicle 2 is an arrangement of roses; this flower dominates the fascicle almost exclusively. But if the imagery promises a certain unity, the poems do not so obviously fulfill it. What seems most characteristic of these early fascicles is the sense of Dickinson suddenly engaged, finding herself as a poet, finding her themes, her images, her voice, and her audience, displaying an enormous amount of wit and intelligence for a correspondent whom she wants to interest. Her *Liebestod* theme continues in several death-of-the-maiden poems, in one of which (58, in Fascicle 3) the maiden of the "loving bosom" has died of deprivation just an hour before "the joy" appeared on the scene.

Fascicle 2 is dominated by the sense of some new presence in her life, so momentous and overwhelming that it unmoors her certitudes, forces her to reassess meanings, sets her off on a dangerous journey through a gothic, horror-filled landscape:

> Through lane it lay—thro' bramble—
> Through clearing and thro' wood—

Banditti often passed us
Upon the lonely road.

The wolf came peering curious—
The owl looked puzzled down—
The serpent's satin figure
Glid stealthily along—

The tempests touched our garments—
The lightning's poinards gleamed—
Fierce from the Crag above us
The hungry Vulture screamed—

The satyrs fingers beckoned—
The valley murmured "Come"—
These were the mates—
This was the road
These children fluttered home. [9]

She is stepping out into dangerous ground here. The fascicle opens
with the fear that she may be forgotten (8), and closes in the last two
poems as "bewildered," "puzzled," "troubled" (48), with the "Baffled"
sense of "Surely, such a country/I was never in!" (17). In 43, a middle
poem in the fascicle, Dickinson expresses a transition "from scene famil-
iar/To an untraversed spot." In a climactic position, as the third poem
from the end of Fascicle 2, the experience is described which generates
these considerations, which is the key to this dislocation of meanings and
values:

Heart! We will forget him!
You and I—tonight!
You may forget the warmth he gave—
I will forget the light!

When you have done, pray tell me
That I may straight begin!
Haste! lest while you're lagging
I remember him! [47]

In Fascicle 3 we seem moved on a month or so in time, to celebrate the
turning of the year, a year of "wondrous" significance to the speaker, in
which she has sensed "A Difference" and accepted her title as "Daisy"
(93). Poem 96 contains "Daisies" and "My Master," the two figures
present in the Master letters. Dickinson's famous Royal imagery begins to
come into prominence in this fascicle. The maiden who dies with love
unfulfilled is "king" in 58, and "You, and I" are recognized as nobility at
the *pompe funèbre* surrounding their funerals (98). Love and death con-

tinue to be associated (92, 88, 50, 51, and 53). The famous poem appears here, "I never lost as much but twice," in which she records two losses by death and now a third loss (49). A suspicion also enters this fascicle that she is somehow out of synchronization with nature: she picks another "flower," but now with a sense that she has wrenched it from its natural setting to make it serve as emblem for her secret love (91). A few poems later she sends her bouquets to "Captives" suggesting freedom to them (95). An ominous poem in this fascicle introduces the serpent into her garden; she is close to her treasure, and fears that "Did but a snake bisect the brake/My life had forfeit been" (11).

Fascicle 4 also seems a fairly unified gathering. Most of the poems exploit one technique, the use of nature as analogue for human emotions, and it seems as if Dickinson is at least partly testing the possibilities here of arranging the fascicles by subject. The sense of time is late winter to early spring, anticipating the return of life and especially of the flowers. Poem 140 inventories the coming of spring and ends with the pronouncement that it answers Nicodemus's question, How shall a man be born again? Several other poems also press on from simple celebration of nature to more inward and spiritual concerns. Flowers are needed to define "extasy," to show "a system of aesthetics/Far superior to mine," in 137. As a brook sustains the life around it, so each person needs an inner "brook of life"; though the brook overflows with plenty in the March thaws, it may dry up in August (136). Here also, expressed again in nature analogues, is the first of her great poems on deprivation as the necessary teacher of the meaning of fulfillment: "Water, is taught by thirst . . ." (135).

There are three poems toward the end of this fascicle which break this unity. Poem 85 is associated with the Master poems and letters:

> "They have not chosen me," he said,
> "But I have chosen them!"
> Brave—Broken hearted statement—
> Uttered in Bethleem!
>
> *I* could not have told it,
> But since *Jesus dared*—
> Sovreign! Know a Daisy
> Thy dishonor shared! [85]

The figures of Dickinson's narrative are in place here, the "Sovreign" and his "Daisy." But the "dishonor" the Sovreign has suffered is unexplained, surely another clue that we as general readers intrude upon a private correspondence not intended for our eyes. A note is also introduced here that Dickinson will bring to full orchestration later in these fascicles, that the life of Jesus will furnish multiple analogues for understanding their experience.

The other two poems turn to investigate the life and death of the obscure housewife: her nobility is totally unrecognized until she dies (144); she ends as a small figure in a rocking chair whose death no one notices, whose life was concerned with "Busy needles, and spools of thread—/And trudging feet from school" (146). This housewife is a stereotype which, for some reason, Dickinson needs to look at closely as she finds her own way. In a letter Dickinson once mentions housework to her friend Mrs. Holland and exclaims: "I prefer pestilence."[4]

Fascicle 5 contains one of Dickinson's most famous poems, "Success is counted sweetest" (67), with its theme of agony and deprivation. The fascicle shows some continuity with the previous fascicles but little unity in itself. Afterlife and the condition of the dead continue to be topics for exploration in ten of the twenty-five poems. A "summer's Day" and its "extasy" are explored in 122, but with no sense that it is the "Day at Summer's full" (322) which will stand as the major marriage poem in Phase Two.

Significant for the plot of the fascicles are suggestions of a personal conflict, with ethical dimensions, now entering the poet's life. Poem 116 explores the sense of God's claims infringing upon her own desires for the first time; but she lightly ends the poem with the intention of taking God to court over the matter.

The fascicle ends with two poems that relate to Dickinson's developing relationship with the Master. In Poem 124 "Daisy" prostrates herself, on an August day, at the feet of her "Immortal Alps," addressed as "Sir." And the final poem (125) senses that the pattern of her life is now fixed: she will have to pay years of sorrow for "each extatic instant." However the experience will develop, these fascicles show that its initial onset opened the gates of poetic inspiration for her and that she began producing at an extraordinarily high level both of quantity and of quality.

Copies of three of these poems in Fascicle 5 were among the fifty-two poems which Dickinson is known to have sent to her friend Samuel Bowles. Two of the poems (114 and 120) puzzle over the meaning of death and the possibilities of immortality; the third (84) is a graceful compliment to Mrs. Bowles, Dickinson's lifelong friend and correspondent. No personal poems or Master poems were sent. Both what Dickinson chose to send Bowles and what she chose not to send him decrease the likelihood that Bowles was the center of her amorous imaginings, as several critics and biographers have conjectured.

With Fascicle 7 the first phase comes to a dramatic climax. Poem 103 is a plea to her silent correspondent: "I have a King, who does not speak." It is quite believable that he may have desired to cool down a relationship that had already brought him six emotionally demanding packages of poetry and an emotionally heated Master letter. In this poem he is characterized as the ruler of her moods: she is ecstatic if she dreams of him, utterly unhappy if she does not.

Poem 102 accepts the nickname "Daisy," offers herself to him, and chides him bitterly for his coolness:

> Great Caesar! Condescend
> The Daisy, to receive,
> Gathered by Cato's Daughter
> With your majestic leave! [102]

The speaker here is Porcia, daughter of Cato Uticensis, celebrated in Addison's *Cato* as the virtuous opponent of the tyrannical Caesar; she is also the wife of Brutus, equally famous opponent to Caesar's tyranny in Shakespeare's *Julius Caesar*. Dickinson is also "Cato's Daughter," daughter of the Hon. Edward Dickinson, who had served in Congress as a representative from Massachusetts and whose name had been put forward for governor of his state. Dickinson's plea to her correspondent to "Condescend" to accept the gift of "Daisy" is thus one of acid hostility, the fury of a woman who feels scorned, the rage which will soften to piteous lament for her rejection in the second of the Master letters.

At other points in the fascicle she assumes a whining child's voice. She is the "little Pilgrim" in 101, who prays to a "Papa above" in 61, and sees April as an argument for resurrection reduced to the level of a child's understanding, at the end of 65.

There seem to be other signs of regression here. Many of the poems are now rhymed, skillfully to be sure, but with the effect of weakening Dickinson's usually taut lines of poetry. There is regression also to a dreamlike state in several poems. She retreats to dreams in the face of unanswerable questions (103); she is confused, "in so dense a Fuzz" that she assumes roles that do not fit her; the fantasy of herself as a "little boat/That toddled down the bay" ends in italicized shock: "My little craft was *lost*!" (107).

All is not well here and the causes of disorder also appear in this fascicle, in feelings of guilt and hostility. Poem 103 ends with the sense that her will goes contrary to God's; therefore he is inaccessible, her certitudes shaken, her questions unanswered. Poem 106 includes her particular persona, the Daisy, who wants to sit at the feet of "Sir," but he rejects her; in the world of the fascicles it is a Master poem and Daisy imagines his devastating accusation: "Wherefore—Marauder—art thou here?" Her demands have become enormous, as she claims "The peace—the flight—the Amethyst—/Night's possibility!" in his presence. Sandra Gilbert and Susan Gubar read this poem as Dickinson's confession of "the depth of her own sexual need for a fiery Master/Lover."[5]

There are death poems in this fascicle also, as there have been throughout the first phase, as if to solicit the Master's pity or threaten him with her own dissolution. The earlier ease with which she assumed resurrection and life after death is now disturbed: she is not sure that there is such a "Morning" and doesn't know where it lies (101).

This fascicle of diverse voices and energies under great pressure is aptly introduced by a poem on Jacob wrestling with an Angel, "a little East of Jordan" (59). Clearly, all is not well in Eden.

Fascicle 8 concludes this first phase with cries of pain and anguish. Some of Dickinson's finest phrases are here: "A *Wounded* Deer—leaps highest/. . . . Mirth is the Mail of Anguish" (165); "To learn the Transport by the Pain—/. . . . This is the Sovereign Anguish" (167). She would bribe an unidentified "Them," importune them until they finally gave her what she wanted and needed (179). There is a poem about the volcano within which bears "appalling Ordnance . . . . smouldering anguish" (175). And there is a poem that expresses the desire—as if she were playing the maddened and impassioned Medea—for the magic potion that would instill some incurable pain in another (177).

The fascicle ends with an allegory about what she wants: an Arctic flower finds itself suddenly transported "To continents of summer—/To firmaments of sun." The point she would make to her correspondent?— "Why nothing,/Only, your inference therefrom!" (180).

Her counselor-correspondent could hardly turn a deaf ear to such eloquent pleas, could hardly avoid the "inference" she suggested.

The first phase of Dickinson's narrative, represented by the poems of these first eight fascicles, is fairly easy to characterize. The relationship seems mainly to have been carried on by correspondence, but not by enough correspondence on his part, according to Dickinson's complaints. One of the aspects of the relationship was that of counselor to counselee. On Dickinson's part the relationship was characterized by great need for continuing reassurances of his concern and help. Some of her solicitations for attention involved the brilliant displays of wit and intelligence in the poems themselves, the sharing of her mental wealth with a well educated man who was prominent in one of the learned professions and to whom an appeal could best be made with religious reflections; others involved outright pleas, threats of her own possible death, the whinings of a small child, the mildly flirtatious advertisements of the early love poems. It is undeniable that among her poems are many whose subjects seem chosen precisely for their interest to a clergyman.

Finally, the energies of the fascicles, the rapid swings of mood, especially toward the end of this phase, would seem to demand some attention, some response, from a careful and sympathetic correspondent who was fortunate enough to be the beneficiary of these fascicles. With such power she wooed him. And, it appears, successfully.

Phase Two: Fascicles 9-13

A new phase in the narrative begins dramatically with Fascicle 9. For the first time Dickinson announces "I'm 'wife'—I've finished that—/That other state/. . . . I'm 'Wife'! Stop there!" (199). This poem, written "about 1860," memorializes a major change in the way Dickinson identifies herself in the fascicles. Exclamation points seem to multiply during this phase, as she exclaims that nothing will "Rearrange a 'Wife's' affection!" (1737, in Fascicle 11). The phase comes to a climax in Fascicle 13 with the central marriage poem, the celebration of the "Day at Summer's full" when the lovers exchanged marriage vows and crucifixes, parted definitively, though with the anticipation of reunion in heaven, and accepted the road to Calvary in this life as justification for their anomalous relationship (322).

Where there is every indication in the first phase that the relationship was carried out entirely by mail, here the indications begin of a first visit from the lover to Amherst, of several meetings there which are recalled for him and reflected upon—not only in Phase Two but throughout the rest of Dickinson's poetic career. It is here that we begin to get "incidents" in her poems, narratives that can be described and tracked through the remaining fascicles.

The only documentation for any sudden new irruption into Dickinson's life at this point, the only known event that can account for the extraordinary change in the narrative, is the visit of Charles Wadsworth to Amherst, apparently his first, in the spring of 1860.

This second phase contains at least a dozen poems which describe actual meetings between the lovers. The intensity of their relationship is vividly narrated in the following poem, where Dickinson analyzes their shifting roles in one emotion-laden evening:

> He was weak, and I was strong—then—
> So He let me lead him in—
> I was weak, and He was strong then—
> So I let him lead me—Home.
>
> 'Twas'nt far—the door was near—
> 'Twas'nt dark—for He went—too—
> 'Twas'nt loud, for He said nought—
> That was all I cared to know.
>
> Day knocked—and we must part—
> Neither—was strongest—now—

He strove—and I strove—too—
We did'nt do it—tho'! [190]

The narrative contains many circumstantial details which would be recognized instantly by her intended correspondent, though we later readers
remain as complete outsiders to the actual event. In a long emotional
conversation she takes the lead initially and then allows him to take the
lead. The conversation lasts all night: they walk home in the dark and
arrive at her house only as "Day knocked." The temptation they avoid is a
sexual one, as indicated by the relief breathed in the last line. They avoid
the temptation only because one is strong when the other's weakness
would persuade them to succumb.

Poem 286 seems to record the same event, in a more abstract way. The
first eight lines read:

That after Horror—that 'twas *us*
That passed the mouldering Pier—
Just as the Granite Crumb let go—
Our Savior, by a Hair—

A second more, had dropped too deep
For Fisherman to plumb—
The very profile of the Thought
Puts Recollection numb—

The Savior's escape from "the Granite Crumb" dates their experience to
coincide with the Easter season (Easter was on April 8, in 1860, close to
the assumed time of Wadsworth's first visit). And the lines express the
lovers' own escape from a moral "Horror" too deep even for Jesus himself
to rescue them from.

And still another poem, in a later fascicle, recalls this night-long
conversation. It celebrates the Victors over temptation, those who wear
white in the Book of Revelation. Any defeat they may have known during
earthly life is "Remembered, as the Mile/Our panting Ancle barely
passed—/When Night devoured the Road—/And we—stood whispering in
the House—/And all we said—was 'Saved'!" (325). "Night" and the
"House," the sense of a lucky escape, together with the exclamation point
at the end, put us in the same narrative as Poem 190.

There must have been more than one recent meeting. At least another
incident, recalled in 203, seems to require an entirely different scenario:

He forgot—and I—remembered—
'Twas an everyday affair—
Long ago as Christ and Peter—
"Warmed them" at the "Temple fire".

> "Thou wert with him"—quoth "the Damsel"?
> "No"—said Peter, 'twas'nt me—
> Jesus merely "looked" at Peter—
> Could I do aught else—to Thee? [203]

Once again there is not enough in the poem for the outside reader to reconstruct the scene satisfactorily; it seems meant for the eyes only of the insider who participated in the event with her and who is addressed in the poem as "Thee." The recoverable aspects of the incident seem to be along these lines: some woman apparently inquired about their relationship; he was unwilling to say in public what he had professed in private, "denied" her as Peter had denied Christ; Dickinson felt betrayed and rejected in the exchange.

Still another version of one of their meetings is narrated in 274:

> The only Ghost I ever saw
> Was dressed in Mechlin—so—
> He had no sandal on his foot—
> And stepped like flakes of snow—
>
> His Mien, was soundless, like the Bird—
> But rapid—like the Roe—
> His fashions, quaint, Mosaic—
> Or haply, Mistletoe—
>
> His conversation—seldom—
> His laughter, like the Breeze
> That dies away in Dimples
> Among the pensive Trees—
>
> Our interview—was transient—
> Of me, himself was shy—
> And God forbid I look behind—
> Since that appalling Day! [274]

The "Ghost" in this poem has most usually been interpreted as Death; in the context of the fascicles the figure is worth a closer look. If one begins explication of the poem from its last words, the subject of the poem becomes clear: the only momentous Day recorded in Dickinson's poetry so far—and from its results it could well be called "appalling"—was the day of her anomalous marriage. The "interview" indeed "was transient." The "Ghost" then is a real human being: he is dressed in "Mechlin," a lace used for liturgical garbs, as a trim for fine shirts, or as a neck cloth. The poem, then, is a portrait of the husband; it is Dickinson's attempt to define the aura of mystery or even of unreality now, surrounding the central event in her poems. The garb could be that of a clergyman, who is described as "Mosaic"—like Moses—in his fashions.

Three other poems in this phase are expressly based on this narrative.
Poem 246 imagines the impossible sequel to their marriage:

> Forever at His side to walk—
> The smaller of the two!
> Brain of His Brain—
> Blood of His Blood—
> Two lives—One Being—now—
>
> Forever of His fate to taste—
> If grief—the largest part—
> If joy—to put my piece away
> For the beloved Heart—
>
> All life—to know each other—
> Whom we can never learn—
> And bye and bye—a Change—
> Called Heaven—
> Rapt Neighborhoods of Men—
> Just finding out—what puzzled us—
> Without the lexicon! [246]

The first stanza is filled with references to the Christian marriage ceremony. The rest of the poem recounts the ideal of mutual sharing and
sacrifice, and the life of joy which is transformed into still finer joy for the
Christian couple in Heaven.

Poem 273 contains another version of this marriage ideal:

> He put the Belt around my life—
> I heard the Buckle snap—
> And turned away, imperial,
> My Lifetime folding up—
> Deliberate, as a Duke would do
> A Kingdom's Title Deed—
> Henceforth, a Dedicated sort—
> A Member of the Cloud.

Marriage as the "Belt," Dickinson seems to be saying, puts limitations on
one's life, but it also gives form and adornment to that life. As the poem
continues, the wife "declines" other invitations because of her exclusive
relationship with the husband.

Every marriage has its anniversaries, and as the final poem in this
sequence, 296 celebrates the first anniversary of Dickinson's anomalous
marriage, with specific autobiographical details:

> One Year ago—jots what?
> God—spell the word! I—cant—

Was't Grace? Not that—
Was't Glory? That—will do—
Spell slower—Glory—

Such Anniversary shall be—
Sometimes—not often—in Eternity—
When farther Parted, than the Common Wo—
Look—feed upon each other's faces—so—
In doubtful meal, if it be possible
Their Banquet's real—

I tasted—careless—then—
I did not know the Wine
Came once a World—Did you?
Oh, had you told me so—
This Thirst would blister—easier—now—
You said it hurt you—most—
Mine—was an Acorn's Breast—
And could not know how fondness grew
In Shaggier Vest—
Perhaps—I could'nt—
But, had you looked in—
A Giant—eye to eye with you, had been—
No Acorn—then—

So—Twelve months ago—
We breathed—
Then dropped the Air—
Which bore it best?
Was this—the patientest—
Because it was a Child, you know—
And could not value—Air?

If to be "Elder"—mean most pain—
I'm old enough, today, I'm certain—then—
As old as thee—how soon?
One—Birthday more—or Ten?
Let me—choose!
Ah, Sir, None!

The poem is a long one for Dickinson, but tightly reasoned, or rather from the tone we might say tightly argued, with a strong sense of the beloved as only audience for the poem and with her unique colloquial voice fully developed. The landmark event in her life is fully accepted as being in the past, datable as one year ago in this anniversary poem. She struggles for definition of the event in the first stanza: "Glory" is even more satisfactory a term than "Grace." The anniversary also looks forward, in the second stanza, to their momentous reunion in heaven, the only occasion on which they will be able to renew their intimacies. The third stanza, the middle one and the longest, introduces the beloved directly, as "You" to whom the argument and the protestations of the poem are made. The protest is a double one: that she was unaware, while the event was taking place, that it "Came once" only, and that she suffered from their separation fully as much as he.

Biographers since George F. Whicher have speculated that Dickinson's love affair, if she had one, was entirely in her mind, that the proper Reverend Wadsworth was unaware of the passion he had aroused and would have rejected with shocked proprieties any sexual overtures from his counselee. The present poem shows that, at least in the versions of their relationship which she recorded in the fascicles, both were fully aware of their mutual involvement and that the situation was fully discussed. More evidence of this mutual recognition will appear later. We might also note that Whicher, author of the first major biography of Emily Dickinson, suspected more than he felt he could divulge to the general reader in 1938; the only clergyman with whom he compared Wadsworth was Henry Ward Beecher, and the reader is left to recall if he can that the most sensational episode in Beecher's life was his trial for adultery with a member of his congregation.[6]

In addition to these marriage poems, this second phase is characterized by more than twenty love poems, of a new intensity and heightened urgency. Poem 162 exclaims, "My River runs to Thee–/Blue Sea–Wilt welcome me?/. . . . *Say* Sea–take me?"

Similar abandonment and commitment are expressed in 202, which progresses from her vase full of "Dew" to her eye still fuller, to the heart fullest of all "For you!" A quieter view of the steady friendship of marriage is developed in 205, where Dickinson would not "dare to leave my friend" lest at death he need her and miss her. But the intensity returns with the brief exclamation of 209:

> With thee, in the Desert–
> With thee in the thirst–
> With thee in the Tamarind wood–
> Leopard breathes–at last!

The exotic "Tamarind wood" seems an Edenic setting (it is the place where the poet dreams in the last line of Poe's "Sonnet–To Science") and for Dickinson it is the place where the fierce energies of the Leopard are finally freed, but only "With thee."

But surely one of her most appealing love poems, and one that has never been recognized as such, is 276:

> Many a phrase has the English language–
> I have heard but one–

> Low as the laughter of the Cricket,
> Loud, as the Thunder's Tongue—
>
> Murmuring, like old Caspian Choirs,
> When the Tide's a' lull—
> Saying itself in new inflection—
> Like a Whippowil—
>
> Breaking in bright Orthography
> On my simple sleep—
> Thundering it's Prospective—
> Till I stir, and weep—
>
> Not for the Sorrow, done me—
> But the push of Joy—
> Say it again, Saxon!
> Hush—Only to me!

The poem is a riddle and the clues are these: it is a phrase that is spoken low but sounds loud; it is an old phrase but sounds always new; it intrudes even upon one's dreams; it offers "Thundering" prospects; it stirs but also causes tears; even though it causes "Sorrow" the speaker would hear it again, spoken privately, for the "push of Joy" it offers. I can think of only one answer to the riddle, the phrase "I love you"; it had been spoken to Dickinson, as she says twice in the poem (lines 2 and 15), presumably by the beloved whose presence is pervasive in the fascicles. And once again her poems record that *he* is the equally conscious agent in their relationship.

Among these love poems one discerns a new eroticism. In fact, one can be more precise and point to Fascicle 10 for the poems that first indicate a major erotic awakening in the poet, not seen before. In 208 she is *voyeur* to a courtship scene where the maiden's cheek blushes red and "Her Boddice rose and fell"; the young man in the scene experiences similar excitement, which is resolved only when the two embrace. A linked perception involving the erotic function of clothes to simultaneously hide and highlight the breast has already been noted, in 210, in the line "As laces just reveal the surge."

Three love poems in this fascicle pointedly describe the awakening of an erotic sensibility. In an Eden setting, "Lips unused to Thee—/Bashful—sip thy Jessamines"—just as the fainting bee, entering the flower, "is lost in Balms" (211). More remarkable still, perhaps, for its compact statement of entering and merging, is the following complete poem:

> Least Rivers—docile to some sea.
> My Caspian—thee—   [212]

The reader finds a new sensibility in this second phase, the sense of release into a new area of experience. This new eroticism is echoed in other poems, later in this second phase, notably in the breathless "Wild Nights—Wild Nights!/Were I with thee" (249).

Many of these love poems in phase two reflect the conditions set at the end of the central marriage poem, 322—the definitive parting of the lovers immediately after their marriage, the long wait until reunion in eternity. But it appears that Dickinson had not anticipated that this separation might involve the absence of all written communication as well.

Poem 217 is one of Dickinson's few prayers, in which she addresses God directly. She brings Him "the departed Heart/I had not strength to hold." It was "The Heart I cherished in my own." But such religious resignation is not visible in other poems. In poem after poem she importunes the absent beloved for his communications, for his "smile" (223). She sends him all she has, her poems, in 224. She fears "My Sovereign is offended" since he doesn't write, in 235. In the absence of any communication from him she breaks into frantic italics:

> If *He dissolve*—then—there is *nothing—more—*
> *Eclipse*—at *Midnight*—
> It was *dark—before—*
>
> *Sunset*—at *Easter*—
> *Blindness*—on the *Dawn*—
> *Faint* Star of Bethlehem—
> *Gone down!*
>
> *Would* but some *God—inform* Him—
> Or it be *too late!*
> Say—that the pulse *just lisps*—
> The *Chariots wait*—
>
> Say—that a *little life*—for *His*—
> Is *leaking—red*—
> *His little Spaniel*—tell Him!
> *Will He heed?* [236]

In 240 the moon and the star are inaccessible to her, a 'firmament" away, but "There is one—farther than you—/He—is more than a firmament—from Me—/So I can never go!" In 245 he is the Jewel she once held in her fingers, which disappeared while she slept. In exuberant extravagance she pounces on the theme of "What would I give to see his face," and offers her life, birds, flowers—all of her poems and treasures—for "*One hour*—of her Sovereign's face" (247). And in similar extravagance she laments that "the sole ear I cared to charm—/Passive—as Granite—laps My

Music" (261). Truly these poems are private communications, for one reader only, lamenting his absence, insisting on her need to communicate with him.

Dickinson must have felt that the cold silence after her lover left was a striking contrast to his ardor when they had struck their marriage agreement. In a fierce poem she argues that if she is "lost" because of their sin, then so is he—he will feel what she feels when "the Savior's face" turns away from him as he has turned away from her (256). She would have been a "Light House spark" to him in his darkness, had he not extinguished that light (259).

But there are moments when she can feel she has gotten over the rejection that followed so swiftly upon her acceptance. In a poem filled with concrete details about their meetings she writes:

> I got so I could hear his name—
> Without—Tremendous gain—
> That Stop-sensation—on my Soul—
> And Thunder—in the Room—
>
> I got so I could walk across
> That Angle in the floor,
> Where he turned so, and I turned—how—
> And all our Sinew tore—
>
> I got so I could stir the Box—
> In which his letters grew
> Without that forcing, in my breath—
> As Staples—driven through—
>
> [293, lines 1-12]

But still later she has decided not to give up her efforts at least to maintain the connection; and she will hope that her persistent knocking will finally draw an answer from him:

> Just so—Christ—raps—
> He—does'nt weary—
> First at the Knocker—
> And then—at the Bell—
> Then—on Divinest Tiptoe standing—
> Might he but spy the hiding soul?
> When he—retires—
> Chilled—or weary—
> It will be ample time for me—
> Patient—upon the steps—until then—
> Heart—I am knocking low
> At thee! [317]

Also in phase two are more details which suggest that the beloved to whom Dickinson writes is a clergyman. Many poems throughout the fascicles embody religious subjects or religious imagery, as if for their special appeal to him. In 324 she opposes her own private religion with Nature to those who "keep the Sabbath in Surplice"—a gibe her recipient would feel especially, since the garb is worn only by the clergy. In 274, as we have already seen, the first physical description that we have of her lover is his "Mosaic" appearance, ornamented in formal "Mechlin" garb rather than the sparer traditional religious costume: "He had no sandal on his foot."

Perhaps even more striking are what seem to be Dickinson's direct responses to his sermonizing. In 234 she addresses "You" directly and can quote passages from his sermon; she follows its reasoning but abandons it as inadequate at the end:

> You're right—"the way *is* narrow"—
> And "difficult the Gate"—
> And "few there be"—Correct again—
> That "enter in—thereat"—
>
> *'Tis* Costly—So are *purples*!
> 'Tis just the price of *Breath*—
> With but the "Discount" of the *Grave*—
> Termed by the *Brokers*—*"Death"*!
>
> And after *that*—there's Heaven—
> The *Good* Man's—*"Dividend"*—
> And *Bad* Men—"go to Jail"—
> I guess—

Apparently, from the diction, his sermonizing had suggested a financial analogy for salvation, which leaves her unconvinced.

Poem 215 presents another response to his sermonizing. She addresses him, "You are sure there's such a person/As 'a Father'—in the sky." She can repeat his description of heaven, based on images from the Book of Revelations, and still wonder if that Eden would be "lonesome/As New England used to be." In another poem she presents a sermon development of her own, on one of the theological virtues, in " 'Hope' is the thing with feathers" (254).

If these letter-poems furnish data for biography, as any letters do, then we must wonder what Dickinson is urging her lover to do in such poems as 292: "If your Nerve, deny you—/Go above your Nerve. . . ." Is she urging him to take the adventurous step of divorcing his wife to marry her, with the necessary loss of his professional standing which that would involve? At least that is the most obvious reading, in the context of the fascicles, of one of Dickinson's most famous poems:

> I'm Nobody! Who are you?
> Are you—Nobody—Too?
> Then there's a pair of us?
> Don't tell! they'd advertise—you know!
>
> How dreary—to be—Somebody!
> How public—like a Frog—
> To tell one's name—the livelong June—
> To an admiring Bog! [288]

Dickinson would be relying on Wadsworth's celebrated sense of humor (described approvingly by no less a humorist than Mark Twain[7]) to take in good spirits the unflattering image of himself as preacher.

One may be surprised at how specific this public and well known poem becomes in the fascicles. But this reading is supported by at least two other fascicle poems. In 366 (in Fascicle 20), addressed to "You, Sir" and describing the married life they might have enjoyed together, she chides him with a similar invitation to abandon his career and his search for public acclaim: "The Dust, will vex your Fame." And in 715 (in Fascicle 23), she reminds him of the moment of death when "Honors—taste dry." Dickinson invites her ambitious lover to be content to be "Nobody" with her. But Wadsworth was commanding the princely salaries of $7,000 and $8,000 during these years, honors of another kind which would be difficult to give up.

It is in this second phase that Dickinson begins to write her martyr poems, as if both subject and sources would appeal to a clergyman correspondent. In 260 she bids him "read—Sweet—how others—strove—/Till we—are stouter—/What they—renounced—/Till we—are less afraid." She must be proposing the eleventh chapter of Hebrews or the seventh chapter of Revelations—both favorite sermon sources—or the great Protestant classic, Foxe's *Book of Martyrs*. She seems herself to have been reading one of these sources and to have taken on the martyr's stance in the poem which begins "Unto like Story—Trouble has enticed me—/How Kinsmen fell—/Brothers and Sisters—who preferred the Glory—/And their young will/Bent to the Scaffold, or in Dungeons—chanted" (295). And poem 325 is about "we" who suffered Anguish and Tribulation but not Surrender or Defeat, and who now are clothed in white like the martyrs in Revelations.

It is in this phase also that we receive more information about the beloved. If he was a clergyman, he was also a married clergyman. At least this is the point which has never been noticed in poem 284:

The Drop, that wrestles in the Sea—
Forgets her own locality—
As I—toward Thee—

She knows herself an incense small—
Yet *small*—she sighs—if *All*—is *All*—
How *larger*—be?

The Ocean—smiles—at her Conceit—
But *she*, forgetting amphitrite—
Pleads—"Me"?

The poem was discussed in chapter 1, for its focus on "Amphitrite," the wife of "Ocean," and is here recalled for its proper place in the narrative sequence.

The relationship between Dickinson and the recipient of these poems, then, was finally an adulterous one, whatever the level of physical involvement or abstention. And there are several poems in this second phase where a new subject is introduced and explored for the first time, that of a crippling sense of guilt. Poem 237 also seems to quote from his sermonizing on the word "forgiven," based on a text from the Sermon on the Mount:

I think just how my shape will rise—
When I shall be *"forgiven"*—
Till Hair—and Eyes—and timid Head—
Are *out of sight*—in Heaven—

I think just how my lips will weigh—
With shapeless—quivering—prayer—
That you—*so late*—*"Consider"* me—
The *"Sparrow"* of your Care—

I mind me that of Anguish—sent—
Some drifts were moved away—
Before my simple bosom—broke—
And why not *this*—if *they*?

And so I con that thing—*"forgiven"*—
Until—delirious—borne—
By my long bright—and *longer*—*trust*—
I *drop* my Heart—*unshriven*!

From the italics and quotation marks Dickinson would seem to be quoting from her correspondent's sermon. The curious turn at the end is her response to it. Though she works her way through a presentation of how those who are "forgiven" will be received into heaven, she ends the poem by choosing to be *"unshriven."* She recognizes her guilt but is not yet ready for repentance.

Another acknowledgement of her guilty heart is in the light poem which presents the picture of the forbidden strawberries on the other side of the fence, which ends with the "guess" that even God would go after them "if He could!" (251). The guilt is lightly dismissed in 267 as well, where the question "Did we disobey Him?" is answered "Just one time!" and the second stanza resolves the problem of guilt by the assertion that we would still love God if *he* erred similarly. But the guilt at other moments is very real and weighs heavily, as in the poem we have already seen, "If I'm lost" (256), with the concluding observation that he shares in her reprobation.

A new kind of suffering enters this second phase as well, intimately tied to Dickinson's anomalous marriage. She settles on the word "anguish" in this phase: twice in 193, where "the drop of Anguish/ . . . scalds me now"; once in 264, where no part of her being is unaffected by it. The cause of this anguish is expressed in the opening of poem 181, "I lost a World—the other day," which ends with a plea to the beloved "Oh find it—Sir—for me!" The poem has been cited as an example of Dickinson's "unassigned symbolism . . . which defies precise interpretation,"[8] but within the fascicle world the imagery is sharply defined: the poem is a love poem, addressed to the same "Sir" as the others are, recalling the Day of her marriage, and lamenting her loneliness without him.

A poem midway through this phase presents still another aspect of the new relationship recorded in Fascicles 9 to 13. It is a poem in which the addressee seems remarkably present, in which the energies of the poet are most strongly engaged. *En route* through the poem we are faced with a much more aggressive lover than conjectures about Wadsworth have allowed. In Dickinson's view he was warm-blooded and insistent, not at all the passive and probably unconscious object of a supposed mental fiction. He must have blackmailed her with a "doubt" about the reality of her love if she held back from physical intimacy with him. Her answer:

> Doubt Me! My Dim Companion!
> Why, God, would be content
> With but a fraction of the Life—
> Poured thee, without a stint—
> The whole of me—forever—
> What more the Woman can,
> Say quick, that I may dower thee
> With last Delight I own!
>
> It cannot be my Spirit—
> For that was thine, before—
> I ceded all of Dust I knew—
> What Opulence the more
> Had I—a freckled Maiden,

Whose farthest of Degree,
Was—that she might—
Some distant Heaven,
Dwell timidly, with thee!

Sift her, from Brow to Barefoot!
Strain till your last Surmise—
Drop, like a Tapestry, away,
Before the Fire's Eyes—
Winnow her finest fondness—
But hallow just the snow
Intact, in Everlasting flake—
Oh, Caviler, for you! [275]

The "Caviler" in the last line is one who would pick a minute point of the total argument to quarrel with. The quibble, from Dickinson's point of view, is her chastity. With total abandonment she offers everything else—still withholding her sexual offering in the last three lines, but promising it in some remote "Everlasting."

Phase Three: Fascicles 13-19

Some overlapping occurs between two phases here. Fascicle 13 contains the single most rich and startling description of Dickinson's marriage experience (322) and thus seems to cap the new sense of wifehood which characterizes the second phase. But that same fascicle also contains Dickinson's clarifications of several new insights into her situation, insights which will be worked out in the next half-dozen fascicles. She is writing rapidly in these poems of 1861-62; urged by the teeming thoughts about her upsetting experience, her poetic output is approaching the average of a poem a day.

Among the new elements in this phase is a crippling sense of her aloneness, the result of the separation that took place immediately after their private marriage ceremony: "So—faces on two Decks—look back/ Bound to opposing Lands—" (322). As she analyzes the relationship and what is left of it she comes upon a new word and a new concept in this phase, "interdicted." Connected with this, many poems now begin to explore the sense that the "crucial experience" in her life has now passed and that she lives in its aftermath. There is as well, in this phase—quite crippling for the poet who writes such ecstatic nature poems—the feeling that because of her guilty relationship she is no longer in harmony with nature. The older harmony is gone.

As in all of the phases and all of the fascicles, there continue to be love poems and poems which reflect on their few intense meetings.

In this third phase Dickinson begins to concentrate on her aloneness after the painful separation of lovers, as if it is a new subject, a new realization of what will characterize her life for the foreseeable future. An early poem in the phase sets the subject:

> You see I cannot see—your lifetime—
> I must guess—
> How many times it ache for me—today—Confess—
> How many times for my far sake
> The brave eyes film—
> But I guess guessing hurts—
> Mine—get so dim!
>
> Too vague—the face—
> My own—so patient—covets—
> Too far—the strength—
> My timidness enfolds—
> Haunting the Heart—
> Like her translated faces—
> Teazing the want—
> It—only—can suffice! [253]

In the first stanza Dickinson assumes that her lover's longing and loneliness are equal to hers. The exercise is a painful one: imagining his face is "Teazing the want—/It—only—can suffice."

The exercise is also futile, and poem 259 piles up "it might have been's" to torment her for separation from her "friend." Surely she recalls this saddest of all sad phrases from John Greenleaf Whittier's famous poem "Maud Muller," in which a rustic beauty is embarrassed by her barefoot charm before the town-bred judge. They meet in the setting of flowers and meadows and she offers him a drink from her nearby spring. But the thought of their difference in social status affects both and prevents their marriage. The well known poem ends with much that would have attracted Dickinson's attention and suggested her borrowing of its most famous phrase:

> For of all sad words of tongue or pen,
> The saddest are these: "It might have been!"
>
> Ah, Well! for us all some sweet hope lies
> Deeply buried from human eyes;
>
> And, in the hereafter, angels may
> Roll the stone from its grave away!

The conditions of her marriage—the long separation until the ecstatic meeting after death—are developed more fully in 577, addressed to "Lover": "If I may have it, when it's dead,/I'll be contented. . . ./Think of it Lover! I and Thee/Permitted—face to face to be—/After a Life." The poem ends with a recollection of the conditions they had set themselves, in 322, that their marriage would only be "Justified—through Calvaries of Love"; according to the present poem they will, in heaven, be able to "look back for Play,/At those Old Times—in Calvary."

Poem 422 laments that "More Life—went out—when He went/Than Ordinary Breath." And the famous poem 299 begins, "Your Riches—taught me—Poverty/. . . . I esteemed All Poverty/For Life's Estate with you." Now she considers herself a "beggar" since he has gone away. She has been lucky to discover his "Gold—/Altho' I prove it, just in time/It's distance—to behold." In 272, to be absent from him is to be "removed from Air" and her life is a kind of death now.

The lonesome conditions of her marriage are recorded in 418; solace from her loneliness is found only in her hope for reunion:

> Not in this World to see his face—
> Sounds long—until I read the place
> Where this—is said to be
> But just the Primer—to a life—
> Unopened—rare—Upon the Shelf—
> Clasped yet—to Him—and me—
>   [lines 1-6]

Those who would see Dickinson's lover as God or Christ, and the love poems as those of a mystic, must run aground on such poems as this: in no theological system is the future unknown to the omniscient deity; but here the two lovers, the "Him" and the "me," view their future life as a "Primer" still "Unopened."

Poem 282 notices that men, like stars, are not fully "noted" until one of them disappears. But 350 charges the "Comrade" to look forward with her to "Eternity."

As this phase progresses one comes upon a famous, frequently anthologized poem which takes on a sudden new richness in the context of the fascicles, as a poem that precisely expresses the anguish of separation that followed their marriage, and the doubt that becomes crucial now regarding life after death:

> If you were coming in the Fall,
> I'd brush the Summer by
> With half a smile, and half a spurn,
> As Housewives do, a Fly.
>
> If I could see you in a year,
> I'd wind the months in balls—
> And put them each in separate Drawers,
> For fear the numbers fuse—

> If only Centuries, delayed,
> I'd count them on my Hand,
> Subtracting, till my fingers dropped
> Into Van Dieman's Land.
>
> If certain, when this life was out—
> That your's and mine, should be—
> I'd toss it yonder, like a Rind,
> And take Eternity—
>
> But, now, uncertain of the length
> Of this, that is between,
> It goads me, like the Goblin Bee—
> That will not state—it's sting. [511]

Poem 339 describes her life now of cultivating her complete fidelity to him even in his absence: "I tend my flowers for thee—/Bright Absentee!" In what seems to the modern reader like an exuberant display of her sexual wares to the beloved, she writes

> My Fuschzia's Coral Seams
> Rip—while the Sower—dreams—
>
> Geraniums—tint—and spot—
> Low Daisies—dot—
> My Cactus—splits her Beard
> To show her throat—
>
> Carnations—tip their spice—
> And Bees—pick up—
> A Hyacinth—I hid—
> Puts out a Ruffled Head—
> And odors fall
> From flasks—so small—
> You marvel how they held—
>
> Globe Roses—break their satin flake—
> Upon my Garden floor—
> Yet—thou—not there. . . .

In his absence, "Her Lord—away," she would prefer not to show herself so "gay." Assuming now the nickname that he gave her, and which she used in the second and third Master letters, she concludes: "I'll dwell in Calyx—Gray—/How modestly—alway—/Thy Daisy—/Draped for thee!"

Finally, in the last fascicle of this third phase, his absence is lamented in her now familiar figure of the Moon and its magnetic relationship to the Sea. They are far apart, yet the moon continues to attract. The poem ends: "Oh, Signor, Thine, the Amber Hand—/And mine—the distant

Sea—/Obedient to the least command/Thine eye impose on me—" (429).

The forbidden aspect of their relationship also begins to emerge for Dickinson's meditation in this phase. If he is the ocean to which her brook would run and merge, still she cannot forget the "Amphitrite" to whom he is married. Their relationship is basically adulterous, forbidden by society, religion, and their own code of morals. In 256 she laments the paradox: that she is "lost" now that she has just been "found."

In poem 239 Dickinson comes on one of the key words to describe their relationship, a word that would spring up naturally in a family of lawyers, "interdicted." Her "Heaven . . . Paradise" is for her "The interdicted Land." In 413 she feels the accusing eye of God wherever she goes, and knows she will even feel its force in heaven. In 240 she writes of "one" who is farther from her than the moon or a star: he is "firmaments" away—one of the biblical terms for heaven.

This new realization of the forbidden aspect of the most important relationship in her life comes to a climax late in this phase in one of her most famous poems.

> I envy Seas, whereon He rides—
> I envy Spokes of Wheels
> Of Chariots, that Him convey—
> I envy Crooked Hills
>
> That gaze upon His journey—
> How easy All can see
> What is forbidden utterly
> As Heaven—unto me!
>
> I envy Nests of Sparrows—
> That dot His distant Eaves—
> The wealthy Fly, upon His Pane—
> The happy—happy Leaves—
>
> That just abroad His Window
> Have Summer's leave to play—
> The Ear Rings of Pizarro
> Could not obtain for me—
>
> I envy Light—that wakes Him—
> And Bells—that boldly ring
> To tell Him it is Noon, abroad—
> Myself—be Noon to Him—
>
> Yet interdict—my Blossom—
> And abrogate—my Bee—
> Lest Noon in Everlasting Night—
> Drop Gabriel—and Me— [498]

To "interdict" another legal term is added, "abrogate." But the poem contains an especially interesting crux at the end. This figure "Gabriel" appears in five other poems, where he can satisfactorily be identified with the archangel who appears to Daniel in the Old Testament, to Mary in the Gospel of Luke. In 195 Dickinson presents as a riddle some human experience that is most like glory in heaven. The answer is marriage, and one of the features of the heavenly bestowal of glory is Gabriel's announcement of it. Poem 336 is another marriage poem in which the crown she receives in marriage is greater than any which Gabriel ever received. Poem 725 is likewise an assessment of their relationship: "Where Thou art—that—is Home." It ends: "Where Thou art not—is Wo—/Tho' Bands of Spices—row—/What Thou dost not—Despair—/Tho' Gabriel—praise me—Sir—." The spices and rowing recall the erotic Eden poems. The previous stanza had stated, "What Thou dost—is Delight," and so the parallel statement must lament the removal of erotic stimuli. Confirmation comes with the final line, where Gabriel's announcement to the Virgin Mary—praise though it was—served likewise to remove all possibilities of erotic fulfillment for her. Finally, two poems refer casually to Robins as "Gabriels": these plain songsters must be angels in disguise (1483 and 1570).

Two things may be noted. "Gabriel" appears most frequently in erotic settings associated with the marriage. And "Gabriel" as an archangel does not fit with any degree of Dickinson's usual exactitude in the poem under consideration, 498. Gabriel here is rather someone with whom she is closely associated in the possible damnation of their souls—hardly the angelic messenger of the Bible.

Identification of this figure comes instead from one of the most popular books of the time, *Evangeline*, by Henry Wadsworth Longfellow. Dickinson had read it, as she mentioned to her school friend Abiah Root in a letter of May 16, 1848.

A reader fresh from Dickinson's poetry will find many echoes in Longfellow's poem. Evangeline's beloved, from whom she is separated until the moment of death, is of course Gabriel. A clergyman has earlier promised her that "the long-wandering bride shall be given again to her bridegroom" in "the Eden of Louisiana." Their final meeting takes place, significantly, in Wadsworth's city, Philadelphia. When Evangeline finally reaches Philadelphia "her ear was pleased with the Thee and Thou of the Quakers," diction Dickinson uses with some consistency in her love poetry. There, in Philadelphia, "many years she lived as a Sister of Mercy," as a nun dressed in white. When she finally finds Gabriel, on his death bed, "then escaped from her lips a cry of . . . terrible anguish." "Anguish" was of course one of Dickinson's favorite words. Finally, after both die, "Side by side, in their modest graves, the lovers are sleeping," as they are imagined doing in several of Dickinson's poems. Longfellow's statement of his theme in the prologue to *Evangeline* could stand, in another idiom, for Dickinson's:

> Ye who believe in affection that hopes, and endures, and is
> patient,
> Ye who believe in the beauty and strength of woman's
> devotion,
> List to the mournful tradition. . . .

Dickinson had redone another recent Longfellow poem, "The Courtship of Miles Standish" (1858), in her own poem 357.

Dickinson had accepted the beloved's code name for her, "Daisy." The lovers would surely delight in the fact that the key to their private code name for him, "Gabriel," was something so public as the middle name of America's most famous living author.

In one of the most interesting articles ever written on Dickinson's poetry, David Porter clearly describes what he feels to be a major defining element in the total corpus of Dickinson's poetry. Porter is able to show convincingly that a large number of Dickinson's poems record her sense of "living in the aftermath," after some "crucial experience" in her life has already passed.[9] It is of special interest to us here that all of the poems which Porter cites appear after Fascicle 8. There are no poems defining her "crucial experience" before the marriage experience recorded in phase two.

But it is in the present phase three that these considerations of living in the aftermath of a crucial experience begin to become most obvious. In expressing mental and nervous exhaustion, in "I felt a Funeral, in my Brain" (280), Dickinson uses verbs in the past tense exclusively. It is only "*After* great pain" (italics added) that "a formal feeling comes" in the famous poem 341, as well as in the less famous 344, where a woman has finished her "road–through pain" and died for love. And in 349 Dickinson proclaims "I *had* the Glory–that will do–/An Honor, Thought can turn her to/When lesser Fames invite" (italics added).

The crucial experience, as well as the marriage, is connected with the often-noticed sense of status achieved in Dickinson's poetry. In 430 Dickinson begins, "It would never be Common–more–I said–/Difference–had begun." But the crucial moment of change is definitely in the past: the poem ends "But where my moment of Brocade–/My–drop–of India?"

In 506 this crucial experience is explicitly connected with her marriage, in an ecstatic love poem:

He touched me, so I live to know
That such a day, permitted so,
I groped upon his breast—
It was a boundless place to me
And silenced, as the awful sea
Puts minor streams to rest.

And now, I'm different from before,
As if I breathed superior air—
Or brushed a Royal Gown—
My feet, too, that had wandered so—
My Gipsy face—transfigured now—
To tenderer Renown—

Into this Port, if I might come,
Rebecca, to Jerusalem,
Would not so ravished turn—
Nor Persian, baffled at her shrine
Lift such a Crucifixal sign
To her imperial Sun.   [506]

Many of these themes come together in 348 and suggest a new theme, which begins to be prominent in this phase. She has now achieved a new status as "Queen of Calvary"—whether through the life-long Calvary of Love the lovers had accepted at the end of 322, or because of the new position of her husband as pastor of Calvary Church in San Francisco. But the experience that put her there is passed and she feels "bereaved." In shame, perhaps from guilt, she now dreads the approach of spring and all of the creatures that used to bring ecstasy. The Robin is "dreaded," she "dared not meet the Daffodils," she wishes the grass would grow tall and cover her from sight, the bees no longer had any word "for me. . . . The Queen of Calvary." This is sad alienation from nature, for our greatest nature poet.

Finally, Dickinson continues to send poems that record and reflect on their few meetings, as well as the love poems to the "Master" which characterize every fascicle. In 271, which her original editors entitled "Wedded," she reflects on the precise conditions of her unusual marriage: she has dropped her life "Into the mystic well—/Too plummetless—that it come back—/Eternity—until." Though "Sages" may call her life, or the confining limits of any marriage, "small," she strongly disagrees: "And I sneered—softly—'small'!"

Another version of what happened on that momentous Day is expressed in 410. Dickinson writes that Night closed that Day, and night has persisted ever since. The results are now that she can no longer "sing"— though the poem itself and several hundred others of the period call this into question. The poem has the further virtue of linking her madness poems with the experience of the marriage day: "And Something's odd–within–/. . . . Could it be Madness–this?"

Another poem in the same fascicle connects one of their meetings with her madness, or at least with her extreme distress, and clearly reflects the role of the beloved in it.

> 'Twas like a Maelstrom, with a notch,
> That nearer, every Day,
> Kept narrowing it's boiling Wheel
> Until the Agony
>
> Toyed coolly with the final inch
> Of your delirious Hem–
> And you dropt, lost,
> When something broke–
> And let you from a Dream–
>
> As if a Goblin with a Guage–
> Kept measuring the Hours–
> Until you felt your Second
> Weigh, helpless, in his Paws–
>
> And not a Sinew–stirred–could help,
> And sense was setting numb–
> When God–remembered–and the Fiend
> Let go, then, Overcome–
>
> As if your Sentence stood–pronounced–
> And you were frozen led
> From Dungeon's luxury of Doubt
> To Gibbets, and the Dead–
>
> And when the Film had stitched your eyes
> A Creature gasped "Repreive"!
> Which Anguish was the utterest–then–
> To perish, or to live? [414]

The program of the poem is fascinating: Dickinson describes a harrowing time of stress, of extreme mental anguish; then God relents and the problem begins to seem resolved, though with a deathlike state of being; and it is only *then* that another person ("A Creature") intervenes with the intention of helping, of giving her "Repreive." The poem ends with a dilemma: to die of the old problem or live with the new problem presents equal "Anguish."

Many have noted the signs of extreme mental suffering and nervous illness in Dickinson during the late 1850s and early 1860s, and John Cody has speculated that someone was called in for counseling during her distress, that the well known phenomenon of transference occurred, producing the love affair whose record we here study. The poem has already been studied briefly in chapter one, but it is worth considering it as a whole at this point, both for the intense imagery of mental suffering, and for the place of the "Creature" who intrudes at the end into what the poet had taken to be a problem involving God, herself, and "the Fiend." Wadsworth saves her, but for a fate more complex still.

This reading of 414 brings out items in the poem which have not been noted in any published criticism. But the reading is fully supported by the program we have seen developing throughout the fascicles. It is also justified by another fascicle poem describing the same situation:

> Of Course—I prayed—
> And did God Care?
> He cared as much as on the Air
> A Bird—had stamped her foot—
> And cried "Give Me"—
> My Reason—Life—
> I had not had—but for Yourself—
> 'Twere better Charity
> To leave me in the Atom's Tomb—
> Merry, and Nought, and gay, and numb—
> Than this smart Misery. [376]

The counsellor has advised "prayer" and she indignantly replies that she has already tried it. Then details of her problem appear, with the same stages we have just seen. He had come to help restore her "Reason," so important and so threatened that she can call it her "Life." But in the process of helping her through a religious and psychological problem, he has left her with another "Misery," so severe that she would prefer nonexistence (being left in "the Atom's Tomb") to this new problem.

Another marriage poem was called "The Contract" by Dickinson's editors in 1891:

> I gave myself to Him—
> And took Himself, for Pay,
> The solemn contract of a Life
> Was ratified, this way—
>
> The Wealth might disappoint—
> Myself a poorer prove
> Than this great Purchaser suspect,
> The Daily Own—of Love
>
> Depreciate the Vision—
> But till the Merchant buy—
> Still Fable—in the Isles of Spice—
> The subtle Cargoes—lie—

At least—'tis Mutual—Risk—
Some—found it—Mutual Gain—
Sweet Debt of Life—Each Night to owe—
Insolvent—every Noon— [580]

This is really another version of the central marriage poem, 322, another version of the "contract" they made that day. The first stanza nicely meshes with the consideration that her life had now entered a state of static immobility. The contract, obviously a marriage contract, is responsible for the change. The major thrust of the poem is that marriage is the crossing of a line: a risk is involved but there is no other way to find out whether the joy it promises is "Fable" or reality. In legal language, sexual intercourse is called "the marriage debt," and Dickinson seems at two points to anticipate it as a nightly occurrence.

In this same fascicle Dickinson once again describes the Lover as the initiator of their affair, as she recalls phrases from their most important conversation:

He showed me Hights I never saw—
"Would'st Climb"—He said?
I said, "Not so"—
"With me"—He said—"With me"?

He showed me secrets—Morning's nest—
The Rope the Nights were put across—
"And now, Would'st have me for a Guest"?
I could not find my "Yes"—

And then—He brake His Life—and lo,
A light for me, did solemn glow—
The steadier, as my face withdrew—
And could I further "No"? [446][10]

The "Yes" she finally gives him is the direct result of his importunings; his is the active role in the affair. This version of their affair is Dickinson's, though her biographers from Whicher to Cody to Weisbuch have asserted that the affair was totally in her mind, possibly with Wadsworth never even suspecting "the passion he had aroused."

A marriage involves the taking of a new name for the bride. Dickinson's version of this, with a larger celebration of the many changes caused by marriage, is 508: "I'm ceded—I've stopped being Theirs'/The name They dropped upon my face/With water, in the country church/Is finished using, now." The poem records her response, as bride, to his proposal, "With Will to choose, or to reject,/And I choose, just a Crown."

Other love poems are not quite so closely tied to the marriage narrative; nevertheless they address the beloved directly and express the intensity of his continued presence in Dickinson's life. Poem 277, noted in the first chapter as being anything but suicidal, is her exuberant threat to die immediately if it will mean "to pass escaped—to thee!" Poem 238 asserts that in her pain she shows more of her love for him: balm and "Jessamine" must be crushed before yielding their perfumes, and the stabbed bird finally tells the depth of her feeling for him in whose bosom her nest was built. Poem 495 expresses to him that her "thoughts—and just two Heart—/And Heaven—above" can make one "almost . . . Content." Poem 334 was apparently accompanied by a flower, described in sensual detail, with the charge that it should stand for them as a kiss: it is "Hid, Lip, for Thee—/Play it were a Humming Bird—/And just sipped—me."

If phase three is largely a lament for their separation, for the impossibility of their relationship in this world, the love poems assert nevertheless his continuing presence to her, the love which she will not let separation cool. The theme becomes a magnificent protest in the last fascicle of this phase:

> Empty my Heart, of Thee—
> It's single Artery—
> Begin, and leave Thee out—
> Simply Extinction's Date—
>
> Much Billow hath the Sea—
> One Baltic—They—
> Subtract Thyself, in play,
> And not enough of me
> Is left—to put away—
> "Myself" meant Thee—
>
> Erase the Root—no Tree—
> Thee—then—no me—
> The Heavens stripped—
> Eternity's vast pocket, picked—   [587]

Phase Four: Fascicles 20-35

Phase four takes in at one sweep by far the largest number of fascicles and poems of all the phases. It surely can be broken down into smaller units, but for the sake of brevity I will present only two major new accomplishments in these poems.

The phase seems to move forward with two new realizations. Dickinson must have known by this point, that she was writing well, and one begins to find assertions here of her achieved sense of professional identity as a poet. Also it must have become clear, especially since Wadsworth had removed himself so abruptly and totally—all the way across the continent—that their separation was for all practical purposes permanent, at least in this life. However, Dickinson could still not "Empty my heart of Thee." Though absent, he is a permanent resident in her mental universe.

These two themes—Dickinson's sense of her status now as a professional poet (to match the professional status of her beloved), and her realization of the beloved's presence-through-absence—merge at times to a new realization: that it is precisely his presence-through-absence and the experiences they have shared which furnish the best subject matter and motivation for her as a professional poet.

Presence-through-absence, probably the more abstract of these conceptions, needs more definition. Dickinson supplies it in Fascicle 31, in poem 546:

> To fill a Gap
> Insert the Thing that caused it—
> Block it up
> With Other—and 'twill yawn the more—
> You cannot solder an Abyss
> With Air.

Dickinson finds that her emptiness can be filled by only one object. By the exact contours of the gap in her life she is always conscious of precisely what is missing. The absence of the beloved is the only form of his conscious presence in her life.

Several analogues are presented to clarify this insight. In 611 "The Love of Thee" remains within her like a "Prism" in a darkened room, displaying the full splendor of light from a distant source. In 674 the beloved is the "Guest" in the soul who keeps her from going out to visit anyone else. (It is interesting to note that this "guest" is called "The Emperor—of Men" in the version Dickinson sent to Sue, making the poem appear to be a religious meditation on the presence of God in her soul. In the fascicle, Dickinson wrote "The Mightiest of Men"—her lover was a real human being.)

A third analogue for the lover's presence-through-absence is taken from her church experience. Her loneliness is prized because its spaciousness is large enough to contain "The Sacrament—of Him" (405). It is precisely the function of a Sacrament to remind the worshipper of an absent and invisible presence.

A fourth analogue presents his presence to her now only as a "dream"; he lives for her only in her lively imaginings of him:

> I could die—to know—
> 'Tis a trifling knowledge—

News-Boys salute the Door—
Carts—joggle by—
Morning's bold face—stares in the window—
Were but mine—the Charter of the least Fly—

Houses hunch the House
With their Brick Shoulders—
Coals—from a Rolling Load—rattle—how—near—
To the very Square—His foot is passing—
Possibly, this moment—
While I—dream—Here— [570]

The dream has the effect of isolating the dreamer as the only person in the world who does not have access to the person she most loves.

Still other analogues are presented in 590: her "Loneliness" is like looking into the the frightening depths of a cave, but even more like looking into the "face" of a loaded cannon. In 620 she employs her bee-rose imagery for another analogue: "Auto da Fe—and Judgment—/Are nothing to the Bee—/His separation from His Rose—/To Him—sums Misery."

The lover's absence is a constant abrading presence, as she describes it in a poem that recounts an actual event:

How sick—to wait—in any place—but thine—
I knew last night—when someone tried to twine—
Thinking—perhaps—that I looked tired—or alone—
Or breaking—almost—with unspoken pain—

And I turned—ducal—
That right—was thine—
One port—suffices—for a Brig—like *mine*—

Our's be the tossing—wild though the sea—
Rather than a Mooring—unshared by thee.
Our's be the Cargo—*unladen—here*—
Rather than the *"spicy isles—"*
And thou—not there— [368]

This is a love poem, springing from a specific occasion, addressed at several points to "thee," and recalling to him at the end the imagery of her earlier love poem "Wild Nights—Wild Nights!" (249). He remains now, to her, as the only person who has ever gained the right to console her. The presence of others only intensifies her need for him.

One of the benefits of reading Dickinson's poems in their fascicle order is demonstrable here. Poem 528 is separated from the one just mentioned by 160 other poems in Johnson's variorum edition; they are actually in two different volumes. But Dickinson copied 528 immediately after 368 in Fascicle 20, on the same sheet of paper.

> Mine—by the Right of the White Election!
> Mine—by the Royal Seal!
> Mine—by the Sign in the Scarlet prison—
> Bars—cannot conceal
>
> Mine—here—in Vision—and in Veto!
> Mine—by the Grave's Repeal—
> Titled—Confirmed—
> Delirious Charter!
> Mine—long as Ages steal! [528]

When this poem is printed and studied by itself it is surely one of those which Jay Leyda called "poems of the omitted center."[11] One catches an almost shrill tone in the series of assertions; there is an intense possessiveness here, but the poem does not indicate what is "mine." Neither verb nor subject is expressed. In the fascicle, however, the poem follows an equally intense poem of possessiveness, obviously addressed to the husband. Thus contextualized, 528 leaps suddenly into focus as another hymn to Dickinson's anomalous marriage, with capitalization of words that have come to signalize that marriage—White, Election, Royal, Scarlet—and its conditions of separation until the lovers meet after death.

Another aspect of his absence, the sexual excitement once awakened but now missing, is frankly acknowledged in 485:

> To make One's Toilette—after Death
> Has made the Toilette cool
> Of only Taste we cared to please
> Is difficult, and still—
>
> That's easier—than Braid the Hair—
> And make the Boddice gay—
> When eyes that fondled it are wrenched
> By Decalogues—away— [485]

The "death" of the beloved, in the first stanza, would be "easier" to bear than the moral and religious imperatives, the "Decalogues," that have separated them from physical contact, from the eyes which can no longer fondle her bodice.

These "Decalogues" receive further expansion in 398. She longs for "his silver Call," for "The looking in his Eyes." But the last two stanzas provide five analogues for the "law" which keeps them apart, and then expands a sixth with the sense of danger in their precarious moral situation:

> But 'tis a single Hair—
> A filament—a law—
> A Cobweb—wove in Adamant—
> A Battlement—of Straw—
>
> A limit like the Veil
> Unto the Lady's face—
> But every Mesh—a Citadel—
> And Dragons—in the Crease—

The analogue of the dream and the pain of sexual deprivation come together in one of the most puzzling poems Dickinson ever wrote:

> Her sweet Weight on my Heart a Night
> Had scarcely deigned to lie—
> When, stirring, for Belief's delight,
> My Bride had slipped away—
>
> If 'twas a Dream—made solid—just
> The Heaven to confirm—
> Or if Myself were dreamed of Her—
> The power to presume—
>
> With Him remain—who unto Me—
> Gave—even as to All—
> A Fiction superseding Faith—
> By so much—as 'twas real—   [518]

If the speaker here is a woman, then the experience does seem to be homosexual, as some have asserted, or quite possibly the dream of one. As the poem progresses, the reality of the experience itself is called more and more into doubt: perhaps the Bride had dreamed both the speaker and the event. So insubstantial is the experience that only God himself seems able to decide its reality. The poem, then, may be the record of a puzzling homosexual dream.

But still another interpretation suggests itself. Dickinson may be recounting an erotic experience from the man's point of view, assuming a masculine voice for this poem. In several poems she writes of things that happened "when I was a boy." And in the poem which follows immediately in the fascicle (355), on the same sheet of paper, she assumes the role of Divinity with regard to the beloved. In still another poem in this fascicle the poet assumes the role of one who has just died (358). The evidence of the fascicles generally seems to argue strongly against a homosexual experience. In all of the love poems the beloved is masculine; the guilt that is undoubtedly there attaches to the fact of his marriage rather than to any other religiously or socially unacceptable relationship.

But the program of the poem needs still closer attention. The dreamer is a man who experienced only the briefest sexual union with his Bride, and then was separated from her. But the experience nevertheless had a religious benefit: it was "for Belief's delight"; the purpose of the experience was "Heaven to confirm." In the last stanza the bold reflection is made that their sexual union provided more evidence for heaven than his Faith ever gave him. In this poem, then, Dickinson enters the mind of her clergyman lover and dreams the sentiments she would hope to find there.

The beloved's presence-through-absence, and the guilt that has required this separation, is intuited in still another way in 532, where Dickinson characterizes her loneliness as "Polar Expiation" by one "Of Heavenly Love—forgot." Her sense of alienation and abandonment begets, it seems, the presence of "Horror's Twin"—another person equally guilt-ridden and abandoned. Some comfort accrues to her loneliness in the knowledge that such another exists. They are linked by their spiritual guilt—but it is precisely that guilt that forbids communication.

Many poems on the theme of the lover's presence-through-absence date this realization from the day of their anomalous marriage. Poem 660 relives the Day which "We thought the Mighty Funeral/Of All Conceived Joy." The lines are majestic in their emphasized capitalizations. The "Woe" she lives today, she says, is continuous with that woe, but greater.

But by far the most important poem in this phase, second in importance in her whole canon only to 322, is 640; it clearly links the marriage theme with the reasons for her lover's presence-through-absence:

I cannot live with You—
It would be Life—
And Life is over there—
Behind the Shelf

The Sexton keeps the Key to—
Putting up
Our Life—His Porcelain—
Like a Cup—

Discarded of the Housewife—
Quaint—or Broke—
A newer Sevres pleases—
Old Ones crack—

I could not die—with You—
For One must wait
To shut the Other's Gaze down—
You—could not—

And I—Could I stand by
And see You—freeze—
Without my Right of Frost—
Death's privilege?

Nor could I rise—with You—
Because Your Face
Would put out Jesus'—
That New Grace

Glow plain—and foreign
On my homesick Eye—
Except that You than He
Shone closer by—

They'd judge Us—How—
For You—served Heaven—You Know,
Or sought to—
I could not—

Because You saturated Sight—
And I had no more Eyes
For sordid excellence
As Paradise

And were You lost, I would be—
Though My Name
Rang loudest
On the Heavenly fame—

And were You—saved—
And I—condemned to be
Where You were not—
That self—were Hell to Me—

So We must meet apart—
You there—I—here—
With just the Door ajar
That Oceans are—and Prayer—
And that White Sustenance—
Despair—

The poem embodies one of the most complete scenarios to be found among Dickinson's poems. The situation is an interview and the argument is pursued with merciless logic, as option after option is considered and then closed off.

The two figures are Dickinson's constant first person "I" and the lover whose identity is hinted at in several places in the poem. The location or setting is also indicated. Central to their conversation is the fact that their marriage by its nature requires separation and loneliness. The poem ends with the "Despair" which several other poems of the same time define more precisely.

The poem creates its own audience and limits it. It is addressed in the first instance, only, to the "You" of the first line and of several lines throughout. There are many poems in these fascicles, as noted in the previous chapter, where we later readers must be considered as Dickinson's audience only in a secondary and removed sense. By historical accident we are present to overhear this dialogue as its author arranged it, solely between the speaker and her audience of one.

Structurally this is an "anatomy" poem, one in which the subject is clearly and exhaustively divided into its constituent parts. Here the parts are her alternatives in view of the marriage event. This anatomy takes the form of considering the stages of life and the options available (or not available, in this case) at each stage.

But we must ask from what formal perspective the human life is anatomized. The stages—living, dying, rising, judgment, heaven or hell— are clearly from the perspective of a clergyman or a deeply religious person, and the arguments at each stage are those that might just have been suggested by such a counselor. The poem is a coolly logical survey of possibilities, in the presence of her beloved. Both accept the Christian view of the human enterprise. She follows the stages of life and the categories of thought a clergyman would propose for solving a personal problem.

It has frequently been suggested by proponents of the case for Wadsworth that the lines "You—served Heaven—You Know,/Or sought to—" are telling, as indeed they are, for establishing his identity as the lover. But the poem offers still more evidence in the case for a clergyman-lover, in a verbal gesture that has been overlooked in all of the commentaries so far published on this poem. In the third line the speaker calls her listener's attention to something within the space, the setting, of their interview, with the words "over there":

> And Life is over there—
> Behind the Shelf
>
> The Sexton keeps the Key to—
> Putting up
> Our Life—His Porcelain—
> Like a Cup. . . .

The setting, then, for the conversation of the poem, is the presbytery, the pastor's study, perhaps in the back of the church or in his nearby home. It contains, for security reasons, a safe or cupboard where the sexton of the church locks up the implements of the Lord's Supper when they are not in use during church ceremonies. The speaker can gesture easily in that direction, calling her listener's attention to this repository for sacred objects within view of them both. With a slight verbal gesture, "over there," the setting of the poem becomes vivid.

Other clues in the poem suggest a clergyman and his study: the detail of "the door ajar" would be suggested by the proprieties and safeguards exercised in a male-female interview; and "White Sustenance" is at least a latent allusion to the communion wafer—if Dickinson is preserving a continuity between her opening description of the communion vessels and this intensely painful abstraction at the end of the poem.

This is a setting with some interesting parallels in other writings by Dickinson. In the second of the Master letters (so numbered in Johnson's edition of the letters, and dated "about 1861"), Dickinson had recalled for the Master some highly specific details of one of their meetings:

> If it had been God's will that I might breathe where you breathed—and find the place—myself—at night—if I (can) never forget that I am not with you—and that sorrow and frost are nearer than I—if I wish with a might I cannot repress—that mine were the Queen's place—the love of the Plantagenet is my only apology—To come nearer than presbyteries—and nearer than the new Coat—that the Tailor made—the prank of the Heart at play on the Heart—in holy Holiday—is forbidden me—.[12]

It is true that Millicent Todd Bingham, when she first published these Master letters in 1955, warned against taking "Presbyteries" any more literally than Dickinson's "Himmaleh—or Calvary."[13] But the metaphorical referents for "Himmaleh" and "Calvary" are obvious in the poems where they occur. Poem 350, for example, in Fascicle 17, contains similar items: "Himmaleh" is a simile and "Gibraltar" is an obvious metaphor. "Calvary," wherever we have seen it, is the state of being into which her anomalous marriage has put her. But the "presbyteries" in this letter is not so obviously a trope for anything else. It seems quite as literal as the "new Coat" which also marks the limit of their physical intimacies. The passage is obviously an impassioned desire to visit the beloved at night, to have "the Queen's place" beside the King. That she can come no closer to him than meetings in an actual "presbytery" is confirmed by the setting of this poem (640), where such a meeting is actually on record.

That this second Master letter is indeed addressed to a clergyman is further suggested by the following statement earlier in the same letter: "I heard of a thing called 'Redemption'—which rested men and women. You remember I asked you for it—you gave me something else." It has been suggested that "Redemption" here is also used metaphorically, but the metaphor has never been successfully explained, and it seems more reasonable to take the statement literally in view of the many other references to a clergyman in Dickinson's work. She had obviously approached a clergyman with her religious problem; the consultation evolved into a more personal relationship.

Poems from other fascicles and sets envisage "You," the audience of the poems, as a clergyman. Poem 1059, addressed to "Sire" around 1865, reports her success in struggling with her pain. The poem ends: "Pause in your Liturgies–/Wait your Chorals–/While I repeat your/Hallowed name–." We must consider again whether "Liturgies" may be metaphorical, but surveying the professions of the men in Dickinson's life none of them seems to be performing liturgies of any kind, literal or figurative, except the clergyman.

Many of these elements stemming from poem 640, "I cannot live with You," appear also in a poem from one of her earliest fascicles, which she put together apparently early in the relationship, in 1859. Here the "Sexton" appears from 640, as well as the woman who calls herself "Daisy"when addressing "Master" in the Master letters:

> Sexton! My Master's sleeping here.
> Pray lead me to his bed!
> I came to build the Bird's nest,
> And sow the Early seed–
>
> That when the snow creeps slowly
> From off his chamber door–
> Daisies point the way there–
> And the Troubadour [96]

The scenario seems imagined, but peopled with three characters from other poems. She addresses the sexton who would have opened the door for her and ushered her into the clergyman's study. The presbytery here is the clergyman's home and she imagines herself being led to his bed ("the Queen's place" in the second Master letter). The poem is playful, a lovely *aubade* sung by herself as Troubadour; no sign of conflict, guilt, or rejection yet appears in this early halcyon stage of their relationship.

And in poem 375, in Fascicle 25, she continues to use the *aubade* genre, inviting her reader to share the view from her bed as she is just waking in her sunny room. The poem inventories the things she can see through her window from that cosy vantage point; the list ends with "the Steeple," marking the place for him of their intense exchanges.

A poem from a fascicle assembled a year later (1860) seems to use the presbytery setting again, but by now the situation has become immensely more complex and intense. Though discussed earlier, the poem can now gain in realism by presentation in its proper context:

> He was weak, and I was strong–then–
> So He let me lead him in–
> I was weak, and He was strong then–
> So I let him lead me–Home.

'Twas'nt far—the door was near—
'Twas'nt dark—for He went—too—
'Twas'nt loud, for He said nought—
That was all I cared to know.

Day knocked—and we must part—
Neither—was strongest—now—
He strove—and I strove—too—
We did'nt do it—tho'! [190]

If one can, at this point, assume a continuity of narrative and the single-ness of the "You" to whom the fascicles are addressed, the episode then reads that he was the weak one who allowed her to lead him "in"— possibly to his study for a long evening's conversation. Sexual temptation was aroused but finally avoided, as the last line indicates, as his strength began to reassert itself, and the episode ended with the gentleman accompanying the lady to the door of her nearby home. But still more seems to have been accomplished in this interview; his silence, in the middle stanza, is satisfying to her, as if she has won the acknowledgement that his feelings correspond to hers.

We would like to know more about what lies behind these poems, what situation led Dickinson to consult a clergyman in his study, to fall in love with him, with painful results, presumably during several interviews. While the answer cannot be given conclusively, there is a conjecture and a solid piece of evidence that bear upon the matter.

The conjecture, persuasively argued, is John Cody's, in *After Great Pain: The Inner Life of Emily Dickinson*. Cody presents a strong case for the threat of intense mental distress hanging over the Dickinson household for several years in the late 1850s and after. In addition to other evidence there are many poems which convince us of Dickinson's experience with severe mental suffering and her knowledge of mental breakdown. Cody points out that we have detailed lists of the physicians who attended the Dickinson family throughout their lifetimes, with the exception of these years. If such a prominent family had need for the services of "alienists" or therapists, it is not likely that they would have left a record of it for the public. And if the problem in Emily's case had religious dimensions, why not call in the services of a learned and prominent clergyman whose connections with the family were already multiple, though slender enough for him to remain, presumably, objective and professional.

Wadsworth appears a likely candidate here. Dickinson had apparently met him in 1855 at the Philadelphia home of her cousins. In early 1858 Mrs. Eudocia Flynt, a close friend of those cousins, recorded in her diary, "sent E Dickinson Mr. Wadsworth Sermon—preached in Phil—."[14] There may have been a heavier traffic in such items than the single notation indicates, in view of the known correspondence between Wadsworth and Dickinson and the many parallels between his sermons and her poems. In 1859, at the Amherst College commencement celebration at her father's home, Dickinson was introduced to the Clark brothers, Wadsworth's close friends, and was surprised to find that they knew him.[15] Dickinson was to carry on an extensive correspondence with them after Wadsworth's death. Such trajectories point to several connections with Wadsworth in Dickinson's life and give substance to the conjecture that the clergyman who is so prominent a figure in the fascicles is a convincing version of Wadsworth.

Did she then meet him initially for therapy or religious consultation in a local clergyman's study? The factual evidence mentioned above bears on this question of the location of their meetings. A visiting minister would logically call upon the hospitality of a brother clergyman for a place to sleep as well as for the use of his study as the proper and professional location for consultation with an unmarried lady. The local clergyman in question was the Reverend Edward S. Dwight, a close friend of the Dickinson family and pastor of their church. Dickinson corresponded with him after he and his family left Amherst in September 1860. When he first preached in Amherst in 1853 Dickinson described him in a letter to her brother Austin and concluded "I never heard a minister I loved half so well."[16] After the Dwights moved to nearby Hadley in 1860 he retained a close contact with Amherst; Dwight was trustee of the college from 1855 until his death in 1890. In December 1861 Emily Dickinson wrote a compassionate letter to Dwight offering consolation because of the recent death (September 1861) of his wife. She recalled that he "always looked so kind to us" as "Dear friend." The letter then sketches an interesting scene: "and so I knock tonight–on that far study door–that used to open kindly–."[17] And we seem to be back again at the setting for poem 640, "I cannot live with you," with her recollection of visits to the pastor's study.

Dwight, though she liked him, was not the object of Dickinson's love, the husband of her marriage. Dwight's wife died in 1861, and he married again a short time later. Dickinson's letters to him regarding both incidents are extant. On the former occasion there was no sense of expectation on her part. Nor, when he remarried, was there any sense of disappointment or betrayal.

But that Dickinson associated the two clergymen closely in her mind is indicated by the sequel to the letter just cited. She accidentally enclosed a poem meant for another person in a letter addressed to Dwight. Dwight replied with some puzzlement and included in his response a picture of his late wife. Dickinson then wrote, on January 2, 1862:

Dear friend,

   I made the mistake—and was just about to recall the note—*misen-veloped* to you—and *your's*—to the other friend—which I just knew—when my "Sister's" face [the picture of Mrs. Dwight]—put this world from my mind—nor should I mention it—except the familiar address—must have surprised your taste—I have the friend who loves me—and thinks me larger than I am—and to reduce a Glamour, innocently caused—I sent the little Verse to *Him*. Your gentle answer—undeserved, I more thank you for.[18]

The connection between the two clergymen is again indicated at the end of this letter, where she adapts the last stanza of 322, her central marriage poem, to the memory of Mrs. Dwight:

> Sufficient troth—that she will rise—
> Deposed—at last—the Grave—
> To that *new* fondness—Justified—
> by Calvaries of love—

The following poem may have been the one she "misenveloped" to Dwight. It is a poem "to the friend who loves me—and thinks me larger than I am":

> Size circumscribes—it has no room
> For petty furniture—
> The Giant tolerates no Gnat
> For Ease of Gianture—
>
> Repudiates it, all the more—
> Because intrinsic size
> Ignores the possibility
> Of Calumnies—or Flies.   [641]

The poem attempts to describe the "size" which her present status has conferred, beyond "petty" considerations, beyond even the reach of lying rumors ("Calumnies"). She seems to be claiming exemption from ordinary norms of behavior on the basis of the lovers' unique personal experience, in the last two lines.

   In the last fascicle of this phase this conversation, alluded to in the letter to Dwight, is once again embodied in a poem directly addressed to the husband. Here he is unequivocally the one who thinks her "Great":

> You said that I "was Great"—one Day—
> Then "Great" it be—if that please Thee—
> Or Small—or any size at all—
> Nay—I'm the size suit Thee—

Tall—like the Stag—would that?
Or lower—like the Wren—
Or other hights of Other Ones
I've seen?

Tell which—it's dull to guess—
And I must be Rhinoceros
Or Mouse
At once—for Thee—

So say—if Queen it be—
Or Page—please Thee—
I'm that—or nought—
Or other thing—if other thing there be—
With just this Stipulus—
I suit Thee— [738]

The poem is directly addressed to the absent "Thee," and it is one of the few poems in which one of their conversations is actually recalled and cited. The poem is a display of Dickinson's wit and humor on the subject of relative sizes, but it is also a love poem. There is another echo of the second Master letter, where she wishes "that mine were the Queen's place"; here she offers herself as "Queen" or as his more distant "Page," whichever suits him better.

The lover's remark about her "greatness" is central to still another poem:

That first Day, when you praised Me, Sweet,
And said that I was strong—
And could be mighty, if I liked—
That Day—the Days among—

Glows Central—like a Jewel
Between Diverging Golds—
The Minor One—that gleamed behind—
And Vaster—of the World's. [659]

The lover here is addressed as "Sweet,"his praise is fondly recalled, and the occasion is dated as the famous "Day" of their marriage.

These links seem neither accidental nor part of a planned literary fiction. Letters to a friend converge with specific details in the poems and in the second Master letter to confirm actual meetings and conversations between Dickinson and her beloved in a local clergyman's study.

Poem 477 is another excursion from the conversation poem 640. Where that poem ended by highlighting the "White Sustenance—/Despair," this poem goes on to describe that state of being more fully. Despair is so vast that only our ignorance of its vastness keeps us going on

through it. Poem 640, with its image of the sexton putting up the communion plate and cup, also furnishes an image for poem 342, where
"Summer folds her miracle—/As Women—do—their Gown—/Or Priests—
adjust the Symbols—/When Sacrament—is done." A further link is here
suggested between the marriage poems: the sacrament of the Last Supper
is also featured in the central marriage poem, 322, in lines 9-12.

There seems, then, to be a remarkable concatenation of identical
figures, key words, and similar situations, all clustered about the great
conversation poem 640—too remarkable to be dismissed as coincidence.
In 640 we have another "center" to the fascicles, linked with and equal in
importance with the great marriage poem 322.

Poem 640 ends with Dickinson's sense of the lover's presence-
through-absence in the compact oxymoron, "So we must meet apart."
Dickinson returns to still another version of the long separation, with the
lover's intensely felt absence, in 313. Dickinson would have been "too
glad. . . . too saved" if she had not been *abandoned* (the meaning of the
word she quotes from Jesus on the Cross—*Sabacthini* [sic]). Though
"Faith bleats to understand," she accepts Calvary and Crucifixion.

But the final aspect of this long separation—and the reason for keeping
the lover as a lively presence in it—is not forgotten. It is part of her
marriage program from the beginning. They will at last meet in heaven as
the reward for separation and fidelity on earth. At least this is the message
of 550, where her death, after a long and painful journey, will be "Reversed—in Victory"; and of the ecstatic poem 625:

> 'Twas a long Parting—but the time
> For Interview—had Come—
> Before the Judgment Seat of God—
> The last—and second time
>
> These Fleshless Lovers met—
> A Heaven in a Gaze—
> A Heaven of Heavens—the Privilege
> Of one another's Eyes—
>
> No Lifetime set—on Them—
> Appareled as the new
> Unborn—except They had beheld—
> Born infiniter—now—
>
> Was Bridal—e'er like This?
> A Paradise—the Host—
> And Cherubim—and Seraphim—
> The unobtrusive Guest—

Surely this poem is written to justify her love in the face of his clerical
advice. If he had counseled that they must look to "Judgment" (in poem

640) and regulate their behavior accordingly, Dickinson here trium-
phantly declares that they can have their love and a successful Judgment
before God as well.

As the second most important theme in phase four, Dickinson now
begins to explore her dedication to Art, her commitment as a professional
poet. While the subject can be stated in these few words, the development
is vast: nearly fifty poems in the fascicles of this phase explore different
aspects of it.

As we survey these poems we shall begin to notice that this subject too
is finally connected with the anomalous marriage. If her marriage was
now a lifelong stasis of separation, it could at least be celebrated in art.
And this celebration would give her a professional standing and identity
similar to her lover's. The perception was to be crystalized in a later phase
where she begins poem 751 as follows: "My Worthiness is all my Doubt—
/His Merit—all my fear."

One of the great poems describing an achieved identity is 1142:

> The Props assist the House—
> Until the House is Built—
> And then the Props withdraw—
> And adequate—Erect—
>
> The House support itself—
> And cease to recollect
> The Scaffold, and the Carpenter—
> Just such a Retrospect
> Hath the Perfected Life—
> A Past of Plank—and Nail—
> And Slowness—then the Stagings drop—
> Affirming it—A Soul—

Many other poems in this phase proclaim an achieved identity. Poem
306 celebrates "The Soul's Superior instants" when she has "ascended/
To too remote a Hight/For lower Recognition." Poem 383 states that
"Exhiliration—is within," and describes the intoxication that "The Soul
achieves—Herself." In 384 she describes the inner freedom of the Soul, no
matter what the outer circumstances may be. These realizations are called
"Moments of Dominion" in 627. In 395 she calls it "That fine Prosperity/
Whose Sources are interior," and in 483 she celebrates "A Solemn thing
within the Soul/To feel itself get ripe."

Dickinson even sets herself up as a kind of master and exemplar to
those who have also "Failed," yet can find, as she has, a sterner, higher
life beyond the killing pain (358). Poem 455 describes, in ascending
order, different kinds of "Triumph"; the poem concludes with a "Severer

Triumph" which one experiences only with an inner sense of moral righteousness. In still another way of expressing this achievement she writes, "Each Life Converges to some Centre—/. . . . Exists in every Human Nature/A Goal"; though it is unachievable, it still must be "Adored," "persevered toward" (680). For models in this new role she returns to the subject of her earlier "martyr" poems, and describes the "Martyr Poets" and the "Martyr Painters" who suffered greatly but taught their admirers to "seek in Art—the Art of Peace" (544). This new identity also involves the beloved. In 388, addressed to "You," she awaits him in a new eternal state "Dressed to meet You—/See—in White."

At least part of this sense of an achieved self-identity is ascribable to her growth as a poet. In 613 she laments, "They shut me up in Prose—/As when a little Girl/They put me in the Closet." But now her medium has been found: "I dwell in Possibility—/A fairer House than Prose." Poetry for her is "The spreading wide my narrow Hands/To gather Paradise" (657). It is in this phase that, with Poe and Emerson, she describes the poet's calling as the highest of all human enterprises:

> I reckon—when I count at all—
> First—Poets—Then the Sun—
> Then Summer—Then the Heaven of God—
> And then—the List is done—
>
> But, looking back—the First so seems
> To Comprehend the Whole—
> The Others look a needless Show—
> So I write—Poets—All—
>
> Their Summer—lasts a Solid Year—
> They can afford a Sun
> The East—would deem extravagant—
> And if the Further Heaven—
>
> Be Beautiful as they prepare
> For Those who worship Them—
> It is too difficult a Grace—
> To justify the Dream—   [569]

It is perhaps then with some amazement that we read Dickinson's own epitaph for herself: "This was a Poet—It is That/Distills amazing sense/From ordinary Meanings" (448). Dickinson here asserts the same strong ego-drive that characterizes all great poets.

Other kinds of imagery are employed to describe this achieved identity as a poet. In 488 she describes herself as a "Carpenter" with simple appropriate tools; when requested to do secular jobs she refuses: "We—Temples build—I said."

Such talent and productivity inevitably bring one face to face with the issue of fame and public notice. Dickinson works through the issue in 406, contrasting those who "Work for Immortality" with the larger crowd who work "for Time"; the former gain a slower but infinitely more valuable reward. And 713 asserts that fame is only true when self-confirmed: "All other Plaudit be/Superfluous." Or, expressed in other words, "The Outer—from the Inner/Derives it's Magnitude" (451).

Resolution of a kind is to reserve the plaudits for her posthumous reputation:

> This is my letter to the World
> That never wrote to Me—
> The simple News that Nature told—
> With tender Majesty
>
> Her Message is committed
> To Hands I cannot see—
> For love of Her—Sweet—countrymen—
> Judge tenderly—of Me [441]

Ultimately, in the personal story we have been following, the profession of poet is presented as a sign of her "worthiness" in the lovers' search for equality. He was esteemed as one of the great clergymen of his era; she would be known as one of its great poets:

> I died for Beauty—but was scarce
> Adjusted In the Tomb
> When One who died for Truth, was lain
> In an adjoining Room—
>
> He questioned softly "Why I failed"?
> "For Beauty", I replied—
> "And I—for Truth—Themself are One—
> We Bretheren, are", He said—
>
> And so, as Kinsmen, met a Night—
> We talked between the Rooms—
> Until the Moss had reached our lips—
> And covered up—our names— [449]

Their professional obligations are stated succinctly here: if one should die for Truth, the other would die for Beauty. Also present in the poem is a serene picture of the lovers' meeting after death.

Where the above poem states it in somewhat abstract and allegorical terms, the following poem expresses their professional equality in unmistakably personal terms:

> You love the Lord—you cannot see—
> You write Him—every day—
> A little note—when you awake—
> And further in the Day.
>
> An Ample Letter—How you miss—
> And would delight to see—
> But then His House—is but a Step—
> And Mine's—in Heaven—You see. [487]

Dickinson devotes much space, in this fourth phase, to the analysis of the work of the poet. He is "The One that could repeat the Summer Day" and thereby is greater than Nature itself, which can do it only once (307). Along the same lines, she addresses the beloved with the boast that she finished two Sunsets while Nature was making only one (308). Most arresting is the sudden shock of realism contained in 675:

> Essential Oils—are wrung—
> The Attar from the Rose
> Be not expressed by Suns—alone—
> It is the gift of Screws—
>
> The General Rose—decay—
> But this—in Lady's Drawer
> Make Summer—When the Lady lie
> In Ceaseless Rosemary— [675]

Pointing to her poems with "this" in the sixth line, Dickinson indicates the exact place where her sister Lavinia would find those poems after Dickinson's funeral.

And so it is especially interesting, in the context of this study, to find an expressed statement of Dickinson's own esthetic, in 669, that the actualities of one's own life are more "enthralling" than any popular romance: " 'Tis Fiction's—to dilute to Plausibility," while life presents the unbelievable dramas. Dickinson denies the restrictions against the "biographical fallacy" long before that term was imagined.

Something of Dickinson's working habits as a poet are also confirmed in this phase. As early as 1858 her father seems to have relaxed domestic discipline so far as to allow Dickinson to write late at night and into the early morning hours, a concession that now seems necessary in view of the amount of time it must have taken to work up the enormous number of poems which were arranged in fascicles beginning in that year.[19]

Three poems mirror this practice of writing at night and early in the morning, when nature and the house are still. Poem 486 begins, "I was the slightest in the House—/I took the smallest Room—/At night, my little

Lamp, and Book–/And one Geranium." In 304 she watches day break at the end of one of those nightly sessions of work, and describes the stages of its coming in clear ecstasy. This nightly vigil with her poetry sets her apart from the rest of men, who rise with Nature and the Sun, and sleep when they sleep (714).

Such dedication also casts her in the role of an outsider, alienated from the normal routines of ordinary people. "Civilization–spurns–the Leopard" she writes to "Signor" (492); and her fears of mental perturbation now become the divine madness of the romantic poet:

> Much Madness is divinest Sense–
> To a discerning Eye–
> Much Sense–the starkest Madness
> 'Tis the Majority
> In this, as All, prevail–
> Assent–and you are sane–
> Demur–you're straightway dangerous–
> And handled with a Chain– [435]

The two major themes of this phase–the beloved's presence-through-absence, and Dickinson's achievement of identity as a professional poet–converge in the following poem:

> The Soul's Superior instants
> Occur to Her–alone–
> When friend–and Earth's occasion
> Have infinite withdrawn–
>
> Or She–Herself–ascended
> To too remote a Hight
> For lower Recognition
> Than Her Omnipotent–
>
> This Mortal Abolition
> Is seldom–but as fair
> As Apparition–subject
> To Autocratic Air–
>
> Eternity's disclosure
> To favorites–a few–
> Of the Colossal substance
> Of Immortality [306]

It is precisely the friend's withdrawl that brings on the poet's "Superior instants." Her exploration of immortality, whether as poet or as lover joined to the beloved, begins with her love.

The two themes converge again in 755:

> No Bobolink—reverse His Singing
> When the only Tree
> Ever He minded occupying
> By the Farmer be—
>
> Clove to the Root—
> His Spacious Future—
> Best Horizon—gone—
> Whose Music be His
> Only Anodyne—
> Brave Bobolink— [755]

She will keep singing her songs, her only solace now that she is bereaved of home and "Future."

There remains only to look at a selection of the love poems in this fourth phase. Some new themes appear, and some older themes with a new intensity. The recipient continues to be addressed as "Sweet," as "Lover." As in earlier fascicles, several of these love poems suggest that the lover should be identified as a clergyman. Poem 376, a poem full of humorous energy, begins with an indignant response to his sober advice: "Of Course—I prayed—/And did God Care?/He cared as much as on the Air/A Bird—had stamped her foot—/And cried 'Give Me.' "

Other love poems present their cases in terms derived from a clergyman's practice. Poem 694 represents a beautiful sky as a sacrament: it "vests . . . in . . . Deity," presenting its "Tabernacle" for the worship of its faithful. And in 387 Dickinson explains her notion of marriage as its own religion, counter perhaps to his more orthodox views: Husband and Wife must both be converts to it; its Churches are "frequent" though small, accommodating only two; failure from this Grace is Infidelity; and so all-absorbing is marriage that a true religionist must consider it a "Heresy." Poem 355 ends with the following quatrain: "To lack—en-amour Thee—/Tho' the Divinity—/Be only/Me—." Such density needs careful unpacking, but at least the following propositions seem latent in these lines: that his first love would be assumed to be God; that she would move in to substitute for God as the object of his love; and that their separation increases his love.

The case for Wadsworth strengthens in some of the poems in which details of the distance between them are given. Poem 474 begins, "They put Us far apart—/As separate as Sea." And 710 proceeds through stages which apply exactly if the speaker and her beloved find themselves at opposite ends of the American continent:

The Sunrise runs for Both—
The East—Her Purple Troth
Keeps with the Hill—
The Noon unwinds Her Blue
Till One Breadth cover Two—
Remotest—still—

Nor does the Night forget
A Lamp for Each—to set—
Wicks wide away—
The North—Her blazing Sign
Erects in Iodine—
Till Both—can see—

The Midnight's Dusky Arms
Clasp Hemispheres, and Homes
And so
Upon Her Bosom—One—
And One upon Her Hem—
Both lie— [710]

Dickinson, at the end, seems specifically to be trying to imagine time zones laid on the face of the globe, with the same heavenly bodies radiating on them all, but recording different stages of the day or night where they strike the earth.

Dickinson still remembers the Day, the moment, of her anomalous marriage. In another group of love poems in this phase she memorializes that Day and gives still other versions of what actually happened. The following poem insists again on the active role that the beloved took in their marriage: "It was a quiet way—/He asked if I was His—/I made no answer of the Tongue,/But answer of the Eyes—" (1053). The poem then develops her lyric response—affirmative—to his question.

Another reflection of that Day, or perhaps of their whole experience together, is recorded in the following magnificent love poem:

We learned the Whole of Love—
The Alphabet—the Words—
A Chapter—then the mighty Book—
Then—Revelation closed—

But in Each Other's eyes
An Ignorance beheld—
Diviner than the Childhood's—
And each to each, a Child—

Attempted to expound
What Neither—understood—

> Alas, that Wisdom is so large—
> And Truth—so manifold! [568]

The lover here is by no means a divine lover (he can be charged with "ignorance"), yet the situation is described for one who would appreciate its being cast in religious terms.

Love poem 643 records still another segment of their marriage conversation:

> I could suffice for Him, I knew—
> He—could suffice for Me—
> Yet Hesitating Fractions—Both
> Surveyed Infinity—
>
> "Would I be Whole" He sudden broached—
> My syllable rebelled—
> 'Twas face to face with Nature—forced—
> 'Twas face to face with God—
>
> Withdrew the Sun—to Other Wests—
> Withdrew the further Star
> Before Decision—stooped to speech—
> And then—be audibler
>
> The Answer of the Sea unto
> The Motion of the Moon—
> Herself adjust Her Tides—unto—
> Could I—do else—with Mine?

The poem dramatizes his proposal and her acceptance, expressed through Dickinson's now conventional imagery of the feminine sea's response to the masculine moon. "Fractions" in the first stanza is the lovers' conception, popular since Plato, that true friendship is the joining of two halves of the same soul. But in Dickinson's case his declaration of love has peculiar overtones; it puts her in naked confrontation with the dictates of morality and religion—"Nature" and "God." Once again, the alleged passivity of Wadsworth, his unawareness of the passion he had aroused, is denied by Dickinson's record of the affair.

More abstractly, the marriage Day is analyzed thus:

> When I hoped, I recollect
> Just the place I stood—
> At a Window facing West—
> Roughest Air—was good—
>
> Not a Sleet could bite me—
> Not a frost could cool—

Hope it was that kept me warm—
Not Merino shawl—

When I feared—I recollect
Just the Day it was—
Worlds were lying out to Sun—
Yet how Nature froze—

Icicles upon my soul
Prickled Blue and Cool—
Bird went praising everywhere—
Only Me—was still—

And the Day that I despaired—
This—if I forget
Nature will—that it be Night
After Sun has set—
Darkness intersect her face—
And put out her eye—
Nature hesitate—before
Memory and I— [768]

Here there is not the same dramatization of their actual words; the poem is rather an attempt to schematize the conflicting emotions caused by the marriage experience. The poem has been taken to represent three different days: the day "I hoped," the day "I feared," and "the Day that I despaired." The reason for assuming three different days derives from the different kinds of weather described: sleet and frost, then warm sun, then the blackness of night. But surely the phenomena are metaphors for emotional weather, the quick shifts of inner feeling she experienced during one highly charged interview. She is protected from this kind of cold by Hope (line 7); and the darkness in the final stage is carefully distinguished into the kind that affects Nature and the kind that affects Memory. This is one day, then, and the only day of such magnitude recorded in the fascicles is the marriage day. It was a day of hope that warmed her against any coldness; it was a day of fear, that chilled her inner soul; and it was, as well, a day of darkness she would not forget even if Nature could.

The Day is memorialized again as "The Day that I was crowned"—a day that is different from other days as diamonds are from coal (356). But it is also the beginning of the long night, the period between the marriage day and the day of the lovers' meeting in Heaven (471).

But if separation was their fate and married life was not to be, still there was nothing to keep Dickinson from imagining what it would be like—or to keep her from putting a bit of pressure on the lover to make him appreciate the kind of devotion he had rejected. Such at least seems to be the purpose of the following poem:

Although I put away his life—
An Ornament too grand
For Forehead low as mine, to wear,
This might have been the Hand

That sowed the flower, he preferred—
Or smoothed a homely pain,
Or pushed the pebble from his path—
Or played his chosen tune—

On Lute the least—the latest—
But just his Ear could know
That whatsoe'er delighted it,
I never would let go—

The foot to bear his errand—
A little Boot I know—
Would leap abroad like Antelope—
With just the grant to do—

His weariest Commandment—
A sweeter to obey,
Than "Hide and Seek"—
Or skip to Flutes—
Or All Day, chase the Bee—

Your Servant, Sir, will weary—
The Surgeon, will not come—
The World, will have it's own—to do—
The Dust, will vex your Fame—

The Cold will force your tightest door
Some Febuary Day,
But say my apron bring the sticks
To make your Cottage gay—

That I may take that promise
To Paradise, with me—
To teach the Angels, avarice,
You, Sir, taught first—to me. [366]

This poem, like 259, is another imitation of Whittier's "Maud Muller," with its melancholy phrase "It might have been." Once again "Sir" is addressed, and line 25 seems to chide his preference for "Fame" over her—a theme she will take up again.

At least one segment of this marriage scenario is real, and is celebrated in 638: "To my small Hearth His fire came—/And all my House aglow/Did fan and rock with sudden light." But other scenes from married life could only be imagined: a winter storm is pleasant if someone loved occupies "the Sofa opposite" (589); and Dickinson sickens at the thought that he might die (648), may already have died (734), without her to comfort his last moments, the final service even Evangeline was allowed to perform for *her* Gabriel.

Toward the end of this phase two poems celebrate the day of Dickinson's marriage in increasingly abstract and spiritualized terms. In Fascicle 32 a strange poem imagines the "Bride" waiting for her new husband to mount the stairs and come into her room for the first time. "Angels" are on the scene, childhood is about to be left behind, and "Eternity" is entered. Perhaps this is Dickinson's deathbed scene, her imagined marriage finally being consummated in Heaven—at least this is suggested by the last line of the poem, with her most typical address to the beloved: "Master—I've seen the Face—before" (461).

In the next fascicle, poem 473 also asserts the reality of Dickinson's marriage. It opens, "I am ashamed—I hide—/What right have I—to be a Bride" and it ends "Baptized—this Day—a Bride." The body of the poem describes the adornments of the bride, especially the preparation of "my Soul" and "My Spirit." There is no sign of the husband in this poem, except in its address to the "Master." It is rather a description of the new spiritual estate gained by a bride through marriage.

The "Master" is also addressed in two other poems late in this phase. Poem 462 is a piteous plea:

> Why make it doubt—it hurts it so—
> So sick—to guess—
> So strong—to know—
> So brave—upon it's little Bed
> To tell the very last They said
> Unto Itself—and smile—And shake—
> For that dear—distant—dangerous—Sake—
> But—the Instead—the Pinching fear
> That Something—it did do—or dare—
> Offend the Vision—and it flee—
> And They no more remember me—
> Nor ever turn to tell me why—
> Oh, Master, This is Misery— [462]

The issues in this poem—doubt and sickness, worry that she has somehow "offended" the Master so totally that he has threatened to cut off all communication with her—these are the exact issues also of the third Master letter, dated at about the same time by handwriting: "Oh, did I offend it— . . . Daisy—Daisy—offend it. . . . A love so big it scares her, rushing among her small heart—pushing aside the blood and leaving her faint and white. . . . Daisy—who never flinched thro' that awful parting. . . . punish dont banish her—shut her in prison, Sir—only pledge that you will forgive. . . ."[20] The only "awful parting" that Dickinson records in the whole range of her poetry is that which occurred immediately after their anomalous marriage agreement. And now the Master seems to have suggested that they refrain even from correspondence.

The Master poem which has gained the most notice also appears late in this phase:

> My Life had stood—a Loaded Gun—
> In Corners—till a Day
> The Owner passed—identified—
> And carried Me away—
>
> And now We roam in Sovreign Woods—
> And now We hunt the Doe—
> And every time I speak for Him—
> The Mountains straight reply—
>
> And do I smile, such cordial light
> Upon the Valley glow—
> It is as a Vesuvian face
> Had let it's pleasure through—
>
> And when at Night—Our good Day done—
> I guard My Master's Head—
> 'Tis better than the Eider-Duck's
> Deep Pillow—to have shared—
>
> To foe of His—I'm deadly foe—
> None stir the second time—
> On whom I lay a Yellow Eye—
> Or an emphatic Thumb—
>
> Though I than He—may longer live
> He longer must—than I—
> For I have but the power to kill,
> Without—the power to die— [754]

The most illuminating criticism of the poem is surely Albert Gelpi's, who recognized the provenance of the poem's imagery and narrative, and expressed it thus: "Dickinson's imagination grasps her situation in terms of the major myth of the American experience. The pioneer on the frontier is the version of the universal hero myth indigenous to our specific historical circumstances, and it remains today, even in our industrial society, the mythic main story of American individualism."[21]

Dispute continues, however, regarding a more detailed reading of the poem. Once again, the most conservative interpretation, illuminated by the fascicle context, seems quite serviceable: the sexual awakening by a Master in the first stanza, a sense of pleasure with him in the second and third stanzas, the lack of sexual intimacy expressed in the fourth stanza, her fierce loyalty to him in the fifth stanza—all of these are elements that have already appeared in different ways even in the same fascicle in which this poem is found.

The sixth stanza presents a paradox that has caused the most dispute. The paradox is usually resolved in terms of the apparatus the critic has already set up. Gelpi sees the stanza as resolution of the conflict between Dickinson and the masculine *"animus"* figure which she has been struggling with in her psyche. Sharon Cameron, in an interpretation which she admits "may sound extreme," reads the stanza as Dickinson's attempt "to disarm any violence against herself which her own violent nature might inspire."[22]

Pursuing a conservative reading of the stanza in the marriage context of the fascicles, the following seems likely. This final stanza begins with a plea that lover and beloved not be separated by the death of one of them. The figurative application of the gun is then made clear: the gun can kill but not die or destroy itself, and the same is true in several senses for the immortal human being. The imagery of the gun, centered in the myth of the frontiersman, serves to focus much in Dickinson's mind regarding her marriage and its aftermath: the loneliness and yet the danger and adventurousness of her enterprise; the violence of her passions matched by the fierce loyalty to the beloved; the fidelity of the wife to her husband, without the license to share his bed; the link that is to be fulfilled in death but which is, at the same time, threatened by the death of one of the lovers.

Still more of Dickinson's most beautiful love poems are found in this fourth phase. Poem 453 is a definition of love with its startling string of verbs: "Love—thou art Vailed—/A few—behold thee—/Smile—and alter—and prattle—and die." Poem 303 celebrates the rare exclusiveness of love, with its celebrated opening "The Soul selects her own Society." Poem 480 begins with an allusion to Elizabeth Barrett Browning's most famous love poem, altered slightly to answer one of the Master's questions:

> "Why do I love" You, Sir?
> Because—
> The Wind does not require the Grass
> To answer—Wherefore when He pass
> She cannot keep Her place.

The poem reasons through several such compulsions in nature, to end, "Therefore—Then—I love Thee."

Poem 456 offers the sophistic argument that she loves him better than Jesus loved mankind: Jesus had to become man and join mankind, whereas she can live separated from him. And 394 offers a similar argument that if "God is Love" then He should be punished—not she, for her love is only participatory in His. Poem 549, addressed to "Sweet," asserts again her choice of "Calvary" in this life, until their meeting in Eternity. Poem 644 paints an exquisite miniature of her exact situation:

> You left me—Sire—two Legacies—
> A Legacy of Love
> A Heavenly Father would suffice
> had He the offer of—
>
> You left me Boundaries of Pain—
> Capacious as the Sea—
> Between Eternity and Time—
> Your Consciousness—and Me—
>
> [644]

And 769 presents the new mathematics of marriage: "One and One—are One."

In still another love poem Dickinson argues that her beloved was to her a "Revelation" of Eternity; since Eternity is the revelation of God, she has had to "adjust" herself to this new idolatry. The poem is argued quite abstractly; but a concrete presentation of the same subject is offered in 649. There a Bride dies on her wedding day. She is carried to the graveyard from her house, which is named "the Homestead"—the name of the house in which Dickinson lived for most of her life.

For all of the intensity of the love poems in this phase, there are still some surprises. One of the edges of Dickinson's hurt, of her sense of betrayal, begins to grow larger. Love changes to disgust. This is the point at which poem 534 arrives. She has begun to "see—Comparatively." Her "loss" has educated her, kept her from "waking in a Gnat's—embrace." The reader supplies an exclamation point here, so far has the lover been reduced.

Perhaps even more startling is Dickinson's glimpse of "Paradise" in 559, which left her "sickened—ever afterward/For Somewhat that it saw." The word appears in 362 also, where some experience has devastated her and "sickened fresh upon my sight—/With every Morn that came." The poem seems to combine equally her experiences with madness and with marriage, and to describe a moral revulsion that continues to the present.

Finally, late in this phase, 464 seems to begin as a love poem, as one of her summaries that moves from the Calvary of this life to the ecstasy of the lovers' meeting in Heaven:

The power to be true to You,
Until upon my face
The Judgment push His Picture—
Presumptuous of Your Place—

Of This—Could Man deprive Me—
Himself—the Heaven excel—
Whose invitation—Your's reduced
Until it showed too small— [464]

The second stanza is not without its difficulties, but it seems to be a definitive substitution—God's invitation totally supplanting the lover's.

Phase Five: Fascicles 36-40

There is every sign, in these last five fascicles, of an affair rounding off to a close, actively being rounded off to a close. Dickinson here works hard to write herself out of a situation which has come to a dead end. She would maintain her dignity, preserve what was truly worth preserving, but still bring the relationship to a kind of conclusion.

The end of the affair is expressed most succinctly in 682: Dickinson felt herself to be just "Thy moment"; it is expressed at more length in 747:

It dropped so low—in my Regard—
I heard it hit the Ground—
And go to pieces on the Stones
At bottom of my Mind—

Yet blamed the Fate that fractured—*less*
Than I reviled Myself,
For entertaining Plated Wares
Upon my Silver Shelf—

The short poem expresses a complexity of insights and emotions: the affair is totally over, in "pieces"; she has accepted this reality in her "Mind"; self-condemnation is warranted for her active participation in the affair; and the realization also dawns that the object of her affections had been false and unworthy of her. With its enlightened bitterness it is hard to imagine a stronger, more tough-minded ending to the experience. Dickinson writes her deliberate *finis*.

In another mood Dickinson can now assess this closed off and finished period with some objectivity. In poem 728, addressed to "you," she reviews the three periods of her life: her life as a child was defined by schoolwork and play, with vague "dreams" of something more; then "you troubled the Ellipse" (the "egg" stage of her life as a child) and opened a freer and larger life: "'Twas my last gratitude/When I slept—at night–/"Twas the first Miracle/Let in–with Light–." But in the third period Dickinson anticipates a closing down of that freedom, a return to the "doomed" loneliness of her childhood.

The beloved had performed a function in her life–contributing to her ripening–and now can disappear as a physical presence. The marriage now becomes a timeless, spaceless perfection. This is serenely expressed in 962:

> Midsummer, was it, when They died–
> A full, and perfect time–
> The Summer closed upon itself
> In Consummated Bloom–
>
> The Corn, her furthest kernel filled
> Before the coming Flail–
> When These–leaned into Perfectness–
> Through Haze of Burial– [962]

An alternative Dickinson preserved for line 7, "These Two–leaned in– Perfection," shows that she had only the two of them in mind as the subject of this poem, though she has not been able to smoothe the assertion into the rhythm of the poem.

Several different effects arise from this realization that the affair was over. Ended it may have been, but she had gone through it and some precious dry residuum was still to be understood, consolidated, retained. On what we may call the professional level, the level of her work, the experience furnished for Dickinson, and would continue to furnish, the central subject of her poetry: "God gave a Loaf to every Bird–/But just a Crumb–to Me–/I dare not eat it–tho' I starve–/My poignant luxury–/To own it–touch it–/Prove the feat–that made the Pellet mine" (791). Their marriage, as now the subject for her art, is condensed to a simple and clear image:

> Autumn–overlooked my Knitting–
> Dyes–said He–have I–
> Could disparage a Flamingo–
> Show Me them–said I–
>
> Cochineal–I chose–for deeming
> It resemble Thee–
> And the little Border–Dusker–
> For resembling Me– [748]

He is the center of her art, she the frame of the whole piece.

The husband as central figure of her art is celebrated in another poem, a famous one in which Dickinson rejects the suggestion (perhaps his) that she seek publication of her works: She responds with some indignation: "Publication—is the Auction/Of the Mind of Man" (709). In the third stanza she analyzes this "mind" which is contained in her poetry: "Thought belong to Him who gave it—/Then—to Him who bear/It's Corporeal illustration." Of the two assertions here, the first is the easiest: the power of thinking is given to us by the Creator, and thus belongs to him. But the second assertion, that it belongs to someone else also, needs closer attention than has yet been given it. Her thought, her poems, also belong to the one whom they corporeally illustrate. Her art now is indeed a private affair, shared only with God and the beloved whom it portrays.

Similar presentation of her marriage experience as concluded but now the primary subject of her poetry is found in 902:

> The first Day that I was a Life
> I recollect it—How still—
> The last Day that I was a Life
> I recollect it—as well—
>
> 'Twas stiller—though the first
> Was still—
> 'Twas empty—but the first
> Was full—
>
> This—was my finallest Occasion—
> But then
> My tenderer Experiment
> Toward Men—
>
> "Which choose I"?
> That—I cannot say—
> "Which choose They"?
> Question Memory! [902]

The first stanza presents a paradox: the day that she began to live was, at the same time, the last day of her life. The second stanza may be construed as an advance on this paradox: the unique day, if understood as her marriage day, was "full"; if understood as separation of lovers, it was "empty." The third stanza may well be the most important editorial statement in all the fascicles. It stands as a reflective moment, in the final fascicle, on the central experience from which the fascicle impulse developed: her love, her anomalous marriage, and the poetic uses she found for it. She assumes here a public role of a poet who has found her vocation and can describe it clearly. The final stanza then considers her relationship to a potentially wider audience than she has yet contemplated. For herself, she is unable to choose between the personal experience and the poetry it generated. As far as "Men" are concerned, whether she has succeeded in her vocation or not will depend on "memory," the place her poems will hold in the minds of readers. At least one reader, finishing the fascicles, has cast his ballot in favor of the success of her fascicle "Experiment."

Another effect of her resolution, her decision that the affair was now closed, was a new kind of commitment, seen at times as a religious dedication. She is, in 722, "The Wayward Nun" whose "service" is now to the everlasting hills. But her service is only to Nature in her "austere" moods, in 743. This is a "Severer Service" than she had performed before; its purpose is "To fill the awful Vacuum/Your life had left behind" (786). In this vacuum she is the total solitary—finding what God will reveal to her now only in the "Caverns" of her soul (777). The enterprise can be described only with an oxymoron: it is "an arid pleasure." She aligns herself again with the "Martyrs" who pursue their pure quest "through Polar Air" (792).

These late fascicles give us the most profound look Dickinson ever took into the subject of adult loneliness, a closer look than most would care to give the subject. The lonely height at which she arrived and her willingness to explore this territory have left us with more information about the subject than any other investigator has provided. The reader witnesses the emergence of a "columnar self," strong with the power which Dickinson identified with the mountains in these late fascicles: cool, permanent, distant, magnificent, solitary. The last fascicles are especially radiant with these qualities.

Loneliness has come, in the course of the fascicles, to characterize the center of Dickinson's life. In the following poem it takes the utmost courage to look at it unflinchingly:

> The Loneliness One dare not sound—
> And would as soon surmise
> As in it's Grave go plumbing
> To ascertain the size—
>
> The Loneliness whose worst alarm
> Is lest itself should see—
> And perish from before itself
> For just a scrutiny—
>
> The Horror not to be surveyed—
> But skirted in the Dark—
> With Consciousness suspended—
> And Being under Lock—
>
> I fear me this—is Loneliness—
> The Maker of the soul
> It's Caverns and it's Corridors
> Illuminate—or seal— [777]

Looking at this kind of loneliness is a ghoulish exercise, like searching among the debris of a grave. Mere sight of this loneliness-spectre is enough to kill the observer, though in the second stanza observer and observed are joined and then split in mutual abhorrence. Once the "Horror" in one's soul is realized, the only way to handle it, according to the third stanza, is to suspend "Consciousness," thereby shutting off an essential part of one's "Being." The last stanza contains a thought-provoking ambiguity: if "The Maker of the soul" is God, then it is He who uses Loneliness either to blind or to illuminate the individual regarding the deeper passageways in his own consciousness; if "Loneliness" itself is "The Maker of the soul," then it can perform these functions of either blinding or illuminating. In either case the experience of Loneliness is a kind of final event in the process of self-knowing and self-building, at once terrifying the soul and showing it the central fact of its existence.

In this new religious phase Dickinson becomes an explorer of the Absolute. She provides her own insight into the nature of God from the beauty of a flower (805). She builds a sense of wonder at human existence from the fact that to the miracle of being alive is superadded the power of willing—which places the human a step nearer the divine (677). She defines high "Truth" as the "Force/That holds without a Prop," which holds up the one who trusts it (780). She writes on "Remorse" (744) and on the "piercing Virtue" renunciation (745). In this high seclusion Dickinson has become truly other-worldly: "The Only News I know/Is Bulletins all Day/From Immortality." (827) But the enterprise produces "Pardon" and religious peace. Jesus tells her, to her surprise, that she is accepted into his "House" (964).

This self-image of the other-worldly recluse is confidently faced and justified in the last poem of the last fascicle:

> Unfulfilled to Observation—
> Incomplete—to Eye—
> But to Faith—a Revolution
> In Locality—
>
> Unto Us—the Suns extinguish—
> To our Opposite—
> New Horizons—they embellish—
> Fronting Us—with Night. [972]

Surely Dickinson knows how others may view the New England spinster: "Unfulfilled," "Incomplete." But "Faith" presents the need to change "locality" in considering questions of fulfillment and completeness. The sun may seem to disappear, to leave us in "Night," but it exists permanently, always embellishing some other "Horizon." The Sun that illuminated her life, the Bliss of her marriage, has suffered "a Revolution/ In Locality"—but waits for her still, permanently, in some other horizon.

Dickinson will continue this pilgrimage toward the Absolute for the rest of a long poetic career. At this point she has written and bound into fascicle form barely half of all the poems that will ultimately compose her canon. Other moods will be explored, but the following poem best expresses her sense of the poet in this mood:

> On the Bleakness of my Lot
> Bloom I strove to raise—
> Late—My Garden of a Rock—
> Yielded Grape—and Maise—
>
> Soil of Flint, if steady tilled
> Will refund the Hand—
> Seed of Palm, by Lybian Sun
> Fructified in Sand— [681]

Such spare asceticism has its rewards: her poetry produces not only the staple necessities, "Grape—and Maise," but some exotic luxuries as well— "Seed of Palm, by Lybian Sun/Fructified."

A repeated effect of closing off and leaving behind the marriage experience is the achievement of a "Columnar Self" (789), a coldly literal version of Emerson's self-reliant person. Having consciously placed her hopes for married love behind her, yet appreciating the growth the experience has promoted, Dickinson discovers a firm and higher identity.

This new self exists in majestic isolation. "Society" is now primarily the soul's cultivation of "His own acquaintance" (746). "Growth" is achieved only within the individual, "Through the solitary prowess/Of a Silent Life" (750). And failure, should it occur, is deeply rooted at the center of an individual being's life (803). Such solitude seems initially impoverishing, but it grows to be a "Banquet . . . . sumptuous enough for me" (773). Such "lonesome Glee . . . . sanctifies the Mind" (774). This is also a moral isolation. Poem 753 asserts that it is only her own Soul which can now declare her guilt or innocence.

Such high achievement of one's own individuality places the self in the largest of contexts: "Behind Me—Dips Eternity/Before Me—Immortality/Myself—the Term between/ . . . . 'Tis Miracle before Me—then— /'Tis Miracle behind" (721). Such largest of conceptions can now be condensed into the smallest of poems:

> No Prisoner be—
> Where Liberty—
> Himself—abide with Thee—
> [720]

But as Emerson had also apprehended regarding the individual on his way toward self-reliance, shyness and awkwardness will dog his steps along the way: "Who Giants know, with lesser Men/Are incomplete, and shy/For Greatness . . . is ill at ease/In minor Company" (796).

In such a course the ineluctable component is "Woe." It rises from her loss and loneliness, fills at times the whole of her horizon, and generates the energy that produces her poetry. If Woe has recognizable boundaries, one can bear up under it (269); but if it has such limits it is not the genuine woe that she is experiencing (686).

The bearing of such woe leaves no energy for life's other activities: "The Cargo of Themselves" is all such sufferers can carry (787). Its benefits can be obtained only by suffering through it: "'tis when/A Value struggle—it exist" (806). Such pain is so concentrated that the individual rises out of any ordinary sense of time. The moment of suffering expands to fill an Eternity, and simultaneously collapses to an intense Now (967). But finally the wisdom of woe is obtained; it derives from confrontation with the highest and most valuable realities: "A nearness to Tremendousness—/An Agony procures" (963).

Such experience with woe exacts its physical toll: "The hallowing of Pain/Like hallowing of Heaven,/Obtains at a corporeal cost" (772). Dickinson now becomes acquainted with insomnia and the effects of narcotics as sleeping drafts. A sense of bereavement follows her night and day; "I tried to drop it in the Crowd—/To lose it in the Sea—/In Cups of artificial Drowse/To steep it's shape away" (784). But she finds, in fact, "No Drug for Consciousness" (786). As she had already recorded in an earlier phase, "Narcotics cannot still the Tooth/That nibbles at the soul" (501). The word is amplified in this last phase: "Memories—of Palm—/Cannot be stifled—with Narcotics—/Nor suppressed—with Balm" (492).

The insomniac then turns the night hours into working hours for the soul at white heat. Poem 783 describes the predawn period from the vantage point of one who is still awake at 4:00 a.m. and watches the progress of day slowly unfolding. In 786 the poet begins her work when Nature's day has gone to sleep. All this in the massive effort to exorcise the beloved from her life and to round off the marriage experience to a terminus.

But this is not possible. One finds the love poems still running constantly through this last phase. Even the last of all the fascicles (Fascicle 40) contains half a dozen of them. There remains their pact that such lovers will meet in eternity. Addressing her clergyman lover (see line 9) she sums up the enduring residue of their relationship:

> You taught me Waiting with Myself—
> Appointment strictly kept—

> You taught me fortitude of Fate—
> This—also—I have learnt—
>
> An Altitude of Death, that could
> No bitterer debar
> Than Life—had done—before it—
> Yet—there is a Science more—
>
> The Heaven you know—to understand
> That you be not ashamed
> Of Me—in Christ's bright Audience
> Upon the further Hand— [740]

There is, in the last lines, serene conviction of their certain union after death. In this conviction she finds "Joy" and "Pardon"; a brief glance into one another's eyes has confirmed their eternal union: "So fleet thou wert, when present—/So infinite—when gone"; he remains a ghostly presence during her earthly life, until the "Haunting actualize—to last—/At least—Eternity" (788). The whole of their acquired marriage wisdom can now be compacted into four lines: "Two—were immortal twice—/The privilege of few—/Eternity—obtained—in Time—/Reversed Divinity—" (800).

And so there is an element in her anomalous marriage experience, as it is winnowed for its essences in this last phase, which she will never renounce. Love is Divine is Eternal was a hard-won equation and still will be celebrated. Poem 725 proceeds through three clearly announced stages: "Where Thou art—that—is Home—/ . . . What Thou dost—is Delight—/ . . . Where Thou art not—is Wo." Poem 729, addressed to "You," to "Sir," protests that she will never "Alter," "Falter," or "Surfeit" of him.

In the third Master letter, Dickinson had begged piteously for some presence in his life: "Low at the knee that bore her once into wordless rest Daisy kneels a culprit—tell her her fault—Master—if it is small eno' to cancel with her life, she is satisfied—but punish dont banish her—shut her in prison, Sir—only pledge that you will forgive—sometime—before the grave, and Daisy will not mind—She will awake in your likeness."[23] The letter must have been followed by silence from the Master. But Dickinson meets his passivity with her own active response, reframing her plea:

> If Blame be my side—forfeit Me—
> But doom me not to forfeit Thee—
> To forfeit Thee? The very name
> Is sentence from Belief—and Home—
> [775]

Dickinson, then, records in the last of her fascicles the latest of her love poems, the final shape her love affair seems to have taken—at least as far as the fascicles are concerned. Poem 961 promises to "Sweet," still a lively presence in her world, that she would do him any service, suffer any humiliation, if only she could be with him. Poem 965 acknowledges the high motivation of their mutual renunciation, but notes as well its tragic outcome: "What Comfort was it Wisdom—was—/The spoiler of Our Home?" As any Bride, she has forsaken all for her husband: "Dropped—my fate—a timid Pebble—/In thy bolder Sea—/Prove—me—Sweet—if I regret it—/Prove Myself—of Thee—" (966, lines 13-16). Poem 986 begins with the consideration that each year until they meet in eternity will bestow some new "trait" on her, then worries in mock panic that she will become so beautiful that he will not recognize her; she resolves the panic with the consideration that such love as hers will always be recognizable. Her Best Beauty is defined at the end of this poem: "The Beauty of Demand—at Rest."

In the traditional marriage service, the marriage vows end with the promise "Till death do us part." The vow in no way fits Dickinson's marriage situation, which will become a reality only *after* death. She revises the vow, then, in 907:

> Till Death—is narrow Loving—
> The scantest Heart extant
> Will hold you till your privilege
> Of Finiteness—be spent—
>
> But He whose loss procures you
> Such Destitution that
> Your Life too abject for itself
> Thenceforward imitate—
>
> Until—Resemblance perfect—
> Yourself, for His pursuit
> Delight of Nature—abdicate—
> Exhibit Love—somewhat—

Dickinson proposes her own marriage as requiring a greater love than the standard marriage, with its promise of love until death.

Surprisingly, granted their physical distance and agreed-upon separation, Dickinson can still assert the lovers' complete union:

> I make His Crescent fill or lack—
> His Nature is at Full
> Or Quarter—as I signify—
> His Tides—do I control—
>
> He holds superior in the Sky
> Or gropes, at my Command

> Behind inferior Clouds—or round
> A Mist's slow Colonnade—
>
> But since We hold a Mutual Disc—
> And front a Mutual Day—
> Which is the Despot, neither knows—
> Nor Whose—the Tyranny— [909]

The poem is near the end of all of the fascicles, and rewards close investigation, especially since it is a later working of her early moon-sea imagery for the lovers. What causes the moon to appear full or crescent, to appear to be high in the sky or behind the clouds, is precisely the position of the earth in relation to it. She then is earth to his moon in this poem and feels that she must influence his feelings as much as he influences hers. But the final stanza puts their relationship in a larger picture. Both moon and earth submit to the stronger influence of the sun. Both lovers stand in relation to the divine presence in their lives, their "Mutual Disk"; the question of which of the lovers controls the other's life then drops into relative unimportance, in the face of this larger power in both their lives. Dickinson resolves religious problems by the artistic manipulation of symbols.

Poem 971 is Dickinson's last statement of her relationship to "the Brave Beloved" in the fascicles. Death, loss of liberty, Distance, Danger—all of these can be borne. They can even be considered "Bounty" in comparison with "Suspense's Vague Calamity." Putting off the fulfillment of her marriage until after death is "Staking our entire Possession/ On a Hair's result"—so balanced are the possibilities for and against such eventual fulfillment.

The poems of the late fascicles become noticeably more private. One objective indication of this is that few of them were published in the 1890s by the original editors, Mabel Loomis Todd and Thomas Wentworth Higginson, who were seeking to popularize Dickinson by presenting her most accessible verse. Most were first published in the collections which began to appear in 1929, when Dickinson's reputation had grown to the point where publication of all her poems seemed timely and desirable, and when family rivalries stimulated collections and counter-collections. Sue's daughter was beginning to publish more of Dickinson's poems, in inaccurate versions and with commentary that, according to Mabel Loomis Todd and her daughter, falsely sentimentalized and mythologized Dickinson's life. They responded with collections of their own, from typescript versions which Todd had made in the 1890s.

Another objective indication of the privacy of these poems is that very few of them have been chosen even by more recent anthologists, who have sought to pick the "best" or the most representative of Dickinson's poems, or at least those whose appeal would be widest. The Dickinson of these late fascicles is mostly unknown to the general reader.

In the latest phase of the fascicles the religious dimension of Dickinson's experience is fully explored, but there is no sign that she renounced human love for divine; rather, she achieved a place for earthly love, even for her heterodox marriage, within traditional religious categories. Though she had been at work on the fascicles for only six years, she arrived here, at the end of them, at that latest stage of artistry where a brush stroke fills a canvas, where an unaccompanied violin can fill a room with more music than a symphony orchestra. The art becomes spare, intense, focused, lean, private, demanding the full attention of the reader.

Thus the fascicles end. The ground for her relationship had been shifting and unstable—the charade-marriage entered into with true love, impossibility mixed with need and fidelity, human incompleteness generating its own dream of wholeness. But during six years of love and meditation, Dickinson created there a foundation of integrity and an achieved sense of the self. The poems grew in an environment that would have seemed ferociously hostile to such rich beauty.

Chapter Three

Life and Letters

By what means, general, can an ordinary woman, without literary reputation, be sustained in the affection of a man she loves when separated from him by distance or a period of years?—Madame de Staël to Napoleon[1]

For Dickinson's admirers, the recovery of the fascicle arrangement of her poems amounts to a new find. The admirer has here not only a more concentrated collection of her poetry but the added authority of Dickinson's own arrangement, as well. As with all new discoveries, these reconstituted fascicles demand careful description and evaluation. The rewards are great, as the admirer comes to appreciate the continuities of mood and perception, the interconnected play of epithets and images, of ideas and narrative scenarios.

But where the first two chapters have faced inward to the fascicles themselves, larger questions now begin to urge themselves regarding possible connections between these fascicle poems and other aspects of Dickinson's life and works. What connections do these fascicles have with the remaining half of Dickinson's body of poetry? In what ways do the fascicles relate to the known and documented evidence in Dickinson's biographies? Can they indeed legitimately furnish any biographical evidence themselves? Do they bear any relationship to her letters and to known figures in her circle of friends and acquaintances? Do later poems and letters throw back any illuminations on the nature of the fascicles themselves, making it still clearer in our minds just what kind of poetry we are here considering? These questions will occupy our attention in the present chapter.

Biography and Criticism

Richard B. Sewall begins his magisterial two-volume *Life of Emily Dickinson* with the observation that Dickinson did not find an enveloping or sustaining vision that holds her poetry together, or at least that the critics had not yet discovered it: "Her vision—dispersed and fragmented among the hundreds of short, tense lyrics that make up her canon—comes to use with none of the wholeness of the plays [of the Athenian or the Elizabethan eras]. It is not surprising that Sophocles and Shakespeare should be closer to us, have clearer shape in our minds, than our near-contemporary, the elusive poet of Amherst." And as late as 1981 David Porter would still assert that "her life and work . . . contain no shapely story."[2]

But the situation has changed with the reconstruction of the original fascicles. When the poems are read as Dickinson grouped them, and when the groupings are read in their original order, what emerges is a remarkable unity. Most of the poems are generated by a single experience or complex of experiences. Each fascicle has a core of poems directly related to Dickinson's love affair and, later, to her anomalous marriage. Other poems radiate from that center or relate to it in some discoverable way. And the fascicles as a whole show many of the characteristics of a suite or a sequence, like Shakespeare's Sonnets, Elizabeth Barrett Browning's *Sonnets from the Portuguese,* or Coventry Patmore's *The Angel in the House.*

The last two examples are suggested because they were works admired by Dickinson and contemporaneous with her. Patmore's poetic suite, marzipan when compared with Dickinson's, was conceived as an anniversary gift. It was addressed to "You, Sweet, his Mistress, Wife, and Muse." For each capitalized word equivalents can be found in the fascicles of Dickinson. And versions of the story were abroad in Dickinson's time that the *Sonnets from the Portuguese* were presented as a gift to Mrs. Browning's husband, celebrating the course of their love, for his eyes only. The story is suggestive as model for Dickinson's fascicles.

A study of the fascicles reveals that there is very little left of Dickinson's "early poetry" or juvenilia. Outside of the fascicles there are only five poems that show her beginnings: valentines from 1850 and 1852, and three poems in letters, one of which Johnson has "arbitrarily established" as poetry from its original prose. These five poems are 1, 2, 3, 5, and 16. It is surely possible that Dickinson destroyed her early efforts from before the time she found her mature artistic voice and the motivation to begin constructing the fascicles; it is also possible that she incorporated earlier pieces she was satisfied with into the fascicles, especially the nature poems which are used to fill them out. In any event, Dickinson appears as a poet quite fully blossomed, with very little preceding her mature work to embarrass or distract later readers from the fascicles themselves.

The poems are individual victories, highly to be prized as such. But the fascicles reveal a larger conception on the part of the poet, a design or a developing organizational system of greater magnitude, such as Sewall suggested.

Dickinson's story in many ways is a retelling of the central story of nineteenth-century literature, of the marriage made in heaven, prevented on earth, but to be celebrated eternally in heaven. Beethoven died leaving among his papers a love letter addressed to the *"unsterbende Geliebte"*; the nineteenth century was thrilled and the twentieth continues to wonder about the identity of this "eternally beloved." Goethe wrote eloquently of the "elective affinities" which draw souls together and bind them immortally, in utter disregard of previously existing earthly ties and obligations. Dickinson knew of the eternally doomed love of Heathcliff and Catherine, in *Wuthering Heights,* by one of the writers she most admired: there is much in the thought and in the diction of this novel which finds verbal echo in Dickinson. Elizabeth Barrett Browning's *Aurora Leigh* has been studied as a rich source for some of Dickinson's diction,[3] and the following scene suggests the kind of atmosphere in which lovers meet. The heroine's father first saw her mother at Mass and it was love at first sight in this charged setting: "Thus, even thus,/He too received his sacramental gift/With eucharistic meanings; for he loved" (*Aurora Leigh,* 1.89-91). In nineteenth-century Romantic diction the perfect human love echoes with reverberations from the religious realm, actually threatening to take it over. The words "Sir" and "Master" are both lovers' terms from *Aurora Leigh,* and it is safe to say that Dickinson learned the language of passion from such passages as the following:

> "I love you, Romney"–
> >   Could I see his face,
> I wept so? Did I drop against his breast
> Or did his arms constrain me? were my cheeks
> Hot, overflooded, with my tears–or his?
> And which of our two large explosive hearts
> So shook me? That, I know not. There were words
> That broke in utterance . . . melted, in the fire,–
> Embrace that was convulsion, . . . then a kiss
> As long and silent as the ecstatic night,
> And deep, deep, shuddering breath, which meant beyond
> Whatever could be told by word or kiss.
> But what he said . . . I have written day by day,
> With somewhat even writing. [*Aurora Leigh,* 9.714-26]

These sentiments could be found closer to home in the American authors whom Dickinson knew. The most famous section of Thoreau's *A Week on the Concord and Merrimack Rivers* (1849) has always been the essay on friendship in the "Wednesday" chapter. A passage from this essay, in which Thoreau advises how a "Friend will address his Friend," establishes in miniature much of the same emotional galaxy in which Dickinson operated:

> "I never asked thy leave to let me love thee,–I have a right. I love thee not as something private and personal, which is *your own,* but as some-

thing universal and worthy of love, *which I have found*. O how I think of you! You are purely good,—you are infinitely good. I can trust you forever. I did not think that humanity was so rich. Give me an opportunity to live."

"You are the fact in a fiction,—you are the truth more strange and admirable than fiction. Consent only to be what you are. I alone will never stand in your way."

"This is what I would like,—to be as intimate with you as our spirits are intimate,—respecting you as I respect my ideal. Never to profane one another by word or action, even by a thought. Between us, if necessary, let there be no acquaintance."

"I have discovered you; how can you be concealed from me?"

The Friend asks no return but that his Friend will religiously accept and wear and not disgrace his apothcosis of him. They cherish each other's hopes. They are kind to each other's dreams.[4]

Significant also in Dickinson's education was the best-selling *Kavanaugh*, a novel by Henry Wadsworth Longfellow, of 1849. The youthful Dickinson and her brother read this book with great pleasure, in conscious rebellion against their father's disapproval. In Longfellow's novel a young clergyman is loved by two women; the plain and sickly girl loses him to her stronger, more beautiful friend. The book recapitulates Dickinson's own *éducation sentimentale*. At school the two girls are deeply in love with one another: "It was, so to speak, a rehearsal in girlhood of the great drama of woman's life" (chapter 8)—a drama that Dickinson played out with the girl who was to be her sister-in-law. Love strikes with powers that elevate its victim to higher realms: "But love it was; and it lifted her soul into a region, which she at once felt was native to it:—into a subtler ether, which seemed its natural element" (chapter 23). Something of the fortunes of both girls are collapsed into the single speaker of Dickinson's fascicle poems: "Ah, what glimpses of home, and fireside, and a whole life of happiness for Cecilia, were revealed in that one word of love and intimacy, 'Arthur'! and for Alice, what a sentence of doom! What sorrow without a name! What an endless struggle of love and friendship, of duty and inclination" (chapter 27).

How closely was Dickinson "influenced" by the novel? In chapter 26 Longfellow introduced one of the sets of symbols which Dickinson found most frequently useful in exploring her own relationship with the beloved: "And, thenceforward, she became unto Kavanaugh what the moon is to the sun, forever following, forever separated, forever sad."

It may be that Dickinson's fascicle poems are an imitation of these symbols and sentiments; but there is evidence that such works provided a whole generation with real-life expectations. One of the overriding themes of Dickinson's fascicles, that of the fated marriage, made in heaven but doomed to frustration on earth, can be cited as current within the circle of Dickinson's family and acquaintances. One of Lavinia's suitors, Joseph Lyman, writing autobiographical letters some years later to his fiancée, used the following commonplace expression: "Poor little soft-lipped Vinnie Dickinson. She thinks I am *so* far off and Life is *so* long! So we have concluded that it was *not* one of those matches made in heaven and not to be made on Earth."[5]

The larger design which is visible in the fascicles has many similarities, then, to the works with which Dickinson was familiar, which she admired most, or to sentiments conventional in her circle. There is no need at this point to affirm that wit and intelligence transformed these home truths from platitude to art.

The reader and student of Dickinson may feel that such a "marriage" as she describes is so eccentric, so many leagues distant from any recognizable center of ordinary human experience, that it thus becomes unavailable, uninteresting, to the supposed modern reader. The experience which generates her poetry, which is celebrated in her poetry, is so far from anything the normal reader has experienced, so far from anything he might wish to experience in his own relationships, that the poetry must necessarily be too idiosyncratic to yield valid insight; Dickinson's poetry, from this point of view, will seem to occupy one of the dark corners of rarely seen human experience, rather than to illuminate significant elements at the center of experience.

But the problem is purely theoretical. The poems have been popular since their first appearance precisely for their illuminations of central human experiences of love, death, joy, pain, loneliness, and despair. Yet these insights into the normal come from a situation which threatens normal life to the utmost. It seems as though there is at least one kind of art which illuminates most only when it takes its standpoint far beyond the borders of human normalcy. Hawthorne felt he conveyed a valid insight into human reality through the story of a minister who hid his face for life behind a black veil. And we are reminded again that American art has traditionally taken its stand at the extreme in order to illuminate the center. In "Bartleby, the Scrivener," "Benito Cereno," and "Billy Budd," the unnamed lawyer, Captain Delano, and Captain Vere all come upon extreme and rare forms of human disorder, with which they finally do not adequately cope; yet each of these stories offers enormously satisfying esthetic experience. "The Beast in the Jungle" has perhaps resonated in the minds of Henry James's readers more than any other of his short stories. In that story James dramatizes the piteous situation of "the man of his time, *the* man, to whom nothing on earth was to have happened," yet every reader comes to identify with him. Hawthorne's Ethan Brand tries to perform the one extreme act never yet performed by a human being, the commission of the "unpardonable sin," and all readers are the wiser for it. One thinks of characters from the larger field of western literature who start midway through life to tour heaven, hell, and purgatory, or of those who start late in life to dedicate themselves to knightly service, and wonders if most great writing does not begin from the eccentric, the bizarre. Dickinson's anomalous marriage is thoroughly within the area in which art operates.

But is it within the area in which *life* operates? In other words, what does a study of the fascicles add to the vexed subject of autobiography in Dickinson's poems? Some years ago the question would have been dismissed as beneath consideration. The legacy of the New Criticism was strong, that the reader absolutize the art object itself, interpreting and evaluating it without the aid of information from history or biography. The yields were high for interpretation, for understanding the mechanics of art, especially in the short intense lyric such as Dickinson wrote.

But too much seemed to be sacrificed and perhaps such pure criticism could be maintained as theory only. Northrop Frye, in a remarkable essay on Emily Dickinson, chided the "vulgarity" of readers who showed an interest in biographical elements in her poetry. But this was only after he had given a detailed summary of her life, satisfying what must have been his own curiosity and what he assumed would be the legitimate curiosity of his readers. William Sherwood called attempts to identify Dickinson's lover "the simpler and more prurient pleasures." But it may be that in the present climate of criticism we are ready to fall back upon Whicher's more generous concession of an earlier era: "Readers of Emily Dickinson who wish to know the most intimate facts of her personal history need offer no apologies for indulging in what is a perfectly natural and legitimate curiosity."[6]

Before the New Critics there was more hospitality to consideration of the artist behind the art. Sainte-Beuve in his essay on Chateaubriand, in *Nouveaux Lundis* (1865), said, "I can enjoy the work itself, but I find it hard to judge in isolation from the person who wrote it." And E.M.W. Tillyard, in his great study of Milton, asserted that the real subject of a great poem is the state of the author's mind at the time of composition: "No one reading through *Paradise Lost* with any degree of seriousness can help asking . . . what were the feelings and ideas that dominated Milton's mind when he wrote it."[7] The New Critics offered a much needed method for reading the poem on its own terms, but their rigid exclusion of all other matters could only be temporary and methodological.

More recently the relevance of biography to the individual text has been argued and brilliantly illustrated by Richard Ellman in a series of biographical sketches. And James E. Miller's study of *T.S. Eliot's Personal Wasteland* is a work of great success and unshakable authority, which perhaps removes the last trace of the problematic from the theory that life helps to understand art. Miller argued that "my illumination of them [the biographical 'springs' of *The Wast Land*] leads not away from the poetry but more deeply into it."[8]

The reader must indeed preserve the distinction between autobiography and lyric poetry; the two genres are distinct and each has its own forms. But this is not to deny that there are raw materials of experience behind each, rough hints and fragments of "actuality" with which the artist builds either autobiography or lyric. There are critics whose methodology has made them reluctant to pursue this rich vein of interpretation. Where John Cody cautiously allows that the love affair may have been manufactured by Dickinson's imagination, and limited totally to her fantasies, later writers have taken the hint without the caution and have declared the whole identity of the lover to be fictitious. Robert Weisbuch, for example, echoing an earlier sentiment of William Sherwood, declares that the three Master letters "were written as fictions," but declines to give a single reason for this opinion.[9]

In the case of Dickinson herself we must consider her own plea to Thomas Wentworth Higginson, in her fourth letter to him, written in July 1862. Dickinson had already sent him eight poems, and now she says, "When I state myself, as the Representative of the Verse—it does not mean—me—but a supposed person."[10] The statement has been taken as reason enough for divorcing the art completely from any traces of autobiography. But just the opposite is true. Dickinson was sending Higginson letters and poems fairly rapidly that spring and summer, and when we look at the poems she sent we may experience the same sudden fear she felt.

The most important of these poems was the central marriage poem itself (322), which she had sent Higginson in her second letter to him. Dickinson must have felt that she had revealed her "guilty secret" amply enough for any discerning eye and was pleading with Higginson—not that her poems were totally free from autobiography, but just the opposite— that there was more of her personal situation in them than she would care to have made public, and that he held her secret in jeopardy. The plea for him to consider her speaker as "a supposed person" is panic, a desperate strategem to keep her personal affairs private.

Brita Lindberg-Seyersted provides more data for biographical readings of Dickinson's poetry from another point of view. In her study of "the voice of the poet," Lindberg-Seyersted found that "about two-fifths of all Emily Dickinson's poems revolve around an explicit 'I' " and that the pronoun would be numerically still more frequent if words like "my" and "me" were included in the count. Asking then how this "I" identifies itself in the poems of a particularly rich year, she found that "in practically all of them the assumed personality when identifiable was feminine, that it owned a dog named Carlo, that it lived in Amherst, and that frequently the poems were actually signed 'Emily' at least in one of the extant drafts.''[11]

Actually, in Dickinson's poetry itself there are statements that sanction a search for the "biographical springs" of her art. A poem in Fascicle 26 argues that fiction "dilutes" reality, that the real "Romance" is the individual's own life (669). A similar perception in 1698 laments that staged "Tragedies" win more applause than those enacted in real life. And there are poems throughout the canon which do not yield their meaning until the story revealed in the fascicles is recalled. The following intensely sexual poem is a case in point:

> Of Life to own—
> From Life to draw—
> But never touch the reservoir. [1294]

This remarkably compressed poem from 1874, fully ten years after Dickinson had finished the fascicles, can only be taken as another late reflection on, an intensely brief scenario from, her state of sexual deprivation after the anomalous marriage. And we have already seen, especially in chapter two, a number of poems which contain concrete, personal details, knowledge of which she assumes in her husband-reader, and which come only from the unique situation Dickinson described as her own.

To whatever extent the restrictions against the biographical fallacy apply in the criticism of public art, the very private case of Dickinson's poetry solicits our caution toward any *a priori* theory. Her poems, as they come to be seen through a reading of the fascicles, are a special kind of communication. They are addressed to one person exclusively, as part of a larger correspondence with him. They recall private conversations, meditate on experiences they alone shared, and chart the surprising turns their relationship took over the years. They also protest against any suggestion of publication for a wider audience. Art though they are, of the highest quality, they seem to be conceived of more as private correspondence. And correspondence has always been taken as one of the first sources of biographical information. Some recent critics, represented by Sandra Gilbert and Susan Gubar, have already begun to return to this sense of the profound connection between the life and work of Emily Dickinson: "The fantasies of guilt and anger that were expressed in the entranced reveries of the fiction-makers like Rossetti and Barrett Browning, and by all the novelists we have considered, were literally enacted by Dickinson in her own life, her own being. . . . Dickinson's life itself, in other words, became a kind of novel or narrative poem.''[12]

Contenders for the Beloved

One of the candidates for the beloved in Dickinson's poetry has been proposed as God. The marriage, in this reading, was between God and the Soul, the poetry is religious poetry of a high order, and Dickinson is a mystical poet. The thesis is held by a minority of critics and biographers, but continues to be found. At times it has even been assumed as the standard interpretation, and criticism has followed upon this assumption.[13]

In 1938 Yvor Winters asserted that at least one poem, "Great Streets of silence led away" (1159), a late poem, was "technically a mystical poem," though his reading of the poem did not justify this impression and he concluded that "there is no reason to believe that Emily Dickinson was a mystic, or thought she was a mystic." But the seed was planted. In 1954 Donald Thackery, refraining from calling Dickinson a mystic "in the technical sense," went on to consider her "mystical attitudes" with reference to discussions in Evelyn Underhill's famous book *Mysticism*.[14]

In his great work of explication in 1960, Charles Anderson thought that several poems were unambiguously concerned with the mystical marriage, that Dickinson's "White Election" was a reference to the state of grace, and her white clothing was "her assumption of the heavenly bridal gown." In the same year the poet Louise Bogan subtly described Dickinson's process of poetic illumination as similar to the experience of the mystics. In 1966 Olive Rabe presented a fully developed essay on "Emily Dickinson as Mystic," and placed Dickinson's marriage poems in the long tradition of Christian mysticism of the experience of the favored soul as the bride of Christ. Michael Dressman gave another census of poems which he felt expressed Dickinson's sense of her mystical marriage with God.[15]

There exists another approach to Dickinson's mysticism, first suggested by Theodora Ward in 1961, that a transition can be seen in her work from poems of earthly love to those of Heavenly love. William R. Sherwood in 1968 accepted this idea of Dickinson's development, adding that in 1862 Dickinson underwent a conversion experience, a sudden influx of grace, which turned her from the love of Charles Wadsworth to the love of God.[16] Ruth Miller followed a similar line, proposing that Dickinson pursued Samuel Bowles both as lover and as publisher of her poems, that he rejected both roles, and that she then turned to God for reassurance of her immortality both as soul and as poet.[17]

One of the poems cited by Miller as mystical is 322, "There came a Day—at summer's full," which I have taken from the beginning of this study to be the central marriage poem. According to Miller, "It is the *Lord* and the *Poet* that combine to make the sealed Church. It is the Lord and the Poet who are permitted to commune. Together they form a private and authentic Church." Miller interprets the parting of lovers, standing on opposite decks, as follows: "The Lord going to where he must; the summer going where it must; and she to where she must."[18]

The reading seems quite vulnerable on several points. Clearly there are more than two personages indicated in the poem. The "two Souls" are linked by such words as "our" and "we" at several points in the poem; and at several points in the poem they come into a *third* presence, the presence of the Divine: their union is described by a simile in the third stanza, as being *like* the quiet joining of the Divine with matter in the Sacrament; and in the next stanza they hope to come into that Divine presence after death, "At 'Supper of the Lamb.' " The final stanza quite unequivocally separates the two human lovers from the divine: Jesus has already risen and will not rise again at the general Resurrection; only the two human lovers will undergo that experience. Other phrases substantiate the poem as a human marriage poem, in Dickinson's unusual experience of that rite. If it were a poem of mystical marriage there would be no need for the restriction that the lovers were "permitted to commune" only one time; and one might also question Miller's understanding of the word "permitted"—from whom is the permission required if one of the parties is God himself? Finally, the poem ends with the anticipation of the future death of both lovers, not an event that the Divine must undergo.

Mystical interpretations of other poems suffer from similar problems and it will be worth a few paragraphs to look at those which have been suggested as examples of the mystical marriage.

Poems 199, 473, 664, 1053, and 1072 are all "Wife" and "Bride" poems. But there is nothing in them to suggest a divine rather than a human spouse. Any interpretation of these poems as mystical would have to rest on an already established proof of Dickinson's mysticism. Instead, the poems of the fascicles show multiple allusions to a human marriage that elevated her to heights of ecstasy, including religious ecstasy.

Poems 306, 393, 513, 564, 593, 1495, and 1581 are undoubtedly moments of rare illumination, of insight into the mysteries of eternity, moments when the soul feels itself solitary before the divine vastness. But none of these poems conveys the still more heightened and personal sense of mystical marriage to this divinity. Actually, the illumination of 593 is produced by the poems of Elizabeth Barrett Browning.

Three other poems have been interpreted as mystical. In 625 the lovers meet in heaven; but the meeting takes place "Before the Judgment Seat of God," indicating God again as a third party apart from the human lovers. In 580 the giving of lovers to each other is "Mutual Risk"; one of the lovers might not realize the inferiority of the other until the commitment is made. Neither would be true in the case of the mystical marriage.

In 579 the speaker suddenly sickens when offered the food she had been longing for for years, a sentiment that can hardly be placed in a mystical context.

There is, in fact, only one unequivocally mystical poem in the whole canon of Dickinson's poetry, but it must be carefully interpreted, both in the light of the situation Dickinson elaborated in the fascicles, and in terms of Dickinson's favorite book.

> Given in Marriage unto Thee
> Oh thou Celestial Host—
> Bride of the Father and the Son
> Bride of the Holy Ghost.
>
> Other Betrothal shall dissolve—
> Wedlock of Will, decay—
> Only the Keeper of this Ring
> Conquer Mortality—   [817]

The first stanza clearly asserts marriage of the soul to the trinitarian Christian God. The second stanza just as clearly distinguishes this marriage from earthly, human marriage, and ends with the assertion that marriage to God is essential to immortality. This is not the marriage of the mystic to God, but the marriage every Christian must experience to be saved. There is little evidence that Dickinson had much exposure to or sympathy with such authors as St. Bernard, Richard of St. Victor, St. Mechthild, and St. John of the Cross, whose statements on mystical marriage have been offered as analogous to Dickinson's.[19] Her undoubted source, cited in numerous poems and letters throughout her life, is the Book of Revelations, where all faithful Christians will, at the end, be seated at the bridal table, at the marriage feast of the Lamb. Dickinson's poem, then, reveals a solid conviction of salvation, of the presence of grace in her soul, not of the more special mystical relationship to God. She has managed the ethical dangers of her situation successfully and the poem is a lyric celebration of that success. As such, the poem finds its place entirely within the synthesis I have been describing, perhaps capping the synthesis at its highest point.

Lesbian candidates for Dickinson's lover have also been proposed, most notably by Rebecca Patterson, who sketched in some detail a picture of the supposed relationship between Dickinson and Kate Scott Anthon. The case seemed thin to most reviewers, and subsequent critics have noted the numerous gaps that Patterson had to fill in with supposition for lack of concrete information. The case had been established on the basis of supposed letters that "must" have been written to stimulate crucial poems, of rejection of obvious interpretations of numerous poems, and of explanation of the masculine figure who dominates the poems as a concession to conventions—though the poems were presumably not for publication. Many of the poems which Patterson cites as indicative of a strong emotional relationship between two women were actually sent to Sue, not to Mrs. Anthon. And of the forty poems overtly addressed to women, Patterson says, "they are of greater biographical importance than the hundreds employing masculine pronouns."[20]

Among the multitude of poems considered by Patterson, there seems to be only one which is not bent, forced, by the requirements of her thesis. Poem 518 is about "My Bride," and begins, "Her sweet Weight upon my Heart a Night." In discussing this poem in its context in Fascicle 29 I have already noted that the scene is presented as "a Dream" and also that there is ample literary precedent for Dickinson imagining what her male lover's fantasies might be in their love affair.

Patterson was undoubtedly right in asserting that "From the days of [Dickinson's] childhood women attracted her emotionally," but she seems to have been too exclusive in continuing "and women alone had the power to wound her" (p. 7). Dickinson's letters, especially of her earlier years, offer numerous examples of an emotional, even effusive relationship with other women. But since Patterson's work, a better context for these letters has been supplied by the research of Carroll Smith-Rosenberg and others. Smith-Rosenberg has studied the letters and diaries of several nineteenth-century American women and found their language far less restrained than modern canons of decorum would allow.[21]

Lillian Faderman has also proposed a homosexual strain, both in the poems and in the letters to the sister-in-law, Susan Gilbert Dickinson. While doubting any actual physical contact, she feels that the homoerotic strain in Dickinson's writings must be acknowledged and reckoned with. This line of interpretation has most recently climaxed in a statement cited approvingly by Adrienne Rich: "I am not wanting to turn Dickinson into a practicing lesbian . . . . What I do want is a lesbian-feminist reading of her poetry and her life as the most accurate way to handle that otherwise confusing constellation of myth and fact surrounding her."[22] Attention is snagged by the phrase "most accurate," and one wonders why this should be so. Responsible criticism will always prefer methods to dogmas in the practice of explication.

But feminist critics have reason to lament some of the published criticism of Dickinson. One male critic asserted that the genesis of Dickinson's poetry lay in severe menstrual distress, and cited such lines as "My period had come for Prayer" (564) and her statement that Pain causes her only "to perceive/New Periods—of Pain" (650).

In the published criticism and biographies the two strongest contenders for the role of Dickinson's lover are the famous newspaper publisher, Samuel Bowles, and the equally famous clergyman, the Reverend Charles Wadsworth. Bowles surely was the most attractive person in the Dickinson circle. Even at a hundred years' distance he charms with energy and intelligence. He was a man with great capacities both for work and for friendship. His biography, which reads like hagiography and was written by an admiring friend, portrays a man active in national politics who turned a provincial weekly newspaper into a daily organ of opinion and reform with a national impact. He was a man with a mission in life, a light that burned clearly and intensely in his age. On several occasions his activities nearly exhausted his physical resources so that he was forced to withdraw, the better to recoup his strength for the next surge forward. The biographies also indicate a man with a not entirely congenial married life, who frequently worked into early morning hours at his office, and who was a magnet to several intelligent and attractive women.[23] The photographs of Bowles show an extraordinarily handsome man, radiant with vitality. One understands instantly Dickinson's exclamation, in a letter to him, that "You have the most triumphant Face out of Paradise."[24] There is much that leads one to cheer on those partisans for Bowles in the quest for a suitable soul mate for Emily Dickinson.

The relationship between Bowles and Dickinson has been related in great detail, especially by Ruth Miller, as a partisan, and by Richard B. Sewall, as a more impartial recorder of the available data.[25] What is apparent in the relationship is an extraordinarily warm friendship, one from which Dickinson especially derived much strength. There is even evidence that Bowles provided the important office of friendly confidant for Dickinson.

When Mabel Loomis Todd was preparing an edition of the letters (1894), she contacted numerous friends and acquaintances of Dickinson asking them for materials, or at least copies of materials, that Dickinson might have sent to them. Among the responses was that of Samuel Bowles, Jr., son of Bowles, who sent to her and Lavinia the poems and letters Dickinson had sent to his father and mother. There is no sign that there was any editing or censoring of the materials he sent. Among the materials were no fewer than fifty-one poems.

Ruth Miller conveniently lists these poems in her book. Actually, several of the poems she cites were sent to Mrs. Bowles, considerably reducing her list of the poems sent to Bowles himself, and because of their sincere protestations of friendship for Mrs. Bowles, considerably reducing the likelihood of that lady's husband being Dickinson's beloved.

Some of these poems had previously been copied by Dickinson into fascicles. A few of these have been looked at in chapter 2 above, and some obvious comments made: in the fascicles where genuine marriage poems or love poems appear, those selected for Bowles were much more impersonal nature poems or observations on life; where love poems were taken from the fascicle context they can easily be read, alone, as protestations of a genuinely warm friendship only, or were in some cases slightly rewritten so that this was the effect.

Among the poems Dickinson sent to Mr. Bowles are many that justify Miller's speculation that she hoped, at least for a while, that he would recognize her talent and advocate the publication of her poems. Some of these are the superb nature poems "These are the days when Birds come back" (130), "Besides the Autumn poets sing" (131), and the sunrise and sunset poems 204 and 1140. Also among the poems sent to Bowles are Dickinson's most obviously finished and public poems, those most accessible to a general readership. Some of these are serious, such as "The Soul unto itself/Is an imperial friend" (683), or poem 121, with its memorable line "Heaven beguiles the tired." Others are lighter or more humorous, such as "Faith is a fine invention" (185), or 329 with its made-up word "Optizan." Poem 829 is on a conventionl subject, a country burial, with conventional rhymes and rhythms.

Only a very few of the poems Dickinson sent to Bowles can be called even flirtatious. I have already discussed in chapter two "The Drop that wrestles in the Sea" (284), an erotic poem in which the speaker would merge herself totally with the beloved, forgetting that "Ocean" is already married to "Amphitrite." But the version Dickinson sent to Bowles was modified slightly to remove the more obviously erotic statements: instead of desiring to be "in Thee," as the fascicle version has it, she would simply move "toward Thee"; and for the version to Bowles she changed the total gift of herself as "Offering" to the blander word "incense." A decidedly erotic love poem (523) was robbed of an innocuous stanza, and it was only that stanza that was then sent to Bowles. Nor was Dickinson "Daisy" to Bowles, as an earlier misreading of one of her letters to him had conjectured.[26]

What the poems to Bowles more accurately suggest is a strong friendship which revealed itself, especially at moments when he was slow to respond, as the continuing need for his high regard. Poem 223 is a clever and teasing plea for his "smile." A stanza from poem 574 celebrates his recovery from a serious illness. Poems 33, 195, 200, and 224 were verses to accompany gifts of flowers, or perhaps of poems. Poems 687 and

921 are reminders to him of her affection, pleas for some response from him. Poem 834 records her joy in anticipation of a visit from him, her sorrow after he has left.

There can be no doubt that Bowles was important to Dickinson, was warmly valued as a friend and, it would seem, as a confidant and advisor. But unless she was also thoroughly a hypocrite she could not have been in love with him as she was with the "Master"; she also sent to Mrs. Bowles the poem of intense friendship which begins "My River runs to Thee" (162).

There is still much to be learned in these letters and poems which Dickinson sent to Bowles, much that defines their relationship more clearly. Dickinson's attention to Bowles waxed and waned. On the evidence of the poems and letters sent to him, that attention was particularly strong during the six months preceding Bowles's departure for Europe on April 5, 1862. Bowles had been a friend of Austin Dickinson's since the 1850s and had visited Austin's home on several occasions during his trips to Amherst. In the months before his departure for Europe, Dickinson sent him no fewer than nine poems and letters, and one to Mrs. Bowles during her husband's brief absence in Washington.

During the fall of 1861 Bowles was in Northampton, less than ten miles southwest of the Dickinson home, undergoing a cure for his sciatica. Dickinson must have sensed a special rapport with him during this period of proximity, and a desire to confide which had to be accomplished before his departure for Europe. Some heavy "freight," as she called it, was burdening her at the time. As she wrote to Higginson in April 1862, just after Bowles left for Europe," I had a terror—since September—I could tell to none" (letter 261). Apparently she told at least some of it to Bowles.

To Dickinson's readers the most startling and important of these letters is surely the following:

> Title divine—is mine!
> The Wife—without the Sign!
> Acute Degree—conferred on me—
> Empress of Calvary!
> Royal—all but the Crown!
> Betrothed—without the swoon
> God sends us Women—
> When you—hold—Garnet to Garnet—
> Gold—to Gold—
> Born—Bridalled—Shrouded—
> In a Day—
> "My Husband"—women say—
> Stroking the Melody—
> Is *this*—the way? [1072]

Here's—what I had to "tell you"—
You will tell no other? Honor—is it's
own pawn— [Letter 250]

Dickinson reveals much here. In the first place it is obvious that this is still another description of the day of her anomalous marriage. The poem is a definition of the particular kind of marriage Dickinson experienced, and several of the themes she established elsewhere regarding that day come together here in still another synthesis: she is "wife," but in no sense that could be celebrated publicly; she is involved in a state of life now best characterized by the term "Calvary"; she senses a difference, a transition, but "without the swoon" that she feels should accompany marriage; and she here uses terms of "royalty" to describe this marriage, as she had frequently in the fascicle poems. One major consideration suggests itself from this letter. If Bowles were the husband of the fascicles he would hardly need to have had this communication sent to him in this way, as a secret she can finally divulge to him, which she entrusts to him in strict confidence, which she was unable to tell him in conversation. If he were the husband of the adulterous relationship defined in the fascicles, there would be little need either to inform him of the fact or to charge him with secrecy.

Other communications from these months, in uncertain chronological relationship, can be seen to revolve about this disclosure. The writings can all be dated by handwriting but there is little to indicate the sequence in which they were sent. What can be done though is to list the issues and subjects that occupy Dickinson's letters to Bowles during this short period.

A series of letters which seem to be in order indicate some great problem which troubles her, even prevents her from seeing Bowles when he visits, and then a sudden outpouring of gratitude for his kindness. In letter 241 she apologizes for not seeing him, perhaps in October when he visited Amherst several times from Northampton, because "something troubled me" and she didn't want to burden him when he was supposed to be recovering from his own illness. In letter 247, which can be dated internally as January 1862, she asks, "Are you willing," and complains, "I am so far from Land," through the context offers no further explanation and she must have been referring to some request for help which she had made in conversation. She hopes, in this letter, someday to be able to return the favor to him. Bowles seems to have proven to be at least a willing listener without yet knowing the subject of her disclosure.

Two other letters would come logically in this sequence, after the secret has been told. Letter 249 is an ecstatic thank-you letter, ending with the great gift of a poem written especially for him:

> [Sh]ould you but fail [at]—Sea—
> [In] sight of me—
> [Or] doomed lie—
> [Ne]xt Sun—to die—
> [O]r rap—at Paradise—unheard
> I'd *harrass God*
> Until he let [you] in! [226]

A second letter (252) reiterates this gratitude: "I cant thank you any more—You are thoughtful so many times. . . ." She ends with a quatrain expressing the difficulty she had in talking with him: *Speech*—is a prank of *Parliament*—/*Tears*—a trick of the *nerve*—/But the Heart with the heaviest freight on—/Does'nt—always—move—."

Still another letter to Bowles fits somewhere in this sequence. It is a letter of explanation and clarification, a self-justification that claims even a high degree of religious achievement:

> Dear friend
>   If you doubted my Snow—for a moment—you never will—again—I know—
>   Because I could not say it—I fixed it in the Verse—for you to read—when your thought wavers, for such a foot as mine—
>
> > Through the strait pass of suffering—
> > The Martyrs—even—trod.
> > Their feet—upon Temptation—
> > Their faces—upon God—
> >
> > A stately—shriven—Company—
> > Convulsion—playing round—
> > Harmless—as streaks of Meteor—
> > Upon a Planet's Bond—
> >
> > Their faith—the everlasting troth—
> > Their Expectation—fair—
> > The Needle—to the North Degree—
> > Wades—so—thro' polar Air! [792; Letter 251]

Somewhere in her disclosures she must have alarmed Bowles, made him doubt her innocence. She reassures him with this poem, which also communicates her sense that the greatest crisis has passed. She communicates to Bowles the same perception she had been exploring in the fascicles, that her life had now entered an unchanging state, that no more momentous changes were to be expected.

Bowles's reason for doubting her "snow" may well have been the "Wife" confession of letter 250, as Johnson conjectures in his biography of Emily Dickinson. But added to this was a further compromising element in their relationship. Dickinson had been having the Bowleses address letters from her to a correspondent whose name has not come down to us. In a letter of March 1862 (letter 256), she asks Bowles to "put the name–on–too" and enclose a letter. She requests this "again," indicating that the practice is not new. In letter 253, she asks Mrs. Bowles to do Bowles's "errand" for her, with regard to "a little note" which she encloses, since Bowles was out of town. As early as August 1861 she was asking Mrs. Bowles for the same service, feeling the need to explain the request apologetically: "We are all human–Mary–until we are divine– and to some of us–that is far off . . . . Can I rely on your 'name'?" (letter 235). In her distress Dickinson may have felt compelled to reveal to Bowles the secret of her marriage, at least partly to justify this questionable secrecy in her correspondence.

Dickinson used other friends, also, to address certain letters and send them on for her. Dr. and Mrs. Josiah Holland were friends of long standing; Dr. Holland was part owner, with Bowles, of the *Springfield Republican*. Dickinson corresponded with the Hollands from 1853 until her death. When their granddaughter, Theodora Ward, came to edit the extant Holland-Dickinson letters in 1951, she stated, "It has always been understood by the Holland family that for many years Emily made a practice of sending Mrs. Holland the letters she wrote to Dr. Wadsworth, to be addressed and forwarded to Philadelphia."[27] Dickinson's surviving letters to the Hollands substantiate this information. Her letter to Mrs. Holland of December 1877 contains the following:

> I enclose a Note, which if you would lift as far as Philadelphia, if it did not tire your Arms–would please me so much.
> Would the Doctor be willing to address it? Ask him, with my love. [letter 525]

In a letter of October 1879 she writes: "I ask you to ask your Doctor [Mr. Holland] will he be so kind as to write the name of my Philadelphia friend on the Note within, and your little Hand will take it to him" (letter 619). Early in 1881 she asks Mrs. Holland, "Will you let me take hold of your Hand to lead this little Note to the mail?" (letter 687). Charles Wadsworth died the following year and no further requests of this nature appear in her letters.

This is a sampling of such requests to address letters to Philadelphia which Dickinson made of the Hollands. They all derive from around 1876 to 1881. Bowles and his wife, as we have seen, were addressing letters for her in the early 1860s.

Relatively few letters from Dickinson to Bowles exist after this period of the early 1860s. Most remarkable, perhaps, are her letters to Mrs.

Bowles, after her husband's death on January 16, 1878. They are full of acknowledged love for "Mr. Sam," but in the context of the love she always felt for Mrs. Bowles as well. Dickinson lost a great friend and confidant in Samuel Bowles, but not, it seems, a husband.

The Case for Wadsworth

Though charged with legend and surmise, as Jay Leyda warned,[28] the very substantial case for the Reverend Charles Wadsworth as Dickinson's beloved should not be underestimated. A large amount of evidence from her poems and letters converges on him to make a more convincing case than that for any other known person in her life.

It is worth asserting at this point that there are several questions that need separate treatment: whether the "you" poems indicate a single addressee to whom the poems were written; whether the identity tags in these poems indicate a clergyman more appropriately than a man of any other profession; and whether, finally, that clergyman can be more specifically identified as Charles Wadsworth. Evidence concerning the first question has already been presented in chapter 1. The other two questions can now be looked at more directly.

Dickinson's fascicle poems (as well as some of the later poems which seem connected to the fascicles by reason of theme, imagery or addressee) contain a number of specific identity tags for the addressee. They all point to the profession of the "You" to whom the poems are addressed as that of a clergyman. It should be emphasized that these are the *only* phrases that seem to identify the activities or the profession of her addressee, and that they *all* point to his identity as a clergyman. Several of these have been noted as they came up earlier in this study; they are repeated here for convenience.

In the first fascicle, in poem 4, he is her "Pilot" who will get her to "Eternity," as if he is her religious counselor. Poem 274 describes him as looking like Moses, "Mosaic," though not to the extreme of wearing "sandals"; he is dressed rather in the "Mechlin" lace of a contemporary clergyman. In 324, if we are correct in concluding that all the fascicle poems are addressed to the beloved, she alludes archly to him as among those who "keep the Sabbath, in Surplice"—a garb that serves to distinguish the clergy from the laity. Poem 336 celebrates the lovers' reunion in heaven after death. It is addressed to "You," to her "Master." In this poem he communicates with "the Raised," i.e., with Jesus, regarding His "Kingdom," in a special way not open to the ordinary person.

Poem 376 opens abruptly, as if it is a direct and indignant response to one of his clerical pieces of advice: "Of Course—I prayed." She chides him: his initial motive in their relationship was "Charity," but he has stirred her and left her in more distress than he found her in. The poem thus represents a relationship that began in counselling, for religious motives, and which proceeded with typically clerical advice long after it had changed to something far more humanly intense and personal.

Poem 433, in Fascicle 19, is also addressed to "You" and begs for the knowledge and strength to forget him—not a sentiment the mystic would feel in reference to God. When this poem was amplified and placed in a later set, the "You" was further identified as "Rabbi of the Wise Book." There are some interesting mysteries here. If in its second version the poem continues to be addressed to the beloved, whom she wants to forget, then he is a "Rabbi" or "teacher" of the Wise Book, the Bible. A further link with the beloved, in Dickinson's mind, seems to be forged from the fact that the most accepted translation of "Rabbi" is "My Master," the term that she uses in her most intense poems and letters to the beloved.

In poem 449 two idealists have died and found themselves buried side by side. The speaker has died for "Beauty," surely identifying Dickinson herself as the poet. Her "kinsman" has died for "Truth." The word may describe Bowles's ideal as a journalist, but it would even better describe Wadsworth's as a clergyman. Poem 487 describes the life of a clergyman with literal exactness: "You love the Lord—you cannot see—/You write Him—every day," whether in sermons or in a religious diary. In this poem the "House" of the Lord "is but a Step" for him, indicating the precise location of a clergyman's home, next to the church he serves.

The great conversation poem, 640, has already been discussed at length, but relevant details can be recalled here. Dickinson anatomizes the stages of her life—life, death, resurrection, judgment, heaven or hell— from the perspective of a clerical counselor. She refers to the cupboard where the implements of the communion service are stored, in the presbytery setting for this conversation. She alludes to the "door ajar" that a cautious counselor would insist on. And she acknowledges his professional duty to "serve heaven" which distinguishes his occupation from the laity's.

In 709 Dickinson mounts her objections to a correspondent who has suggested publication, for money, of her poetry. Her climactic argument would appeal strongly to a clergyman, would perhaps not even be understood by anyone else. This is the phrase, towards the end of the poem, where she offers him an analogy to the sale of her poems: "Be the Merchant/Of the Heavenly Grace." The argument here is that publication would be equivalent to one of the greatest sins in his profession, "Simony," the sale of graces and indulgences for money.

Poem 740 anticipates union with the beloved in "Christ's bright Audience." The "You" to whom it is addressed is therefore not Christ.

The poem climaxes with "The Heaven you know" in some special way not available to everyone. Once again, the identity tag would apply most normally to a clergyman, whose studies and personal experiences would justify this phrase.

Poem 1059, in one of the later sets, addresses "Sire" and begs him to listen to her songs: they may be sad but they sing only of him. The poem ends, "Pause in your Liturgies–/Wait your Chorals–/While I repeat your /Hallowed name." Liturgies and chorals are not metaphors which apply readily, with any ease, to the professional work of any of the other possible contenders for Dickinson's love. But they apply with literal accuracy to the clerical Master of her songs, whose professional status she has felt to compete with her for his attention.

If a writer selects subject matter for its strong appeal to the audience, it becomes quite clear that Dickinson's addressee is an intensely committed religious practitioner. Among her fascicle poems are definitions of faith, hope, charity, and repentance, discussions of the afterlife, judgment and paradise, developments of sermon topics on Biblical stories. Five poems (260, 295, 325, 544, and 792) suggest that she and her addressee model their behavior on the Christian martyrs; classic sources in a clergyman's sermon repertory would be the martyr chapters in the New Testament, Revelations 19, and Hebrews 11; a book he would be sure to know and recommend would be the classic of Protestant Christianity, Foxe's *Book of Martyrs*. In fact, within the whole range of Dickinson's subject matter, reference, and allusion, nothing so predominates as the religious, as if that was the area in which she most hoped to interest her addressee. Unless we are to propose some figure totally unknown to the careful students of Dickinson's life, Wadsworth most clearly fits the description.

Still another class of poems recalls snatches from his sermonizing or from conversations regarding their dilemma. In 215 Dickinson quotes from a sermon on "Paradise" which compares it to "Eden" and further links it with the "Farmers" of "Amherst." It is addressed to the "You" of the fascicles. The poem ends with some reservations regarding the persuasiveness of the sermon, as if it has been spoken directly to her and requires her response. Poem 234 also quotes directly from her addressee's sermonizing and responds with her running commentary:

> You're right–"the way *is* narrow"–
> And "difficult the Gate"–
> And "few there be"–Correct again–
> That "enter in–thereat"–
>
> '*Tis* Costly–So are *purples*!
> 'Tis just the price of *Breath*–
> With but the "Discount" of the *Grave*–
> Termed by the *Brokers*–''*Death*''!

> And after *that*—there's Heaven—
> And *Good* Man's—"*Dividend*"—
> And *Bad* Men—"go to Jail"—
> I guess—

In the first stanza Dickinson accepts her clergyman's text, from the Sermon on the Mount (Matthew 7.14), and the conclusions he derives from it, as unimpeachable. Her own reflections follow, with what must be ironic comment that the purchase price of the Christian's reward is "discounted"—diminished or made less—by "Death." The "*Brokers*" here must be the clergy, the middlemen between God and the soul, who would stand with St. Paul in attempting to minimize the sting of death, the victory of the grave (I Corinthians 15.55)—a text to which Dickinson will return on other occasions. The poem has been described as an example of Dickinson's "scandalous frivolity" regarding orthodox notions of the Last Judgment.[29] But without succumbing to the shock of scandal, and seriously questioning a frivolous tone here, the reader nevertheless notes Dickinson's reluctance, in the last two words of the poem, to accept the pattern of life thus thrust upon her by her orthodox counselor. Love for him does not force her acceptance of his mercantile metaphors.

A few poems later in this same fascicle Dickinson returns to the question of afterlife, now phrased as "how my shape will rise," with a text from Matthew (10.29) for added consideration:

> I think just how my shape will rise—
> When I shall be '*'forgiven*"—
> Till Hair—and Eyes—and timid Head—
> Are *out of sight*—in Heaven—
>
> I think just how my lips will weigh—
> With shapeless—quivering—prayer—
> That you—*so late*—"*Consider*" me—
> The "*Sparrow*" of your Care—
>
> I mind me that of Anguish—sent—
> *Some* drifts were moved away—
> Before my simple bosom—broke—
> And why not *this*—if *they?*
>
> And so I con that thing—"*forgiven*"—
> Until—delirious—borne—
> By my long bright—and *longer—trust*—
> I *drop* my Heart—*unshriven!* [237]

This poem also responds to words from his sermonizing, which she quotes back to him, again disagreeing. There appear to be two problems in the poem. The first lies in identification of the "you" of lines 7 and 8. If the poem is isolated from the fascicles it can be read as a prayer, with the "you" who cares for her as God. The biblical citation regarding the "*Sparrow*" would support that interpretation, even though such direct address to God is unusual for Dickinson. But in the context of the fascicles, especially following so closely upon the dialogue on the same subject in the poem just considered, it is entirely possible that her religious counselor is the one whose "Care" she appreciates.

This reading seems all the more likely in view of the ending of the poem, where the second obscurity occurs. The second half of the poem moves through the search for some escape from the guilt she feels, the "Anguish" her guilt causes, and the need to be "*forgiven*." In answer she argues that her "Heart" is the guilty organ, and since she leaves it behind at death she leaves behind her guilt as well. There is no need to repent in the meantime. No real skill in rhetoric is needed here to detect the obvious equivocation. The argument, if addressed to God, is the transparent sophistry of one who refuses to repent but wants to be saved anyway. But if it is addressed to the lover it is another hyperbolic protestation of her love as absolutely unchangeable. In the context of the fascicles, the "you" of lines 7 and 8 is surely the beloved and the poem as a whole is a love poem addressed to him. The final word of the poem is as much a rejection of his pious platitudes as it is a triumphant claim to his love.

Finally, one of the most conclusive pieces of evidence that the beloved is a clergyman is presented in poem 944. This is Dickinson's imagined view of what their married life together would be like:

> I learned—at least—what Home could be—
> How ignorant I had been
> Of pretty ways of Covenant—
> How awkward at the Hymn
>
> Round our new Fireside—but for this—
> This pattern—of the Way—
> Whose Memory drowns me, like the Dip
> Of a Celestial Sea—
>
> What Mornings in our Garden—guessed—
> What Bees—for us—to hum—
> With only Birds to interrupt
> The Ripple of our Theme—
>
> And Task for Both—
> When Play be done—
> Your Problem—of the Brain—
> And mine—some foolisher effect—
> A Ruffle—or a Tune—

The Afternoons—Together spent—
And Twilight—in the Lanes—
Some ministry to poorer lives—
Seen poorest—thro' our gains—

And then Return—and Night—and Home—

And then away to You to pass—
A new—diviner—care—
Till Sunrise take us back to Scene—
Transmuted—Vivider—

This seems a Home—
And Home is not—
But what that Place could be—
Afflicts me—as a Setting Sun—
Where Dawn—knows how to be—

The poem presents the imagined and idealized life of the married couple. The reader's attention will immediately be drawn to the delicately and tantalizingly unfinished stanza, where the three unwritten lines draw a curtain of privacy over the most intimate aspects of their marriage. The life is imagined in which both enjoy a considerable amount of leisure together. His profession is described as work "of the Brain" and evidently is both lucrative and undemanding enough to support hours of "Play" in the mornings, as well as "Afternoons—Together spent" and long evenings "Round our new Fireside" together. His profession is one in which she is expected to participate, as his wife—unlike the lawyer's work of her father and brother or the journalistic work of Bowles. It is the visitation side of the pastor's work, and is called explicitly "Ministry" in the poem.

In describing the difficult problem of Dickinson's relationship with the Reverend Charles Wadsworth, there are reasons for beginning toward the end of Dickinson's life, with the letters she wrote to the Clark brothers, friends of Wadsworth. These letters contain her most overt references to the clergyman.

James C. Clark had initiated the correspondence in the summer of 1882, carrying out Wadsworth's deathbed request to have a copy of his published sermons sent to Dickinson. No fewer than twenty-one letters from Dickinson to the Clark brothers remain, written during the last four years of her life.

A sampling of phrases from these letters tells us much about the relationship between Dickinson and Wadsworth. It was "an intimacy of many years. . . . I cannot conjecture a world without him"; he is "the beloved Clergyman" in this letter (letter 773). She thanks Clark for sending her a photograph of Wadsworth, and says she expects Wadsworth to "assist me in another World" (letter 776). In letter 807 Wadsworth is "my dearest earthly friend. . . . my lost friend." As James Clark was dying Dickinson wrote to his brother Charles, "Perhaps the one has called him, of whom we have so often talked, during this grieved year" (letter 818). In letter 827 she thanks Charles Clark for "a paper which mentioned Wadsworth," according to the editor of the *Letters*: "Thank you for the paper. I felt it almost a bliss of sorrow that the name so long in Heaven on earth, should be on earth in Heaven." In letter 859 Wadsworth is referred to as the "Fugitive, whom to know was Life." In letter 872 Wadsworth is "the great friend." In letter 880 he is "The Heaven that evanesced." Barely a month before she died Dickinson addressed two letters to Charles Clark asking for still more information about Wadsworth, requesting current news of his children. From the death of Wadsworth to her own death she was aggressively persistent in maintaining contact with the only people she knew who had been close to him.

During these last years of her life she referred to Wadsworth in letters to other correspondents as well. To her friend Judge Otis P. Lord she wrote on April 30, 1882, "My Philadelphia has passed from the earth" (letter 750). Wadsworth had died April 1. Her phrase recalls *Antony and Cleopatra*, where the enamored Antony addresses his forbidden beloved as "My Egypt"; Dickinson mentions the play in a letter to Lord from about the same time (letter 791). She wrote to Lord again of the death of "My Clergyman" in December of the same year.

These many statements by Dickinson late in her life force us back into the existing record for the intervening years, from the time she stopped binding her fascicles until these late references to Wadsworth. Some anchor points exist during these years, marking off convenient divisions. In 1862 Wadsworth abruptly decamped, moving himself and his family from a successful practice in Philadelphia all the way to the frontier city of San Francisco, where he was installed as pastor of the Calvary Church in November of 1862. In 1869, after seven years of this exile, he returned to Philadelphia, to the Third Reformed Dutch Church there. In 1873 he was prominent in the news again, for the last time in his professional career. He led his flock out from the Reformed Church into the Presbyterian fold. Five years of dispute followed in the Philadelphia law courts regarding title to church property formerly held by the Reformed Dutch Church.[30] The next fully documented event in the Wadsworth-Dickinson relationship is his sudden and unexpected visit to Dickinson "Twenty years later" in the summer of 1880. Finally, as we have seen, Wadsworth's death in April 1882 elicited numerous comments from her. These dates will guide us through this section of our study of Dickinson's poems.

We begin, then, with the first period, the time between Wadsworth's departure for San Francisco in 1862 and his return to Philadelphia in 1869. During this period Dickinson was in her middle to late thirties; she began corresponding with Thomas Wentworth Higginson about her poems; she twice spent seven months in Boston (1864 and 1865) for treatment of an eye problem, perhaps psychosomatic in origin. The period is interesting poetically for the breakdown of her practice of collecting poems into tied booklets. She continued to gather current poems but was apparently unable to select and arrange them satisfactorily, nor did she tie them with string as she had the fascicles. Franklin, in his 1981 edition, has called these gatherings "Sets," and has found that there are fifteen of them. Also from this period are individual poems which exist in unique manuscript drafts.

Several remarkable love poems are found among these sets and poems. Poem 663 recalls one of the rare interviews the lovers had enjoyed. The surviving evidence records only one visit by Wadsworth (in spring 1860) before his second recorded visit much later (in August 1880). But if he is the beloved husband, then the first word of this poem, dated by handwriting "about 1862," requires other visits, or perhaps a series of several meetings during a protracted visit by Wadsworth to Amherst in the spring of 1860.

Again—his voice is at the door—
I feel the old *Degree*—
I hear him ask the servant
For such an one—as me—

I take a *flower*—as I go—
My face to *justify*—
He never *saw* me—*in this life*—
I might *surprise* his eye!

I cross the Hall with *mingled* steps—
I—silent—pass the door—
I look on all this world *contains*—
Just his face—nothing more!

We talk in *careless*—and in *toss*—
A kind of *plummet* strain—
Each—sounding—shily—
Just—how—deep—
The *other's* one—had been—

We *walk*—I leave my Dog—at home—
A *tender—thoughtful* Moon
Goes with us—just a little way—
And—then—we are *alone*—

Alone–if *Angels* are "alone"–
First time they *try* the *sky!*
Alone–if those "vailed faces"–be–
We cannot *count*–on High!

I'd give–to live that hour–*again*–
The *purple*–*in my Vein*–
But *He* must *count the drops*–*himself*–
My price for *every stain*!

The first two lines insist that this is not the first visit; that it is a visit from the husband who has conferred a new "*Degree*" upon her, a higher status in life; and that his remarkable "voice" has the power to move her. Even Dickinson's sister Lavinia responded to that unusual voice; in one of the letters to Charles Clark (in mid-April 1886) Dickinson included the following item in describing Wadsworth's last visit: "The last time he came in Life, I was with my Lilies and Heliotropes, said my sister to me, 'the Gentleman with the deep voice wants to see you, Emily' " (letter 1040). In a poem from 1871, she recalls "the Voice that stands for Floods to me" (1189).

The circumstance alluded to in the poem would surely be understood by the beloved to whom it is addressed, but we who stand outside are presented with a puzzle. The first word of the poem insists on at least one previous visit, yet line 7 says "He never *saw* me–*in this life*." Solution to the problem must come from Dickinson's frequent analysis of the "new life" conferred on her by her marriage, and this recorded visit then becomes the first one they enjoyed after the marriage event had taken place.

The poem also connects the beloved with the addressee of the "Master" letters. The second of these letters, which dates from somewhere within the period 1858-1861, contains the following plea: "Couldn't Carlo [her dog] and you and I walk in the meadows an hour–and nobody care but the Bobolink–and *his*–a silver scruple?" (letter 233). The request is in the context of a protestation of her love–that she has expressed it to him numerous times as clearly as she knows how, and that if she were the man and loved as strongly, then she would surely come to visit him. The poem describes the kind of walk she has in mind, in its fifth stanza. But where the letter is anguished longing, the poem is joyous fulfillment. One wonders whether the second Master letter had its intended effect, or whether the poem substitutes for an impossible reality, a potentially compromising scenario for a married clergyman to take a part in. The letter goes on to a plea that the Master "come to New England . . . to Amherst"; the poem, then, with its realistic details, would persuade us that she celebrates the answer to that plea.

Another memorable love poem, from Set 5, also comes out of this second Master letter. The letter begins with Dickinson's description of herself as a wounded bird, who would tell less than the truth about herself if she denied her wound:

Master.
　If you saw a bullet hit a Bird—and he told you he was'nt shot—you might weep at his courtesy, but you would certainly doubt his word.
　One drop more from the gash that stains your Daisy's bosom—then would you *believe*? Thomas' faith in Anatomy, was stronger than his faith in faith. [Letter 233]

The poem likewise brings together the wounded bird and the doubting Thomas:

> Split the Lark—and you'll find the Music—
> Bulb after Bulb, in Silver rolled—
> Scantily dealt to the Summer Morning
> Saved for your Ear when Lutes be old.
>
> Loose the Flood—you shall find it patent—
> Gush after Gush, reserved for you—
> Scarlet Experiment! Sceptic Thomas!
> Now, do you doubt that your Bird was true?
> [861]

The poem has been taken as a generalized statement on the esthetics of song. But it is surely rather a lover's protest of eternal fidelity, no matter what the pain, and a loving complaint that such fidelity can be doubted. Both the letter and the poem insist on the reality of her love and the depth of her devotedness, in the face of his incomprehension. And the imagery of the fatally wounded bird surely connects the two. The dull beloved is addressed as "You" in no fewer than five of the eight lines of the poem and the final line clinches the fact that the genre is surely the love poem. The tunes are "scantily dealt" to the world at large (exactly Dickinson's practice); they are mainly "saved for your Ear." The love is a painful one, with images of surgical destruction in the first stanza and the "Scarlet Experiment" in the second. The poem is not about poetic theory but about her love for her husband.

A similar claim is also made in the following poem:

> Bind me—I still can sing—
> Banish—my mandolin
> Strikes true within—
>
> Slay—and my Soul shall rise
> Chanting to Paradise—
> Still thine. [1005]

Both singing and being slain as proofs of her love are the themes of this poem also. The unique audience is again the beloved addressed in the second person.

Dickinson's unique "marriage" situation, as we have come to understand it through the fascicles, is reflected in many of the poems of this period. In 493 the fact of the marriage is reasserted, along with its effect of heightening her formal dignity as an adult: "The World—stands—solemner—to me—/Since I was wed—to Him." The poem is unequivocal assertion of her married state.

But the marriage has unique conditions. Poem 433, in its 1865 version in the sets, is addressed to "You" and asks for the wisdom to forget. The poem ends with a direct address identifying the husband as a clergyman and asking him for his advice on how to forget him: "Rabbi of the Wise Book/Dont you know?"

Four other poems from this period present more abstract reflections on the marriage situation. Both husband and wife must now play the role of homeless exile. In 1010 both of them have accepted "Homelessness" as a substitute for "Home" in order to "Spotless be from blame." In 1017 her homeless situation is described in paradoxes: "To die—without the Dying/And live—without the Life." And in 1022, to bear the lonely pain would be impossible without her assurance that "Another bear it's Duplicate/In other Continent." Poem 944 records with gratitude that at least her imagination has been flooded with new experience because of her marriage: "I learned—at least—what Home could be."

The beloved remains intensely present in these sets, once again identified as "Thee" to whom the poems are addressed, a "Thee" so intensely personal and individualized that the general reader is unable to find himself in the world of the poem itself, surely not as the one so intimately addressed. The reader must still view the poems from outside, as a privileged observer.

This beloved "Thee" is frequently spoken of in terms that describe Wadsworth, now self-exiled in San Francisco. Poem 1022 imagines his bearing the same pain "In other Continent." Poem 808 protests that no day is dark "So set it's Sun in Thee," and imagines the ships that touch his distant shore as links between them. A poem written in 1864 (846) protests that for two years Nature had been bountiful, but not to her; Wadsworth had left two years earlier, in 1862. Poem 863 sees their separation as created "not of Mile or Main" but by "The Will," by their own choice. The presence of "Thee" in her life is now relegated entirely to dreams, in 939: "I arise—and in my Dream—/Do Thee distinguished Grace—/Till jealous Daylight interrupt." In 1029 she protests that their union will not be hindered by Mountain or by Sea. In a poem that begs for an "Answer" from "Thee," she complains, "Somewhere thy sweet Face has spilled/Beyond my Boundary'' (881). The beauties of nature now terrify her, ''Thou from Here, so far'' (956). Most striking of the love poems addressed to the absent ''Thee'' is surely the following:

> 'Twas my one Glory—
> Let it be
> Remembered
> I was owned of Thee— [1028]

But even its power is matched by the prayer that concludes 882: ''O God/Why give if Thou must take away/The Loved?''

The theme that becomes most urgent during this period of Wadsworth's absence in San Francisco, most the point of anchorage for the pattern her life has now assumed, is that of lovers meeting for endless marriage in heaven. Poem 925 acknowledges that she was ''Struck. . . . Maimed. . . . Robbed'' by the beloved; paradoxically, ''Most—I love the Cause that slew Me.'' But each now looks forward to ''the infinite Aurora/In the other's eyes.'' In another set, in poem 850, she waits to join the other at death, and uses the intervening time to ''sing.'' According to poem 1040, those who love on earth are doomed to eventual separation: ''Division is Adhesion's forfeit''; but ''On High'' this will not be so. In 1046 the present ''Paralysis'' will surely give way ''To Being, somewhere,'' though it be centuries away. The four brief lines of 1001 state her situation exactly:

> The Stimulus, beyond the Grave
> His Countenance to see
> Supports me like imperial Drams
> Afforded Day by Day.

The editors of *Poems* (1896) did not understand the last line as a reference to the Marriage Day, and they altered it to read ''Afforded royally.'' And 897 repeats the needed fulfillment:

> How fortunate the Grave—
> All Prizes to obtain—
> Successful certain, if at last,
> First Suitor not in vain.

Progressing to the next major period in Wadsworth's life for which we have some documentation, one comes upon a date listed in most of Dickinson's biographies, October 16, 1869, the date Wadsworth left his church in San Francisco and moved his family back to Philadelphia, where he accepted a call to become pastor of the Third Reformed Dutch Church. The Dickinson family's favorite newspaper, the *Springfield Re-*

publican, carried a notice of this transfer on the date noted above.[31] The move had been announced in the papers several months earlier. Dickinson had felt doubly estranged from Wadsworth by his move to San Francisco, where they were separated by a vast continent. It is also an established matter of Dickinson's biography, mentioned earlier in this chapter, that she corresponded steadily with Wadsworth during this time, reportedly using others to address her letters.

The period from Wadsworth's return to Philadelphia until his last visit to Dickinson covers about eleven years, from 1869 to 1880. Just over three hundred of Dickinson's poems survive from this period, numbered by Johnson 1136 to 1464. The relatively small number has been taken to indicate a diminution in her creative powers, from the peak productivity of about the same number in the single year 1862. But the record of these years displays some oddities which need fuller pondering.

The poems of these years fall into three categories. Some are found in the late "Sets." A second noticeable category contains finished occasional poems which Dickinson sent to Sue and to other friends, many of which exist both in pencilled worksheet drafts and in the final form which she sent, and which were later retrieved from the recipients. A third category contains poems relating to her marriage themes. The oddity of this category is that there are very few poems in it and that nearly all exist in pencilled worksheet drafts. It is tempting to argue by analogy with the second category, that she sent finished versions of these remarkable poems also: the established fact that she continued to correspond with Wadsworth increases the temptation. A clergyman's professional correspondence would be sealed and probably destroyed shortly after his death, to protect the privacy of those who sought his counsel. In the absence of any of Wadsworth's professional papers one comes to the melancholy conclusion that whatever Dickinson sent him must have been destroyed.

A few of the poems from this last category are in finished form and are described by Johnson as "folded as if enclosed in a letter"–they are poems which Dickinson may have decided not to send, for reasons that can be determined in some cases from their content. It is important to recall that Dickinson sent Wadsworth her poems all along, just as he sent her copies of his sermons, and that each responded to the other's work in creative ways. At least twelve poems from a long span of years have been noted as similar to passages from Wadsworth's printed sermons. Though the question of dates presents some uncertainty, it seems that the influence was mutual: each inspired the other, on occasion, to a telling sequence of words or imagery.[32]

Among the worksheet marriage poems written during this period of Dickinson's life are several "Thee" poems. Virtually all of these pencilled drafts assume the presence of the beloved still in her life, an active presence though they are separated physically and geographically. In 1145 the poet imagines "thy long Paradise of Light" where she will feel no need for "Earthly Play" or other Company. In 1155 she defines "Distance" as "Until thyself, Beloved." In 1171 memory recalls "the World you colored" as better than that which Nature colors. A brief poem begins as an *aubade* but ends with the terrors of separation: "Let my first Knowing be of thee/With Morning's warming Light—/And my first Fearing, lest Unknowns/Engulph thee in the night—" (1218). A final "Thee" poem from very late in this period (it is dated tentatively as from some time before Christmas 1879), seems to indicate a new surge of sorrow, shortly before Wadsworth's 1880 visit, perhaps stimulating that visit:

> One thing of thee I covet—
> The power to forget—
> The pathos of the Avarice
> Defrays the Dross of it—
>
> One thing of thee I borrow
> And promise to return—
> The Booty and the Sorrow
> Thy sweetness to have known— [1464]

The intense compactness of the poem and the oxymoronic turn of thought are among the qualities that reward connoisseurs of Dickinson's late poetry. She asks the power to forget while fiercely retaining the right to remember. The beloved is surely a lively presence in the poem, spoken as it is immediately to him.

The same mood pervades 1132, with its striking images of sexual deprivation:

> The smouldering embers blush—
> Oh Cheek within the Coal
> Hast thou survived so many nights?
> The smouldering embers smile—
> Soft stirs the news of Light
> The stolid Rafters glow
> One requisite has Fire that lasts
> Prometheus never knew—

The poem is dated "about 1868," and Johnson speculates that "it is possible that ED wrote the poem upon learning that Charles Wadsworth was leaving his San Francisco pastorate and returning to the East." Clearly that return held at least the hope of renewed intimacy, of at least a nearer proximity to the beloved.

Johnson has also suggested another of the poems as Dickinson's response to the news that Wadsworth was returning home from San Francisco to Philadelphia in 1869. Both dating and content lead one to concur:

> Oh Sumptuous moment
> Slower go
> That I may gloat on thee—
> 'Twill never be the same to starve
> Now I abundance see—
>
> Which was to famish, then or now—
> The difference of Day
> Ask him unto the Gallows led—
> With morning in the sky [1125]

The sense of their mutual exile is strong in all of these marriage poems and may suggest the answer to a puzzle in 1290. Evidently the beloved was not as diligent a correspondent as she:

> The most pathetic thing I do
> Is play I hear from you—
> I make believe until my Heart
> Almost believes it too
> But when I break it with the news
> You knew it was not true
> I wish I had not broken it—
> Goliah—so would you—

The addressee of this poem is called "Goliah," a puzzling designation for the beloved until one discovers that the glossaries for several nineteenth-century editions of the King James Version of the Bible speculated that the name of David's gigantic opponent means "Exile."

In addition to these marriage poems there are many others of the period which recapitulate or extend themes from the fascicle years. Poems 1175 and 1239 continue Dickinson's considerations of the "risks" involved in the wager she had made: life would not be as exciting "If we had ventured less," even though "Risk is the Hair that holds" the heavy weight suspended over our heads. The River-Sea imagery of earlier poems continues as a useful trope: poem 1210 argues a complex proposition that the brook waits to postpone its flowing to the sea until it can mature to be a Sea itself, even though it involves the risk that the Sea will not then be ready to accept its lover as equal; but 1237 acknowledges the prior fact that "My Heart so ran to thee" and "Basks" there, even though the rest of her has not yet caught up. It is as if she is sending the beloved her latest considerations on the imagery of her earlier erotic sea poems.

The ethical imperative to "Forget his Morning Forces" is repeated in

1280, with its rationale, "He has obligation/Who has Paradise," given in 1348. Such forgetting is not passive but a consciously imposed denial, a painful abstention: in 1240 Bread is a Divine thing "Disclosed to be denied"; in 1291 "Sahara" is content until it hears of the existence of "Caspian," and then its desert dies for lack of water; the condition is named "sumptuous Destitution" in 1382 and "The Banquet of Abstemiousness" in 1430. In one of her most powerfully sexual poems Dickinson wrote an exact statement of her condition in three lines:

> Of Life to own—
> From Life to draw—
> But never touch the reservoir—
> [1294]

She possesses sexual capacity to beget children, has actually drawn her own life from that capacity, but she is doomed never to "touch" that capacity in her own life. But erotic pleasure can be re-awakened: poem 1383 begins, "Long Years apart—can make no/Breach a second cannot fill," and ends: "The embers of a Thousand Years/Uncovered by the Hand/That fondled them when they were Fire/Will gleam and understand."

A sense of guilt still pursues her and she would "flee from memory" in 1242; in 1377 she remembers how "luscious" is "Forbidden Fruit." A very difficult poem ends with a surprising evaluation of her religious status, as a Judas: in 1297 she charges her soul to meet some fate that competes with duty—"Go boldly—for thou paid'st his price/Redemption—for a Kiss."

During this time Dickinson turns again, in two poems, to raging hostility against the beloved who has allowed her to starve. Poem 1282 begins: "Art thou the thing I wanted?/Begone—my Tooth has grown—/Supply the minor Palate/That has not starved so long—." She ends this poem with olympian aloofness, preferring to "dine without Like God." And poem 1378 makes the stinging charge that "His Heart was darker than the starless night."

One poem stands out as still another reflection on the marriage Day:

> Had this one Day not been,
> Or could it cease to be
> How smitten, how superfluous,
> Were every other Day!
>
> Lest Love should value less
> What Loss would value more
> Had it the stricken privilege,
> It cherishes before. [1253]

The diction grows more abstract, but the intense recollection of that Day is not thereby diminished. Her anomalous marriage is the only situation which contextualizes the poem satisfactorily.

One is aware that an industry was being conducted at the Homestead. Dickinson habitually worked from late evening after the family had retired until the early morning hours. Working in a room of her own for several hours each night, Dickinson brought the poems and correspondence from draft to final form, rejecting much in the process. The pieces described as "folded as if enclosed in an envelope" must have been returned either to her or to her editors after Dickinson's death, or else aborted by her at the very last moment when the decision was made not to send them. There is no evidence to support the first hypothesis in regard to the poems under consideration. In regard to the second hypothesis, some internal evidence must be considered.

Poem 1339, for example, remains an unsent note "without salutation or signature" as if to avoid incriminating anyone:

Sweet is it as Life, with it's enhancing Shadow of Death.

> A Bee his burnished Carriage
> Drove boldly to a Rose—
> Combinedly alighting—
> Himself—his Carriage was—
> The Rose received his visit
> With frank tranquility
> Witholding not a Crescent
> To his Cupidity—
> Their Moment consummated—
> Remained for him—to flee—
> Remained for her—of rapture
> But the humility.

The poem is one of Dickinson's most frankly sexual poems. Little is left to imagination: the rose surrenders totally, consummation takes place, the bee leaves, and all that is left for the rose is humility. Dickinson surely knew the difference between *humility* and *humiliation*, and she chooses here a word that signifies the lover's devout submission to the beloved, rather than any charge of exploitation of the female by the male. The stages of the encounter are calmly narrated in a clear program mirrored and heightened by the regularity in meter and rhyme. The poem may not have been sent because of its frank eroticism, its potential embarrassment of a married lover; but another reason for witholding it may appear in its cool objectivity, the implied criticism of the man who had loved her and left her.

Finally, for the 1869-80 period, a superb love poem remains, but one that grows clearly from her unusual experience. In a poem of forty lines (epic length for Dickinson), the last meeting of lovers until eternity is a moment lifted "Above Mortality." Eternity is then the subject, with one of Dickinson's finest quatrains to celebrate their love: "Significance that each has lived/The other to detect/Discovery not God himself/Could now annihilate" (1260, lines 9-12). The short period of their physical closeness stands now in her mind as "the Realm of you," and his face obscures for her everything now but "Immortality." This intense love poem, also addressed to "thee," repeats the lovers' heresy of earlier poems in the fascicles: Heaven will be "A Residence too plain/Unless in my Redeemer's Face/I recognize your own."

The next landmark in the Dickinson-Wadsworth relationship can now be looked at, the final meeting in Amherst some two years previous to Wadsworth's death in 1882. In her letters to the Clark brothers, Dickinson twice mentions Wadsworth's last visit, dating it around the summer of 1880. In her first letter to James D. Clark she writes:

> I saw him two years since for the last time, though how unsuspected!
> He rang one summer evening to my glad surprise—"Why did you not tell me you were coming, So I could have it to hope for," I said—"Because I did not know it myself. I stepped from my Pulpit to the Train," was his quiet reply. [Letter 766]

When James Clark died, Dickinson continued the correspondence with his brother Charles. In mid-April of 1886 she described to him the same visit, as if reauthenticating her claim to an interest in Wadsworth:

> The last time he came in Life, I was with my Lilies and Heliotropes, said my sister to me, "the Gentleman with the deep voice wants to see you, Emily," hearing him ask of the servant. "Where did you come from," I said, for he spoke like an Apparition.
> "I stepped from my Pulpit [from] to the Train" was my [sic] simple reply, and when I asked "how long," "Twenty Years" said he with inscrutable roguery—but the loved Voice has ceased. . . . [Letter 1040]

The two descriptions certify a meeting between Wadsworth and Dickinson around the summer of 1880. The visit had been preceded by a lapse of twenty years. But obviously they had not forgotten each other; a tone of frank and natural ease with one another is conveyed by both descriptions. The two descriptions give us warrant, as well, to search the private poems written around that time to see if the 1880 meeting stimulated new poetic observations on the relationship.

The first poem to claim our attention does so because it takes up the detail mentioned in both of Dickinson's letters to the Clark brothers, Wadsworth's arrival by *train:*

> I thought the Train would never come—
> How slow the whistle sang—
> I dont believe a peevish Bird
> So whimpered for the Spring—
> I taught my Heart a hundred times
> Precisely what to say—
> Provoking Lover, when you came
> It's Treatise flew away
> To hide my strategy too late
> To wiser be too soon—
> For miseries so halcyon
> The happiness atone—   [1449]

The poem is a redoing of the visit, now with the chance to anticipate Wadsworth's arrival by train which, she said, had taken her by surprise. It is addressed playfully to "Provoking Lover . . . you," and the innocence and joy of earlier love poems seems to be recaptured. She presents herself as being in agony over the slowness of his train's arrival; she rehearses her comments for the meeting many times and then abandons them, finding that the emotion of simple "happiness" dominates. This is another poem which exists only as a "Pencilled worksheet draft," tempting us again to wonder about the existence of a fair copy and its destination. It is dated by handwriting "about 1878," but Johnson in his introduction to the three-volume variorum was the first to admit that his chronology was "tentative . . . only a calculated guess" (I: lxi-lxii), leaving us free to see the poem as a commentary on the 1880 visit.

Of some seventy other poems which can be dated by handwriting at around the time of Wadsworth's last visit, more than half were written in letters to family or friends, as condolences or to accompany small gifts, or simply as gifts themselves. Among the remaining poems, however, at least five are descriptions of an important meeting.

Like many of the late love poems, 1507 exists only in a worksheet draft, as if it were a private record which did not need polishing for a recipient, or as if the polished version had been sent off but never retrieved:

> The Pile of Years is not so high
> As when you came before
> But it is rising every Day
> From recollection's Floor
> And while by stepping on my Heart
> I still can reach the top
> Efface the burden with your face
> And catch me ere I drop

The first two lines set up a time scheme which corresponds to the known visits of Wadsworth: Dickinson was in her late twenties when he first visited, but she had not had to wait quite so long for the present visit. The remainder of the poem seems relatively calm, a graceful compliment: as the years of separation pile up they become like a wall separating the lovers; directly addressing "you" she asks for his presence to remove that wall.

Another description of the interview may be contained in poem 1495: "The Thrill came slowly like a Boon/for Centuries delayed. . . ." The substance of the meeting is also conveyed in two other poems. Poem 1500 indicates a change in their roles, during this meeting:

> It came his turn to beg—
> The begging for the life
> Is different from another Alms
> 'Tis Penury in Chief—
>
> I scanned his narrow realm
> I gave him leave to live
> Lest Gratitude revive the snake
> Though smuggled his reprieve

The reversal of roles seems to indicate Dickinson's sense that she was the beggar originally, perhaps in her demands for more of his time and attention, if not for actual marriage. Now he is the beggar for the same kind of "life," and his begging only reveals the "Penury" of his life. Whatever it was that he begged for, her response is in the second stanza, where she seems to relish the upper hand in the game of sexual politics. But so private is the poem—so specific to the actual interview—that there is no telling exactly how she answered the question: it had to be in some way that would not evoke his "Gratitude" and thus stir the temptation ("snake") back to life; but still it had to smuggle in "reprieve" for him, grant him some diminution of their sentence of separation. Clearly Dickinson felt in control of her emotions and of the situation, though she is not interested in conveying details to readers a hundred years later.

This poem seems linked to another poem of the same period by the word "reprieve." Poem 1473 records a meeting and features the word as important:

> We talked with each other about each other
> Though neither of us spoke—
> We were listening to the seconds Races
> And the Hoofs of the Clock—
> Pausing in Front of our Palsied Faces

> Time compassion took—
> Arks of Reprieve he offered to us—
> Ararats—we took—

It seems to be a special kind of meeting, where meaning is communicated in several modes of speech and silence, where their awareness of the quick passage of time is alarming. The earlier wording of one line introduces a significant thought: for "Time compassion took," Dickinson had written "Time's Decision shook," as if at least at one point she considered the interview as a dangerous moment during which the lovers thought of reversing the decision, recorded in the fascicles, to remain apart. But in the final version of the poem, Time is compassionate in offering them at least a temporary "reprieve" to their long sentence of separation.

A fifth poem presents the most circumstantial description of this meeting:

> His voice decrepit was with Joy—
> Her words did totter so
> How old the News of Love must be
> To make Lips elderly
> That purled a moment since with Glee—
> Is it Delight or Woe—
> Or Terror—that do decorate
> This livid interview— [1476]

Research by Vivian R. Pollak has recently turned up the information that even as early as his tenure in San Francisco (1862-69) Wadsworth suffered severe speech difficulties, a crippling ailment for one of the most noted pulpit orators of his day. Pollak cites obituary notices of Wadsworth which indicate that during his last years as a clergyman his congregation had dwindled to a handful because of his speech impairment.[33] If Dickinson was moved initially, in their 1880 interview, by Wadsworth's noticeably changed voice, she turned it gracefully to humorous parody which included herself, in the opening lines. But if this is the beginning of the poem, it is finished by an abrupt shift, which is also stimulated by the reminder of aging and mortality: the poem turns from the "glee" of the opening lines to the progression of "Delight . . . Woe . . . Terror . . . livid" in the final lines. The visit, she told the Clarks, was a surprise, and certainly several different reactions had to be sorted out, as they are in the poem. Along with the initial joy of seeing him, she surely notices his age: Wadsworth was sixty-six and she was fifty. But still the old Woe of the past as well as the long-standing Terror for the future reasserted itself. Her final impression of the interview, in this poem, was painful: until well after Dickinson's time the word "livid" was associated exclusively with the black and blue colors of a bruise; her dictionary defined it as "discolored, as flesh by contusion."

The old doubts about immortality reasserted themselves again in several poems during this period. Her own and Wadsworth's immortality was the exact point of the wager of long ago. St. Paul's first letter to the Corinthians (15.35), which indirectly provides a strong assurance of their bodily resurrection, is seized upon as subject for a poem. Paul's verse reads: "But some man will say, How are the dead raised up? and with what body do they come?" Dickinson's poem moves from this starting point:

> "And with what body do they come?"–
> Then they *do* come–Rejoice!
> What Door–What Hour–Run–run–My Soul!
> Illuminate the House!
>
> "Body!" Then real–a Face and Eyes–
> To know that it is them!–
> Paul knew that Man that knew the News–
> He passed through Bethlehem– [1492]

Not only immortality but full sensuous enjoyment seems promised by the phrase in Paul, and Dickinson's wager will be won.

If Wadsworth was the "Husband" of the marriage poems, then his death in April 1882 provides us with a final date for examining Dickinson's poems. The event would surely stimulate further assessments of her peculiar marriage situation, since it marked the first real change in that situation in almost twenty-five years. The many references to him, in the letters to the Clarks and to Judge Lord, show that she kept him very much in her mind during these last years. Some caution must be exercised here in light of her relationship to Judge Lord. I omit poems here that could apply equally well to the death of Judge Lord in 1884, though it should be noted that the intensity of that relationship has recently been called into question.[34] Though Dickinson showed great affection for Judge Lord, she is on record several times as refusing his invitations to intimacy and to marriage.[35]

A poem, dated by handwriting "about 1882," the year of Wadsworth's death, begins with calm reflection on the program I have been describing through the whole course of this study: "My Wars are laid away in Books–/I have one Battle more–" (1549). The "Books" are surely the fascicles she has put together recording her mental life during the experience that stimulated the greatest of her poetry. The remaining "Battle," as is clear from the rest of the poem, is her own death. The sense of a past war in which "we" were slain appears also in another poem from this time. Poem 1529 begins, "'Tis Seasons since the Dimpled War/In which we each were Conqueror/And each of us were slain. . . ."

Another poem from the same time reflects on the experience from another point of view:

> I groped for him before I knew
> With solemn nameless need
> All other bounty sudden chaff
> For this foreshadowed Food
> Which others taste and spurn and sneer—
> Though I within suppose
> That consecrated it could be
> The only Food that grows   [1555]

The "him" of the first line must be the husband of the marriage poems; only the male figure of the fascicle poems so completely fulfilled her needs. The early lines in the poem indicate some surprise, some unexpectedness in the sudden intense nature of the relationship. The crushing restriction sensed throughout the fascicles is reiterated near the end of the poem: such love must be "consecrated" to be enjoyed.

The same restriction appears in poem 1554:

> "Go tell it"—What a Message—
> To whom—is specified—
> Not murmur—not endearment—
> But simply—we—obeyed—
> Obeyed—a Lure—a Longing?
> Oh Nature—none of this—
> To Law—said sweet Thermopylae
> I give my dying Kiss—

The action which set her life into its unchangeable pattern was that they rejected "a Lure—a Longing," and obeyed the "Law." Her "death," the changeless mode her life took after the marriage, was like the death of the Spartans at Thermopylae: it was in strict conformity to "law" as she and her times understood it. At this point in her life, then, she particularizes the Christian sense (again from St. Paul) of life as a warfare; her war was fought, and dubiously won, in the marriage decision many years ago.

Still another poem of 1882 revives the experience. Poem 1548 begins, "Meeting by Accident,/We hovered by design," and goes on to assert that "Destiny" allows such relationships only rarely. She seems here to return to the idea of their marriage made in heaven, ratified by heaven even though it cannot be enjoyed on earth. It is possible that some of these poems were written in the light of Dickinson's current relationship with Judge Lord, though little is known about this late friendship and the conceptual framework and idioms of the poems I select tie the poems back to the earlier relationship explored in the fascicles. That she was writing poems with Wadsworth in mind during these years is clear from the fact that she included two poems about him (1543 and 1576) in the letters she was writing to the Clark brothers.

Half a dozen poems from these last years in Dickinson's life, the years after Wadsworth's death, are written explicitly to "Thee," as if he were still guest of her solitude, available now perhaps in a new mode of presence to her. Poem 1534 returns to an older theme of her life and her poetry; the poem reads in its entirety:

> Society for me my misery
> Since Gift of Thee.

Poem 1556 addresses an implied "Thee":

> Image of Light, Adieu—
> Thanks for the interview—
> So long—so short—
> Preceptor of the whole—
> Coeval Cardinal—
> Impart—Depart—

The first line of this poem of 1882 commends the deceased to God, with an epithet that places him very close indeed to the divinity. The "interview" of line 2, which she mentions around this time to James Clark as having taken place some twenty-two years before, must now seem very "long" ago, has always been lamented as having been too "short." The marriage, as we have seen frequently, gave her a sense of "whole"-ness and maturity. The two words in the fifth line seem to be adjectives, asserting their relationship from the same moment in time ("Coeval") and acknowledging in him a certain superiority: he is "Cardinal," pivotal, in her life. The poem, a small compendium of the marriage themes, ends with acknowledgement of his importance in her life.

Another "Thee" poem of 1882 responds to his death with a similar memorial, contrasting "night" with the "Image of Light" in the previous poem:

> Within thy Grave!
> Oh no, but on some other flight—
> Thou only camest to mankind
> To rend it with Good Night— [1552]

A short quatrain from this year, also addressed to "Thee," sets up an enormous puzzle:

> Tried always and Condemned by thee
> Permit me this reprieve
> That dying I may earn the look
> For which I cease to live— [1559]

The first line establishes the scene as a law court, with "thee" as both prosecutor and judge. But what possible human situation could fit the allegorical scene? Is it his high religious standards which she cannot live up to? It is possible that here the "thee" is the divine judge, and the "reprieve" she asks for is excuse from his condemnation of her adulterous wishes. But the last line has connections twenty years old and more, with the sense of death as the state of her life after the anomalous marriage. It is also a plea for the fulfillment in heaven of the union she has sacrificed on earth. If God is the figure at the beginning of the poem, she quickly shifts her attention to the earthly lover, now dead, who has filled her whole inner world for more than two decades.

Poem 1560 is also a "Thee" poem:

> To be forgot by thee
> Surpasses Memory
> Of other minds
> The Heart cannot forget
> Unless it contemplate   Unless] Until
> What it declines
> I was regarded then
> Raised from oblivion
> A single time   single] royal
> To be remembered what—   for one must recollect
> Worthy to be forgot   before it can forget
> Is my renown

The poem is a worksheet draft, though the shape has begun to emerge strongly; I have included some of the variants because they seem to clarify obscurities. The central event of the poem is the recollection of having been "regarded/Raised from oblivion a single time." That she has in mind her marriage is clear from the "royal" variant. The paradox of the ending is perhaps more clear from the variant: remembering is passive; but forgetting is an act of the will directed, in this case at least, toward a person somehow raised in worth. The poem is a series of four packages; each expresses the same basic thought, the importance of keeping their union alive in memory. The intention behind the poem seems to be to hold firmly in place the reasons for the beloved never to forget her, even though they now stand on different sides of the experience of death.

Two other "Thee" poems survive from the last year of Dickinson's life, when she felt battered by many deaths and sensed her own weakening physical condition. The first is quite finished:

> So give me back to Death—
> The Death I never feared
> Except that it deprived of thee—
> And now, by Life deprived,
> In my own Grave I breathe
> And estimate it's size—
> It's size is all that Hell can guess
> And all that Heaven was—
>   [1632]

The poem looks back over a long stretch, acknowledges a recent important change, and anticipates an event soon to occur. The program is clear. The long stretch is her frequently affirmed attitude toward death, that it holds nothing for her to fear as long as it offers final union with the beloved. The recent important change is the death of the beloved: she is "by life deprived," so that under no circumstances could their marriage now be celebrated on earth. And the anticipation of a near event in the future is the resignation of the first line—the death she has "never feared"—carried forward now to a state of imminent fulfillment—she already "breathes" easily in the Grave. The poem ends with a new consideration in the final two lines: if there is no union with the beloved after death, then all of human speculations about hell are fulfilled; if there is union, then it will be the heaven she has already experienced. The "risk," inherent in her situation from the beginning, remains a lively torment to the end.

The last of these "Thee" poems is an unfinished worksheet, represented as follows in the Johnson edition:

> Extol thee—could I—   Then I will
> by saying nothing new—
> But just the anti fair—averring—fairest—truest truth
> that thou art heavenly
>   tritest—brightest truth—
>   sweetest
>   that tritest eulogy
>   that thou art heavenly
> Perceiving thee is evidence
> That we are of the sky
> Partaking thee a guar t y   guaranty
> of immortality [1643]

While the poem is not complete, it obviously falls into the class of love poems which "extol" the qualities of the beloved. Mainly, Dickinson would make an advance on the "trite" statement that the beloved is "heavenly" by asserting it now as literal truth. Her union with him, perceived in all of the marriage poems, is still unbroken, arguing then to her own "guaranty—of immortality."

It should be noted that all of these are private poems. So far as is known they were not sent to anyone nor was any attempt made to publish them. Many of them have no outside referents; that is to say, they make no sense apart from the narrative program so fully developed in the fascicles. Within that program they make a great deal of sense. A prime example, from these final years, is the following poem, begun before the death of Wadsworth and finished shortly after he died:

> The farthest Thunder that I heard
> Was nearer than the Sky
> And rumbles still, though torrid Noons
> Have lain their missiles by—
> The Lightning that preceded it
> Struck no one but myself—
> But I would not exchange the Bolt
> For all the rest of Life—
> Indebtedness to Oxygen
> The Happy may repay,
> But not the obligation
> To Electricity—
> It founds the Homes and decks the Days
> And every clamor bright
> Is but the gleam concomitant
> Of that waylaying Light—
> The Thought is quiet as a Flake—
> A Crash without a Sound,
> How Life's reverberation
> It's Explanation found—   [1581]

Mysterious questions urge themselves. What kind of Thunder continues to rumble through long sunlit days? What kind of Lightning initiated it, striking only one person who still lives to tell about it? Why was that bolt so valuable that she would not exchange it for anything? What kind of Lightning founds Homes, decks days, and brightens everything else that happens? Finally, what is such Thunder and Lightning that it crashed "without a Sound" and yet gave "Explanations" to all of life's meanings and questions? Whatever possible range of allegorical meanings might be suggested here, none fits better than the narrative program fully displayed in the fascicles. And whoever the beloved might be supposed to be, it must also be significant that the poem was brought to completion just after the death of Wadsworth.

A final worksheet poem from this era, after the death of Wadsworth, provides still further light on their relationship. The poem seems very much still in process, though its central conception is clear. Johnson displays the worksheet thus:

> The Bobolink is gone— the Rowdy of the Meadow—
> And no one swaggers now but me—
> The Presbyterian Birds can now resume the Meeting
> He gaily interrupted that overflowing Day
>   boldly
> When opening the Sabbath in their afflictive Way
> He bowed to Heaven instead of Earth
>   to every Heaven above
>   to all the saints he knew
>   every God he knew
> And shouted Let us pray—
> and bubbled let us pray—
>
> He recognized his maker—overturned the Decalogue—
>
> He swung upon the Decalogue
> And shouted Let us pray—
>
> When supplicating mercy
> In a portentous way—   portentous way
>
> Gay from an unannointed Twig   Sweet from a surreptitious
>   Twig
> He gurgled— Let us pray—
>   bubbled [1591]

Dickinson here is working with the materials of a very popular poem of her day, William Cullen Bryant's "Robert of Lincoln," first published in 1855. Bryant celebrates the bird as "Braggart and prince of braggarts"; he is "Rowdy of the Meadow" in Dickinson's poem. Contrasting with this feature of the Bobolink in Bryant's poem is the domestic peace of home and garden, with its sure appeal to Dickinson: "Snug and safe is that nest of ours,/Hidden among the summer flowers." Two items, however, distinguish Dickinson's poem and stamp it with characteristics of her fascicle narrative: first of all, the recharacterization of the bird as clergyman, of a particular religious denomination; and secondly, her insistence, in two different ways in the draft, on working in her clergyman-bird's tampering with the "Decalogue." This is a key word, one will recall, in an undoubted marriage poem; 485 had lamented that the "eyes that fondled [her bosom] are wrenched/By Decalogues—away."

Still mysterious in the scenario is another line of reference: this clergyman-bird had somehow thrust himself into the midst of "Presbyterian" birds, "interrupted" their staid ceremonies, and insisted on praying in his own enthusiastic way. Now that he is gone they can "resume" their former calm ways.

Key to the mystery is provided by the fact that, in the winter of 1873-74, Wadsworth distressed many religious sensibilities in Philadelphia by leading his flock out of their Reformed Dutch affiliation and into the Presbyterian church. Jay Leyda provides the following documentation: "NEW YORK, JANUARY 22. 'Religious Intelligence' in the Independent: Yet another large society in Philadelphia, Dr. Wadsworth's, has left the Reformed (Dutch) Church, this time to join the Presbyterians. The Reformed Classis is angry and has deposed the minister. But Dr. Wadsworth and the Presbyterians snap their fingers at them, and do not see that he preaches any the worse for the deposition." Wadsworth's biography in the Encyclopaedia of the Presbyterian Church adds the following details: "In 1873 [Wadsworth's Reformed Dutch Church] united with the Western Presbyterian Church, under the new name of Immanuel Presbyterian Church. The court, having decided that this church could not hold property of the Third Reformed Church, in February, 1878, Immanuel Church was united with the Clinton Street Church, under the name of the Clinton Street Immanuel Church, and Dr. Wadsworth was installed as its pastor, March 25, 1879, continuing to be so until his death, April 1st, 1882."[36] The case had taken five years to be settled.

The focus of the poem thus shifts: it is not a poem primarily about a species of New England songbird; it is rather a celebration of the personality of the recently dead husband as it was revealed in one of the major incidents of his career.

The Pregnancy Sequence

A major subject remains requiring our attention, a subject intimately connected with the marriage theme that pervades Dickinson's poetry.

There is sufficient cause, in the narrative we have followed to this point, for the tenderness, the devotion, even for the pain and suffering of the love poems. But is there sufficient cause for the rage and guilt, the sense of abandonment? Permeating Dickinson's poetry is, as well, the expressed need for secrecy, the sense of betrayal, the sense of being one of the "lost." To this must be added her need to assert some unbreakable link to the beloved, a striving to set herself "righteous," and a lifelong awe of the father in whose house she continued to live. Fully recorded also was a crippling shyness in all her encounters, an embarrassment so acute that it either prevented her from meeting people outside the family or left them (as it did Higginson) with a sense of being "drained" by her intense discomfort during their meetings. So shy was Emily Dickinson, so intense was her agoraphobia, that she was unable to appear in church after she reached her maturity; she could not even bear to have her measurements taken by her dressmaker, and had her sister stand in as model with the seamstress for her famous white dresses; even when delivery boys appeared from stores in town, she would vanish and let someone else answer the door; her closest friend and sympathizer outside the family, Mabel Loomis Todd, never set eyes on her until the day of Dickinson's funeral.

We may well ask if our story has sufficiently incorporated all of these biographical and literary facts, if we have listened closely enough to Dickinson's poetry to hear all of her themes and all of her subjects. What still needs to be considered is a large class of her poems, beginning in the fascicles, in which the subject of pregnancy is central.

Was Emily Dickinson ever pregnant? The question may offend for its too close inquiry into a private life, its too close linking of biography with poems. It cannot, however, be ruled out of literary analysis, as if there were *a priori* limitations to the subjects an author might be expected to treat, whether as real phenomena or as groundwork for a trope. The obligation of the reader is to remain open, attentive to whatever topics these poems bring forward. Is there still another event remaining to be considered, naturally linked to the marriage narrative we have been following?

In a chronological reading of Dickinson's poems there is an important crux in the developing narrative. Early poems state resistance to, refusal of, sexual intercourse. A private poem (213) which did not find its way into the fascicles begins, "Did the Harebell loose her girdle/To the lover Bee," and resists intercourse on the traditional grounds that the lover would lose his respect for her afterward, and for himself as well. The poem is dated by handwriting at about 1860, the year of Wadsworth's first visit.

Poem 190 (placed in Fascicle 9 and also dated about 1860) describes a nighttime meeting with the beloved (it is addressed "we"), the strength of the sexual forces which attracted them both, and their alternating weaknesses to resist. It ends with what seems to be a sigh of relief, with some humor in it, that they had resisted the final sexual intimacy: "We did'nt do it—tho'!"

Another poem (in Fascicle 13, dated about 1861) considers climbing a fence for the "Strawberries" on the other side, but worries about "stain-[ing] my Apron" in the process. She *seems* here to be resisting the temptation, even though God himself probably would not (251). She continues her resistance in poem 275 (dated about 1861 and copied into Fascicle 12). The poem is a strong protest of her love and an offering of the greatest proofs of that love. She offers him "the Life/Poured thee, without a stint/The whole of me—forever." The poem continues: "What more the woman can,/Say quick, that I may dower thee/With last Delight I own." But she does present a restriction to her offering, phrasing it as a plea to him: "But hallow just the snow/Intact, in Everlasting flake—/Oh, Caviler, for you!" In this last line she rejects as a petty quibble his physical desire for her.

Finally, in 340 (dated "early 1862" and found in Fascicle 18) she argues by metaphor that her foot wants Bliss even though it is a muddy Abyss which would soil her shoe. The foot should win the argument by the logic of the poem, by following its natural impulses toward sensuous fulfillment; but the poem ends with another refusal, a concession to proprieties: "Verdict for Boot!"

But concurrently with these poems denying herself a fall from virginity, there is a fascination with the prospect. Poem 211, "Come slowly— Eden" (dated about 1860, in Fascicle 10), imagines that the bee, enticed ever closer to the flower, finally "Enters—and is lost in Balms." And at one point in this chronology the reader can recognize an abrupt change, a reversal of these negations. One can recall the pent-up power in Dickinson's volcano poems and witness its release in poems that celebrate the fullness of sexual union.

The scene is played in 446 (dated about 1862, in Fascicle 16), where "He showed me Hights I never saw" and "secrets"; he invites her to "Climb . . . with me," to "have me for a Guest." The poem ends "And then—He brake His Life—and lo,/A light for me, did solemn glow—/The steadier, as my face withdrew—/And could I further No?"[37] The poem records some final acquiescence after long resistance. The same scene is played out in 643 (also dated about 1862, in Fascicle 33):

> I could suffice for Him, I knew—
> He—could suffice for Me—
> Yet Hesitating Fractions—Both
> Surveyed Infinity—
>
> "Would I be Whole" He sudden broached—
> My syllable rebelled—
> 'Twas face to face with Nature—forced—
> 'Twas face to face with God—
>
> Withdrew the Sun—to Other Wests—
> Withdrew the furthest Star
> Before Decision—stooped to speech—
> And then—be audibler

> The Answer of the Sea unto
> The Motion of the Moon—
> Herself adjust Her Tides—unto—
> Could I—do else—with Mine? [643]

The poem also records initial resistance of the female to the male's demands. But at the end of the poem the woman's acquiescence is couched in one of Dickinson's strongest marriage symbols: she could no more resist him than the sea could resist the pull of the moon.

Poem 580 imagines marital relations as "The Daily Own—of Love/ .... Sweet Debt of Life—Each Night to owe—/Insolvent—every Noon." The poem (dated about 1862 and found in Fascicle 15) begins, "I gave myself to Him." The alternative she proposed for this first line underscores the totality of the gift: "I gave Him all myself."

The moment of something very much like consummation is then recorded in poem 506, in Fascicle 17:

> He touched me, so I live to know
> That such a day, permitted so,
> I groped upon his breast—
> It was a boundless place to me
> And silenced, as the awful sea
> Puts minor streams to rest.
>
> And now, I'm different from before,
> As if I breathed superior air—
> Or brushed a Royal Gown. . . .

The experience was deeply unsettling. In 503 (from early 1862, in Fascicle 18) Dickinson tries to describe a bird's spontaneous song; but her real concern breaks through the telling with thoughts of "Eve's great surrender/. . . . Eve—and the Anguish." The poem is a nature poem, but Eve's sexual life intrudes.

Many years later, about 1875, the scenario was replayed once more:

> A Bee his burnished Carriage
> Drove boldly to a Rose—
> Combinedly alighting—
> Himself—his Carriage was—
> The Rose received his visit
> With frank tranquility
> Withholding not a Crescent
> To his Cupidity—
> Their Moment consummated—
> Remained for him—to flee—
> Remained for her—of rapture
> But the humility. [1339]

The sexual "consummation" is explicit. The poem was copied out and folded as if Dickinson had considered sending it, headed by a note which is almost impossibly enigmatic to later readers: "Sweet is it as Life, with it's enhancing Shadow of Death." We have seen Dickinson's poems of this time mirroring her depression before the last visit of Wadsworth. It must have been tempting to try to rekindle his love with such a reminder; but the temptation was rejected if the poem was not sent.

Poems such as these leave us with little warrant to suspect that the affair did not proceed to its natural conclusion. As a minimum they require a highly awakened sexuality, a noticeable transition from latency to activity. The change that occurs—from denial of sexual intimacy to affirmation and participation—is found in poems which Dickinson copied into the fascicles of 1862. The presumptions are always, in dating her poems, that the handwriting gives only an approximate date and that the copies that survive may be from still earlier versions—though the ordering within the fascicles themselves is quite firm. But it should also be noted that biographers have found 1861-62 to be the years of Dickinson's greatest mental and emotional crisis. Simultaneously, these years were the height of her sexual interest and the period of her greatest poetic output.

Dickinson's poems in which pregnancy appears, either as trope or as main subject, must be seen in this sequence of natural events. The factual question of Dickinson's pregnancy cannot be satisfactorily answered in the absence of medical records or the testimonials of her family or others in whom she may have confided. One recalls the fate of her correspondence with her closest confidantes. It was destroyed in the case of the Norcross sisters, her cousins, who held back from Mabel Loomis Todd what they considered to be too personal for publication, and the last surviving sister burned all of their letters from Dickinson before she died. In the case of Dickinson's other confidante, Mrs. Holland, a gap exists for the years 1860-65, in an otherwise steady correspondence.

But factual matters outside the poetry are not essential to our inquiry. Our enterprise is to follow the linear chronology of these poems. The staging of subjects is quite clear: from refusal of sexual intimacy, to acquiescence and surrender, to poems in which the subject of pregnancy appears. Where several poems vividly present the flower as ravished by the bee, several other poems force considerations of the biological consequences of such an encounter, whether real or as an imagined continuation of a process thus set in motion.

The pregnancy and childbearing metaphors do not begin to appear in Dickinson's poetry until 1861, in Fascicle 11, and then in only one poem. This is 1737, a poem destroyed by Dickinson's family, though fortunately not before Todd had made a copy of it. It is Dickinson's protest of undying and unchangeable love for the husband, beginning "Rearrange a 'Wife's' affection!" The final stanza reads: "Big my Secret but it's *bandaged*—/It will never get away/Till the Day its Weary Keeper/Leads it through the Grave to thee." Her secret, expressed as "it" in each of the four lines, seems to be couched in a metaphor of pregnancy and parenting (the Secret is also a "Burden—Borne" in the previous stanza). The natural syntax of the first line is wrenched around to feature the word "Big"; one of the prevailing historical uses of this word is in the phrase "big with child." The "it," we should also notice, is a person: one does not "bandage" or "lead" an inanimate object, or keep watch over it lest it "get away." The metaphor latent in the last two lines suggests a parent leading a child through the experience of death, to reunion with its father. There are three, then, to meet beyond the grave: "Thee" to whom the poem is addressed; the "I" who speaks the poem; and the personalized, secret "it," who links the two together. *"Bandaged"* is underlined in the text, as if to suggest a specialized meaning, as *"wife"* is in the first line of the poem. The most obvious meaning would be the dressing of a wound; but Dickinson's underlining would push us to other meanings, such as the swaddling of a newborn infant. All of this, of course, only surrounds and highlights the central word of the stanza, her personified "Secret" which they share and which must be kept from public exposure, and which the family tried to hide by destroying the poem.

The next fascicle, Fascicle 12, contains a large number of Dickinson's pregnancy poems. One of these is 217:

> Father—I bring thee—not Myself—
> That were the little load—
> I bring thee the departed Heart
> I had not strength to hold—
>
> The Heart I cherished in my own
> Till mine—too heavy grew—
> Yet—strangest—heavier—since it went—
> Is it too large for you?

The poem seems to be one of confession and repentance. The crime being confessed is that of "cherishing" (or "carrying," in the version sent to Sue) another Heart inside of her. It may be that the poem laments the loss of the husband after the anomalous marriage ceremony, but Dickinson's diction and imagery build a metaphor out of the subject of pregnancy and childbearing. And the death of the newborn is implied in the metaphor, if it is a metaphor, since the newborn is now with God, according to the last line.

The following poem too, also dated "about 1861," suggests that the subject of her writing is no longer alive. The "Heart" of the previous poem becomes a "face" here:

> Jesus! thy Crucifix
> Enable thee to guess
> The smaller size!
>
> Jesus! thy second face
> Mind thee in Paradise
> Of our's! [225]

Interpreters have suggested a variety of meanings for this poem, but we must note that Dickinson sent a copy of it to Samuel Bowles when his wife was under doctor's care during a difficult pregnancy, suggesting the area of meaning in which the poem operated for Dickinson.[38] The poem itself describes great suffering, like that of Jesus, in the first stanza. The presence now in heaven of some deeply beloved face, will remind Him of "our's"—as if guilty parents plead for remembrance because of a likeness to their dead child.

These matters come together in an exceedingly troubled and difficult poem in this fascicle:

> A single Screw of Flesh
> Is all that pins the Soul
> That stands for Deity, to Mine,
> Upon my side the Vail—
>
> Once witnessed of the Gauze—
> It's name is put away
> As far from mine, as if no plight
> Had printed yesterday,
>
> In tender—solemn Alphabet,
> My eyes just turned to see,
> When it was smuggled by my sight
> Into Eternity—
>
> More Hands—to hold—These are but Two—
> One more new-mailed Nerve
> Just granted, for the Peril's sake—
> Some striding—Giant—Love—
>
> So greater than the Gods can show,
> They slink before the Clay,
> That not for all their Heaven can boast
> Will let it's Keepsake—go [263]

The first stanza presents three again: the "I" who speaks the poem, the beloved "soul" who "stands for Deity" to her, and "A single Screw of

Flesh." This last mysterious entity is described in the rest of the poem as *pinning* the two of them together, as having a "name" but now "put away" from her forever, "smuggled . . ./Into Eternity," as offering her "More Hands—to hold," as "Clay." All of these require that it be a human being who has just died. This entity is also her "Keepsake"—in Vergil's *Aeneid*, Dido appeals to Aeneas for just such a "Keepsake," a child of theirs to play in her courtyard and remind her of him after he has gone. All of these descriptive items identify a human being rather than an inanimate object.

The most troublesome word in the poem is "Screw" in the first line, until one remembers that in Dickinson's time, in common household use, the word meant a small package. On would buy a "screw" of tobacco or spices, for example, the purchase rolled in a loose sheet of paper with the ends twisted. Dickinson's poem, then, memorializes a small human being, intimately connecting her and the "thee" of the fascicles, taken out of this world before its time.

Parenthetically, we may here have the solution to the mystery of the many poems which refer to a deeply loved person as already dead, already in the presence of God and waiting for her there. Critics have noticed these poems for decades now without being able to identify the death of anyone in the Dickinson circle close enough to warrant them. One of these poems, 482 in Fascicle 22, describes such a mysterious death, of someone deeply loved by Dickinson:

> We Cover Thee—Sweet Face—
> Not that We tire of Thee—
> But that Thyself fatigue of Us—
> Remember—as Thou go—
> We follow Thee until
> Thou notice Us—no more—
> And then—reluctant—turn away
> To Con Thee oer and oer—
>
> And blame the scanty love
> We were Content to show—
> Augmented—Sweet—a Hundred fold—
> If Thou would'st take it—now— [482]

The death of some person intimately close appears frequently in Dickinson's poems of 1862, and the burial in the following poem, from Fascicle 28, is indeed a secret one:

> Unit, like Death, for Whom?
> True, like the Tomb,
> Who tells no secret
> Told to Him—

> The Grave is strict—
> Tickets admit
> Just two—the Bearer—
> And the Borne—
> And seat—just One—
> The Living—tell—
> The Dying—but a Syllable—
> The Coy Dead—None—
> No Chatter—here—no tea—
> So Babbler, and Bohea—stay there—
> But Gravity—and Expectation—and Fear—
> A tremor just, that All's not sure.   [408]

It is curious that *two* are buried here, and that they are indentified as mother and child, "the Bearer—/And the Borne," and that the tomb "tells no secret." The last two lines intensify the moral and emotional atmosphere in which the mysterious burial takes place.

Other poems in Fascicle 12 seem attracted into this galaxy. Poem 264 describes a "Weight" that invades the whole body, though when standing by itself the poem can be a more generalized definition simply of "Anguish." Poem 267 questions "Did we disobey Him?/Just one time," and the range of possibilities becomes narrow in the context. In the next fascicle, in poem 256, she feels herself "lost—now" and accuses the beloved "You . . . Sir" of being lost equally. In Fascicle 15, in poem 410, the Day had been "a thing/So terrible"; but it was followed quickly by "A Day as huge/As Yesterdays in pairs/[Which] Unrolled it's horror in my face." Once again the range of referents seems sharply limited, especially since the poem ends by describing the discovery of the second Day: "And Something's odd—within."

This "Something odd—within" is the subject of an extremely personal poem of the same year, 1862. It survives in two slightly different versions. It was not placed in any of the fascicles that were being assembled this year, but Dickinson retained the copies in two of the "Sets." What seems to be the later of the two versions is as follows:

> While it is alive
> Until Death touches it
> While it and I lap one Air
> Dwell in one Blood
> Under one Sacrament
> Show me Division can split or pare—
>
> Love is like Life—merely longer
> Love is like Death, during the Grave
> Love is the Fellow of the Resurrection
> Scooping up the Dust and chanting "Live"!   [491]

To be noticed here is the lack of metaphoric signals; the poem is a definition of, an arrangement of attitudes toward, the concrete "it" at the center of the poem's focus. This seems to be the same "it" as in the poems just discussed. In the earlier version of this poem, "it" is emphasized as having a specialized meaning by the use of quotation marks in the first and third lines. In the first stanza "it and I lap one Air/Dwell in one Blood," and the description most naturally fits the mother and the unborn child she carries. The first two lines set in question how long "it" is to remain alive. And the fifth line attempts to place "it" within the framework of the anomalous marriage: mother and child dwell under one sacrament. In such a situation Dickinson had to see herself as married, in some way or other, to legitimize what she was carrying—as she tried to explain in her statements to Bowles already seen, that she was "innocent" because she was "wife."

As we listen for the reverberations of this experience over the years we come upon numerous echoes in the Sets. Poem 924 begins with the following quatrain: "Love—is that later Thing than Death—/More previous—than Life—/Confirms it at it's entrance—And/Usurps it—of itself—" (924). The poem then is a definition of love, contextualized by the process of procreation. An act of love initiates life (line 2); the love of husband and wife is "confirmed" at the birth of the child (line 3); and this love act of the two then forcefully binds the child to the parenting couple. As the poem continues, Love "tastes Death" first, depositing the life "with God" after a "little interval." Granted the obscurity of the poem, its elements once again bring together love, pregnancy, birthing, and the early death of the child.

Perhaps this sequence is not so mysterious. The historian Carl Degler has recently assembled information from a surprisingly large number of sources from throughout the middle of the nineteenth century in America, testifying to the widespread availability of abortions through drugs or surgery, whether procured through doctors or self-induced by widely advertised drugs or other means.[39] There was some range of social tolerance here, larger than we would suspect. Even the ordinarily conservative Catholic Church permitted early abortions until 1869.

The solution seems unthinkable in the case of Emily Dickinson, until we recall that 1861 and 1862 were the years of her greatest emotional and mental crisis, that Dickinson was sick and bedridden for a whole summer at this time, that there was something profoundly shattering in her experience of "marriage," that she nevertheless had compelling reasons to assert repeatedly that she was married, that the family doctors and the family medical histories for all the Dickinsons are recorded except for these years, and that Dickinson's sister-in-law next door, Susan, was routinely procuring abortions from the year of her marriage in 1856 until the birth of her first child in 1861.[40] Nor should we exclude from this sequence the fact that in 1862 Wadsworth abruptly and unaccountably (considering his professional success in Philadelphia) put a whole continent between himself and Dickinson—surely a prudent move for a professional man, to remove himself from possible scandal.

We must acknowledge this stratum of imagery, deep within the most intense and passionate of Dickinson's poems, which includes pregnancy, a lengthy confinement to bed, a death and a mysterious burial, and consuming guilt. A poem from Fascicle 28 describes a program composed of many of these features:

> My first well Day—since many ill—
> I asked to go abroad,
> And take the Sunshine in my hands,
> And see the things in Pod—
>
> A'blossom just when I went in
> To take my Chance with pain—
> Uncertain if myself, or He,
> Should prove the strongest One.
>
> The Summer deepened, while we strove—
> She put some flowers away—
> And Redder cheeked Ones—in their stead—
> A fond—illusive way—
>
> To cheat Herself, it seemed she tried—
> As if before a child
> To fade—Tomorrow—Rainbows held
> The Sepulchre, could hide.
>
> She dealt a fashion to the Nut—
> She tied the Hoods to Seeds—
> She dropped bright scraps of Tint, about—
> And left Brazilian Threads
>
> On every shoulder that she met—
> Then both her Hands of Haze
> Put up—to hide her parting Grace
> From our unfitted eyes.
>
> My loss, by sickness—Was it Loss?
> Or that Etherial Gain
> One earns by measuring the Grave—
> Then—measuring the Sun—   [574]

The poem describes a whole summer of "sickness" (this final version was recorded in the handwriting of "about 1862"), unexplained in any biography. She links "child" and "Sepulchre" as relevant images in this poetic world, in the fourth stanza. The poem moves from the sense of separation from Nature to the attempt to reinsert herself into a harmony with Nature; Nature, however, at the end, hides "her parting Grace/From our unfitted eyes." The concluding stanza then concentrates on "My loss, by sickness," and produces the possibility that her life has been spared in order to recoup her moral losses.

We may be able to specify this particular summer more closely from an existing document. In the fall of 1861 Susan Dickinson sent Dickinson a note: "If you have suffered this past Summer I am sorry."[41] Another letter exists which also refers to events of the early 1860s. It is not precisely datable because the handwritten original had disappeared. In condolence with Kate Scott Anthon, whose first husband had died, Dickinson wrote, "I, too went out to meet the 'Dust' early in the morning, I, too in Daisy mounds possess hid treasure" (letter 222). One senses that Dickinson intends to conceal more than she reveals here; but it is interesting that she finds the husband's nickname for her intruding upon the recollection.

If Dickinson suffered a painful abortion which left her sick and bedridden for a whole summer, then two poems record vividly remembered details. Poem 861 garishly asserts that her love for the "you" of the fascicles was proven "Gush after Gush" in a "Scarlet Experiment." And poem 762 reintroduces the mysterious "it" from poems we have just seen, describing its birth in images of a surgical abortion: "The Whole of it came not at once—/'Twas Murder by degrees—/A Thrust—and then for Life a chance—/The Bliss to cauterize—."

The second Master letter (Letter 233) attracts our attention at this point. Dickinson protests to Master that she is shattered, seriously damaged. She had asked him for redemption and he had given her "something else. . . . I knew you had altered me." She mentions another figure, "this stranger" in their lives, who was so dear to her that she would have traded her life for his. Parodying the Lord's prayer, she addresses the Master as "Father." Then in the middle of the letter comes the allusion to a question he must have asked in a letter; her answer is outrage and sarcasm: "I dont know what you can do for it—thank you—Master—but if I had the Beard on my cheek—like you—and you——had Daisy's petals— and you cared so for me—what would become of you?" There is something almost stereotyped in the image of the married man who has begotten a child outside of his marriage, who is genuinely concerned to do the "right thing," yet who finally can retreat behind the safety of his own marriage. As the letter continues, Dickinson pleads for at least another visit from him, to see him just one more time. The third Master letter then is a shocked response to his decision that they should see no more of each other. Recalling one of their intimate moments she pleads,

"Low at the knee that bore her once unto wordless rest Daisy kneels a culprit . . . punish dont banish her. . . ."

The mysterious death continues to haunt the poetry of Emily Dickinson in the late fascicles and beyond. In 784 she is obsessed, waking and sleeping, by a mysterious grave on which no human parentage is recorded; not even narcotics will give her relief. In 876 she is not able to visit this grave publicly, but she will meet the dead one again at the Resurrection. In 482 and 908 the mysteriously buried person is called "Sweet," as if named after the husband of the fascicles. Poem 860 begins, "Absence disembodies—so does Death"—indicating that Dickinson has become lonely in two ways, through an absence and through a death. Poem 935 returns to the mysterious "it" whose death "leaves Us homesick." The speaker has not had sufficient opportunity to get to know the dead person, but its absence leaves an overwhelming sense of "something lost." Poem 936 focuses on "This Dust," which had died before its "Mind" achieved more than "a too minute Area," before "This World, and it's species" could attract its attention.

Poem 1030 describes again the world of "Us," and asserts that a death involving them both is likewise their "Certificate of Immortality." Poem 1059, a love poem addressed to "Sire," to "You," describes her suffering and twice memorializes the "Death" which has caused it, but which is, paradoxically, her only sign of "Wealth." This is the poem which identifies the beloved addressee as a clergyman: "Pause in your Liturgies—/Wait your Chorals." If a fair copy of this poem was sent, then the guilty father had another reminder of the outcome of their affair:

> Sang from the Heart, Sire,
> Dipped my Beak in it,
> If the Tune drip too much
> Have a tint too Red
>
> Pardon the Cochineal—
> Suffer the Vermillion—
> Death is the Wealth
> Of the Poorest Bird.

The lines seem to be saturated with sarcasm, as they remind him of the kind of "sickness" he has caused her to suffer. In the same set, in poem 662, she expresses their mutual "embarrassment" with one another and before God as well.

Poem 1712, from Fascicle 24, dated about 1862, presents many problems. The poem seems to have been tampered with even before it reached Mabel Loomis Todd. The first 17 lines were destroyed by the family and survive only in transcripts made by Todd and her copyist. The remaining lines had become attached to other poems in the course of publication.[42]

A Pit—but Heaven over it—
And Heaven beside, and Heaven abroad;
And yet a Pit—
With Heaven over it.

To stir would be to slip—
To look would be to drop—
To dream—to sap the Prop
That holds my chances up.
Ah! Pit! With Heaven over it!

The depth is all my thought—
I dare not ask my feet—
'Twould start us where we sit
So straight you'd scarce suspect
It was a Pit—with fathoms under it
Its Circuit just the same
Seed—summer—tomb—
Whose Doom to whom

'Twould start them—
We—could tremble—
But since we got a Bomb—
And held it in our Bosom—
Nay—Hold it—it is calm

The poem presents a situation of ultimate moral danger: heaven and hell loom on the scene as immediate consequences. The setting is the "Pit" which looks very much like the grave of the many poems we have just been studying. The moral danger involves the two lovers: " 'Twould start *us;*" it also involves a strong community reaction: " 'Twould start *them*" (italics added). The dangerous moral situation remains vague, until a metaphor for it is introduced in lines 20-21: "We got a Bomb—/And held it in our Bosom." The metaphor surely derives from conception ("we got"), gestation, and nursing. A mysterious line in the poem (line 16) seems to have no bearing on anything at all, inside the poem or out, unless one notes the linking of the male "seed," the "Summer's Day" of the marriage experience, and the "tomb" which is at the center of this and of several other of Dickinson's pregnancy musings.[43]

When one comes upon the famous poem 493 in this context, one senses that the poem has not yet been read in its entirety:

The World—stands—solemner—to me—
Since I was wed—to Him—

>A modesty befits the soul
>That bears another's—name—
>A doubt—if it be fair—indeed—
>To wear that perfect—pearl—
>The Man—upon the Woman—binds—
>To clasp her soul—for all—
>A prayer, that it more angel—prove—
>A whiter Gift—within—
>To that munificence, that chose—
>So unadorned—a Queen—
>A Gratitude—that such be true—
>It had esteemed the Dream—
>Too beautiful—for Shape to prove—
>Or posture—to redeem!

It is undoubtedly a wedding poem, a description of her "marriage" and its effects. It is on the same sheet of paper as 491, discussed earlier, "While it is alive," a sheet of poems she transcribed in 1862 but set aside without binding into a fascicle. In this context one comes to focus on "that perfect—pearl—/The Man—upon the Woman—binds—/To clasp her soul—for all." Is Dickinson disguising or revealing here, for the perfect reader who knows her thoughts, who has shared her experience, and has read her favorite book? We have earlier discussed Dickinson's deep involvement in the story of *The Scarlet Letter*, and "Pearl" is Hester's and the clergyman's illegitimate child there. Dickinson's own Dimmesdale would be acutely sensitive to these lines.

Once this train of allusions is started, one wonders if the last two lines have ever yet been read. Why does Dickinson concentrate on her changed "Shape," as something that has now come to be mismatched with the ideal beauty of her "Dream"? What physical condition could Dickinson possibly describe, except pregnancy, which "posture" could not "redeem"? Does she, with the exclamation point ending the last line, call attention to her own daring in pointing to her uncontrollable pregnancy? It is no wonder she remained, to the end of her life, of two minds about the publication of her poems, when so many of her best are privileged communications about her deepest secrets.

Poem 1180, from a late set, memorializes "my Guest 'Today in Paradise.' " She has the guarantee of this from Christ's promise to the thief on the cross. Unless it is her child, the epithet "my Guest" does not seem to describe any of the deaths in Dickinson's recent experience. In the same set another poem, addressed "we," shares a thought with the beloved: the "marauding Hand" of Death has taken away *someone* who would have made earth a heaven for them (1205). Finally, in this set, poem 1230 makes the following statement: a death would not have occurred if Love had been prompt enough to step in and prevent it:

It came at last but prompter Death
Had occupied the House—
His pallid Furniture arranged
And his metallic Peace—

Oh faithful Frost that kept the Date
Had Love as punctual been
Delight had aggrandized the Gate
And blocked the coming in. [1230]

Again the range of situations to which the poem can refer narrows to one.

Beyond the fascicles and the sets, in the later years of her life, Dickinson continued to return to this subject. One of these poems exists only as a rough worksheet dated "about 1876." The beginning and ending of the poem are firm, while the middle stages are still fluid. Johnson displays the worksheet thus, and an investigation of the surviving manuscript scraps confirms his arrangement:

[*stanza 1*]
Summer—we all have seen—
A few of us—believed—
A few—the more aspiring
Unquestionably loved—

[*stanza 2*]
But Summer does not care—
˙She takes her gracious way
   goes   *spacious*
          subtle—
          simple—
          mighty—
          gallant
As eligible as the moon
As unperverted as the moon

To the Temerity—
    a
    our

She goes her sylvan way—
      her ample way—
        perfect

as undiverted as the Moon
As eligible as the Moon—
    unavailing
from her Divinity
to our extremity—
    adversity—
By our obliquity.

[*stanza 3*]
Deputed to adore—
Contented
The Lot to be adored
   Doom

Created to adore—

The Affluence evolved—
      conferred—
      bestowed—
      involved—

Unknown as to an Ecstasy
The Embryo endowed— [1386]

The first stanza progresses clearly to an unquestionable love, which occurred during a memorable "Summer." One recalls the marriage on "a Day—at Summer's full" (322). We are firmly situated in Dickinson's constellation of marriage poems. The final two lines of the poem are equally clear: the conclusion of the poem forges a surprising link between "Ecstasy" and "Embryo." The ending then is also firm and one needs to comprehend the work of the intervening lines to see if this Embryo is not metaphoric.

In stanza 2, Summer, though the setting for their love, is indifferent to it. It is not to be "perverted" by "our obliquity" or our "Temerity." Dickinson cannot decide here whether to focus on the sinfulness or the rashness of the lovers' action, qualities that could hardly apply to one's admiration of summer. Creeping into this stanza, and then deleted, is Dickinson's frequent trope of herself as moon to the beloved's "divine" sun.

The first two lines of the last stanza are also still in flux. A clear consideration is that she must adore someone. She is also adored in turn; but here the neutral word "Lot" is changed, on further consideration, to "Doom." Summer passes away indifferent to the lovers, who remain "unknown" to it. But the permanent residue of the experience is the "Ecstasy/The Embryo endowed." It becomes most likely, then, that "Embryo" is not a metaphor for anything within the world of this poem; it is rather the very subject of the poem itself. It appeared during a loving summer, causing doom, making the speaker realize how indifferent Nature and its processes are to the embarrassed human.

The poem was not finished, so far as is known, for anyone but the poet herself. The major elements of her experience are there, but the un-finished state of the poem will protect her secret, should her papers be found and looked into after her death. It is one more private clarification, many years later, of the biological effects of her "marriage" experience. A retrospective view, from fifteen years later, can show the experience to have been alarming, but rich and valuable nevertheless.

Such a reading gains credence from another poem of the same year, 1876. Poem 1387 describes two aspects of a butterfly: its bright colors, and its "prone"-ness to "shut it's spotted Fan/And panting on a Clover lean/As if it were undone." In the literature written in English "undone" has virtually only one meaning: to become pregnant outside of marriage.

In the next year Dickinson wrote the following poem, this version of which also disappeared; it exists only in Todd's transcript:

> To the unwilling dust
> We soft commit thee.
> Guile if it hath,
> Inviolate to thee—

Breezes caress and firmament salute thee,
Nothing affront thy secrecy. [1402]

The poem describes a secret burial. The "We" of the love poems are the agents of the affair. "Guile" is involved in the situation, but not in any way that could touch the one being buried. The baby has become a harmonious part of nature; its secret will be kept.

Also from 1877 the following worksheet survives:

> [*stanza one*]
> Crisis is sweet and yet the Heart
> Upon the hither side
> Has Dowers of Prospective
> Surrendered by the Tried–
> Withheld to the arrived–
> Debarred–
> denied
> *To Denizen denied*
>
> [*stanza two*]
> Inquire of the proudest Rose
> fullest
> *closing*
> Which *rapture*–she preferred
> triump[h]
> Hour–
> moment
> And she ~~would~~ tell you sighing–
> answer
> will point undoubtedly
> And she will point you fondly–
> longingly
> *sighing*
> The transport of the Bud–
> rapture
> To her surrendered Bud
> rescinded
> *The Hour of her Bud*
> session of
> *to her rescinded Bud*
> receding
> Departed–
> Receipted Bud
> Expended [1416]

Once again the movement of the poem is clear, though the selection of words is incomplete. The first stanza generalizes on "Crisis" with an oxymoron: it is "sweet," but one finds something even better afterward. The second stanza carries this out through an example curiously applicable to the story we here follow. The rose, when asked "which rapture— she preferred," answers only by pointing *To her rescinded Bud.*" The moment of losing her child has left her, at least, with pride in having had the child.

Dickinson returned to her secret once again in a worksheet poem of 1879:

> "Secrets" is a daily word
> Yet does not exist—
> Muffled—it remits surmise—
> Murmured—it has ceased—
> Dungeoned in the Human Breast
> Doubtless secrets lie—
> But that Grate inviolate—
> Goes nor comes away
> Nothing with a Tongue or Ear—
> Secrets stapled there
> Will emerge but once—and dumb—
> To the Sepulchre— [1385]

The last line contains a surprise: her secret will not appear finally *in* the grave, it has gone *to* the grave.

Finally, from 1877, a letter poem survives which Dickinson had written to Kate Scott Anthon, an acquaintance from former years whom she now refused to see. Apparently shocked by her own rudeness, Dickinson penned the following explanation, but then, shocked by too much self-revelation, she never sent it; not this version, at least. The paper on which she had written it was turned into a worksheet.

> I shall not murmur if at last
> The ones I loved below
> Permission have to understand
> For what I shunned them so—
> Divulging it would rest my Heart
> But it would ravage their's—
> Why, Katie, Treason has a Voice—
> But mine—dispels—in Tears. [1410]

If her fault were "Treason," still she would tell it, even though it is, according to Dante, the worst of the crimes. Hers is, she says, even worse, and divulging her secret would "ravage" a trusting friend's heart.

The Legend of the Broken Heart

One of the continuing aims of Dickinson biography has been to discredit and dispel what has been called "The Legend of the Broken Heart," the theory that Dickinson was seduced and abandoned, and that such an event had something to do with her poetry. It was Millicent Todd Bingham who rode out against this biographical heresy, mainly in hostile response to the writings of Susan Dickinson's daughter, Martha Dickinson Bianchi. Madame Bianchi (as she came to be called) had published an overheated version of Dickinson's romance in her *Life and Letters of Emily Dickinson*, in 1924. The affecting and offending scene was presented thus:

> It was on a visit to the same Eliza, in Philadelphia, that Emily met the fate she had instinctively shunned. Even now, after the many slow years she has been removed from us in the body, her spirit hinders the baring of that chapter in her life which has been so universally misunderstood, so stupidly if not wantonly misrepresented. All that ever was told was a confidence to her Sister Sue, sacredly guarded under all provocation till death united them—the confiding and the listening—in one abiding silence.
>
> Certainly in that first witchery of an undreamed Southern springtime Emily was overtaken—doomed once and forever by her own heart. It was instantaneous, overwhelming, impossible. There is no doubt that two predestined souls were kept apart only by her high sense of duty, and the necessity for preserving love untarnished by the inevitable destruction of another woman's life.
>
> Without stopping to look back, she fled to her own home for refuge— as a wild thing running from whatever it may be that pursues; but only a few days later Sister Sue looked up from her sewing to see Lavinia, pallid and breathless from running, who grasped her wrist with hurrying hand, urging: "Sue, come! That man is here!—Father and Mother are away, and I am afraid Emily will go away with him!" But the one word he implored, Emily would not say. Unable to endure his life under the old conditions, after a short time he left his profession and home and silently withdrew with his wife and an only child to a remote city, a continent's width remote, where echo at least could not mock him with its vain outcry: dying prematurely, the spell unbroken.
>
> And Emily went on alone in the old house under the pines. On the wall of her own room hung a picture in a heavy oval frame of gold— unexplained.[44]

The attention here is to "fine" writing and the description contains some major discrepancies: the house next door was not yet built "a few days" after Dickinson presumably met Wadsworth in Philadelphia, nor was he the father of just one child, nor did he leave his profession or die prematurely. Other items, however, are familiar from the poems presented in this study. Bianchi played with her readers, telling part of the story but deliberately distracting attention away from its true subject. In 1924 she surely felt the need to protect Wadsworth's son, the Reverend Charles Wadsworth, Jr., whose many important offices and benevolent activities in Philadelphia are listed in his biography in *The National Cyclopaedia of American Biography*. The younger Wadsworth was even more prominent than his father and was at the height of his career when Bianchi was writing.

Millicent Todd Bingham, whose mother had warred bitterly with the ladies of the Dickinson family, reacted strongly against this passage, as would anyone concerned even merely with the health of English prose, and took the opposite extreme. In 1945, having waited for the death of anyone who could have challenged or corrected her, she lamented that Bianchi's *Life and Letters* had "revived the legend of the broken heart." She asserted that "Emily did not need a man to write poems," that "her primary interest was her poetry." But she concluded that "the legend of a broken heart has withstood all attempts to uproot it."[45]

Bingham was still exercised by the "legend" in 1954, in her *Emily Dickinson: A Revelation*, where she published for the first time the materials relating to Dickinson's relationship with Judge Lord, asserting that these (somehow) discredited or disproved the legend. The relationship with Lord, though acknowledged to be late in Dickinson's life, argued against the legend of Dickinson as a recluse "because of youthful love for a married man."[46] It became clear that polemics against the "Legend" had become confused and were really directed against Susan Dickinson and her daughter, Madame Bianchi, who seemed to have more information, though they teased with it, than did Mrs. Todd's daughter.

Later readers of these Dickinson materials can enjoy a delicious irony. The legend of the "Broken Heart" derives from Dickinson herself, who used the phrase to describe herself and her situation in nearly a dozen poems. As a further irony, one finds that the most prominent and celebratory of these "broken heart" poems exists only in the unique copy made by Bingham's mother. The original had been destroyed by Dickinson's family and the only extant version was Todd's transcript, in the possession of Todd's daughter at the time she was attempting to discredit the legend of the broken heart. The poem in question reads as follows:

> Proud of my broken heart, since thou didst break it,
> Proud of the pain I did not feel till thee,
>
> Proud of my night, since thou with moons dost slake it,
> *Not* to partake thy passion, *my* humility.

> Thou can'st not boast, like Jesus, drunken without companion
> Was the strong cup of anguish brewed for the Nazarene
>
> Thou can'st not pierce tradition with the peerless puncture,
> See! I usurped *thy* crucifix to honor mine!   [1736]

The poem is undatable because it does not exist in Dickinson's handwriting, but its accuracy can be presumed from Mrs. Todd's high standards of copying. It obviously derives from the marriage experience: the exchange of crucifixes instead of wedding rings, a prominent feature of poem 322, is recalled in the final line of this poem. The lines are a protest of love and separation, but of companionship in suffering, exactly fitting the diction of other marriage poems. Prominent in the strong push of the first line is Dickinson's own proud claim to a "Broken Heart."

Two early poems connect the broken heart with Dickinson's husband of the marriage poems. Poem 85 is addressed to "Sovreign" from "Daisy," asserting that she shares the "Broken hearted statement" of Jesus: "They have not chosen me . . ./But I have chosen them." And 151 is a "Master" poem from the same year as the first Master letter (1859), acknowledging that she is "broken," hiding herself under his "Ermine." An undated poem, preserved only in a draft by Susan Dickinson, asserts that one can expect sympathy only from another who has suffered in the same way:

> Unto a broken heart
> No other one may go
> Without the high prerogative
> Itself hath suffered too   [1704]

Two late poems, from 1873 and 1874, reflect on the marriage as an event with continuing effect on her life. The first one laments the one-sidedness of the correspondence. She is the one who "breaks" her own heart with the pretense that he is still in communication with her, but he is equal agent in this heartbreak (1290). The other late poem (1304) analyzes the possible causes of her broken heart:

> Not with a Club, the Heart is broken
> Nor with a Stone—
> A Whip so small you could not see it
> I've known
>
> To lash the Magic Creature
> Till it fell,
> Yet that Whip's Name
> Too noble then to tell.

Magnanimous as Bird
By Boy descried—
Singing unto the Stone
Of which it died—

Shame need not crouch
In such an Earth as Our's—
Shame—stand erect—
The Universe is your's.

The cause of the heartbreak is once again the small mysterious word, surely "love" in this case. What makes this poem unusual, though entirely congruent with Dickinson's marriage situation, is the celebration of a "shame" in the final stanza. Dickinson's first editors dropped this stanza in their 1896 collection of her poems, perhaps jarred by such an intrusion. But in the long retrospect, shame has been incorporated, absorbed into the larger synthesis of her marriage experience. Perhaps there is bitterness in this ending: since the universe is filled with shameful deeds, hers need not stand out for special censure. The insight is as old as two other heartbreak poems, of 1861 and 1862, the years of greatest marriage crisis. In 237 she had worried about forgiveness "Before my simple bosom—broke." Now, after the heartbreak, she feels an ecstasy that somehow she will still get to heaven though "unshriven." And in 428 Ideals and Crowns are *broken, fractured, splintered*—but reappear as whole in Glory.

Resistance to the legend of the broken heart has been renewed recently in a new form in the feminist critique of Suzanne Juhasz, who objected to the notion of any man assuming a position of importance in Emily Dickinson's life: "Both approaches are phallocentric: that (a) Emily Dickinson wrote poetry because she did not have a sex life or (b) the only explanation for such poetry was an active (albeit secret) sex life. Both interpretations lodge the male at the center of a woman's creativity."[47] Surely this is to attack all love poetry and the attempt to understand the world it defines and the characters it describes. In the case of Dickinson it would remove an essential dimension from the corpus of her poetry, a dimension she built into it by her intense sense of the addressee of her poems, and the loss of which removes the poetry into utter abstraction.

Preferable are the more genial allowances made by Sandra Gilbert and Susan Gubar. Commenting on "The Daisy follows soft the Sun" (106), an early love poem addressed to "Sir," they write: "In the intensity of her final longing, however, for 'The peace—the flight—the Amethyst—/Night's possibility!' Dickinson not only brings her narrative conceit to a satisfactorily romantic conclusion, she also confesses more openly than elsewhere in the poems the depth of her own sexual need for a fiery Master/

Lover.'' The poem in this case is read without prevenient theories that would rule such considerations out of order on *a priori* grounds. Commenting more generally on Dickinson's love poems, Gilbert and Gubar seem to redress the balance tipped by Juhasz: "Mothered by Awe, [Dickinson] might sometimes abase herself to her distant Master in a fever of despair, but she could also transform him into a powerful muse to serve *her* purposes."[48]

Conclusion

The whole of Emily Dickinson does not appear in this book. Some of the missing dimensions can quickly be listed. I have not included a chapter on Dickinson's life before she began the fascicles, which would discuss her earlier sentimental friendships with girls her own age, her early loves and flirtations, her posturings for a religious position before that subject was preempted by the stronger demands of her love affair.

Missing also, though not entirely, are the psychological intricacies of her suffering, treated sensitively by John Cody, and the philosophical reverberations of her lonely and meditative suffering analyzed by authors as different as Clark Griffith and Inder Nath Kher. Missing as well is Dickinson's extraordinary humor, well captured in the first act of William Luce's *The Belle of Amherst*, an exuberant joy which leads to outreach in the numerous directions recently suggested by Karl Keller.[1]

There are also dimensions of Dickinson which have yielded valuable insight to feminist, sociological, and lesbian critics; but that side of Dickinson does not appear here. Nor have I noted Dickinson's susceptibility to the analyses of current rhetorical criticism, an area explored by Roland Hagenbüchle, Robert Weisbuch, and Sharon Cameron. Each of these persuasive parts has been taken for the whole, but an easygoing syncretist may find that many of them blend to a composite, the complexity of which supplies the needed sense of a convincingly real person behind the poems.

The foregoing study has begun, rather, from the narrative characteristics of the fascicles and the sets, and has led in other directions. Such a study presents a portrait, as promised in the introduction, somewhat altered, somewhat enlarged when compared with previous studies. What emerges is a portrait of Dickinson as the American poet of romantic love *par excellence*, with some notable irregularities to distinguish her from other poets of that inclination. An ironic temperament, for example, surely provides a framework of steel for these potentially fluid and vaporous emotions. Such a portrait has attracted the general reader to Dickinson's poetry for nearly a hundred years now, while it has been almost universally resisted by Dickinson's critics and biographers.

The fascicles and sets can now be seen as the absolutely essential constructions which Dickinson herself built to house the poems. The poems of these collections are remarkably unified by the unmistakable "I" who speaks most of the poems, as well as by the deeply loved singular "you" to whom they are addressed. Remarkable as well is the story they had both lived through and continued to live through; reflections on those events contain the numerous "narrative patches" I have concentrated on, events that need not be spelled out elaborately for a general reader because they were written in the first instance "for your eyes only."

The story that these poems tell includes the following items and stages. Dickinson, in her mid-twenties, was badly disturbed by psychological problems which had a serious religious component. For counseling and therapy a well known clergyman was called upon, a man whose credentials were impeccable, who had already attracted Dickinson's confidence, but who was not so publicly connected with the Dickinson family that his attendance could cause gossip.

The counseling was carried on, in its initial stages, mostly by correspondence. There exists a note, in Wadsworth's handwriting, offering his sympathies and stating himself ready to help in whatever way he can.[2] But by 1858 Dickinson had become deeply attached to her counselor. She began to send him little booklets of her poems, keeping the drafts of these "fascicles" for herself. She also wrote him the first of the Master letters, complaining that he had not read her poems carefully enough to see their true meaning, and already anticipating union with him in heaven. The poems are private communications addressed to "you," who is further identified by such words as "dearest," "sweet," "Sir," and "beloved." The addressee was also identified, in numerous ways, as a clergyman.

When Wadsworth did come to Amherst, the local pastor's study was used as an appropriate conference room, though Wadsworth also visited Dickinson in her home.

During the interviews in the spring of 1860, their attraction was mutually recognized and sexual stimulation was high. The beloved is portrayed as equally conscious of their mutual infatuation. But because he was already married and well established in his profession, divorce was not a practical consideration. Thus guilt, because of the adulterous nature of their love, was an important dimension in the relationship. In the absence of legal marriage, the couple pledged spiritual marriage, which involved union in heaven as their reward for separation during life.

At some point in this sequence, at the urging of the male, the relationship seems to have been consummated, with pregnancy or the deep fear of pregnancy as the result. The crisis disturbed Dickinson physically and mentally during a whole summer, probably the summer of 1861, led her to confide in Higginson vaguely about the "terror—since September

[1861]—I could tell to none,"[3] led her to confide also in the intense letters and poems sent to Samuel Bowles in the winter of 1861-62. During this summer of 1861 she wrote the second Master letter, telling Wadsworth that she was deeply "wounded," that she did "tell you all." To his apparent question, "What can I do about it?" she responded sarcastically, "I dont know what you can do for it—thank you." She then called upon his masculine sense of responsibility and said that she would do her duty if their roles were reversed. The third Master letter, from the winter of 1861-62, recalls their intimate moments, records "that awful parting," protests that her love will never die, and pleads for some part in his life, some continued proximity.

Though the affair was relatively brief and based on only a few personal intimacies, it was maintained over the years by a steady two-way correspondence. Numerous phases in this relationship can be determined through the poems which reflect on the awakening of first love, deprivation, loneliness, and the religious dimension of their situation. Later poems and their dates coincide remarkably with the known movements and events in the life of Wadsworth. A brief renewal of intimacy occurred during Wadsworth's later visit to Amherst in 1880. And a final series of poems records her reactions to his death in 1882.

Most marriages go on to children, to financial and domestic matters, to growing daily tenderness, to the working out of personal frictions, and half of them in our day to the consuming pain of divorce. This marriage was arrested in its first stage. Dickinson preserves a moment in the process, presents a frozen section for microscopic scrutiny. The price was separation and its attendant pain, but it drove her deeper into her own mind, where she found the kind of wisdom the mind has always valued. Meditation on *her* marriage led, as do all great artistic conceptions, to the exploration of other themes: immortality, love, death, the phenomenon of adult loneliness, the precise kind of fulfillment the beloved provides, the higher forms of consciousness produced by love, the natural world as our symbolic context, the problem of knowlege ("Perception of an object costs/Precise the Object's loss" [1071]), the relationships subsisting among knowledge, language, and reality. What she thought out for one dear lover has entered the mainstream of our acquired wisdom.

Appendix A

The Problem
of the Sets

The poems of Emily Dickinson survive in three categories: the forty fascicles, which furnish the main subject of this book; the fifteen sets, which will now occupy our attention briefly; and the hundreds of loose single poems found among her papers after her death or retrieved from her correspondents.

The sets are markedly different from the fascicles. They are almost all from the decade after Dickinson stopped the fascicle-binding process, although there is some overlapping. Where the fascicles average 20 poems each, the sets vary widely from only one poem to 129 poems. Finally, where the fascicles are tied, the sets are only loosely gathered and no signs remain indicating their original internal order. It is obvious that the sets represent a much less organized and finished form of collection than do the fascicles. But they do preserve 333 new poems from the years 1862 to 1877, at a high stage of completion.

Nor can the sets be considered under a single category. Sets 1, 2, 3, and 4a are obviously related to some of the later fascicles. They contain poems that were considered for individual fascicles, but for some reason were rejected in the final selection.

The seven poems of Set 1 are written on the same stationery as was used for Fascicles 29, 30, and 31, and are dated by their handwriting at the same year as the poems of these fascicles, 1862. It may have been that Dickinson did not consider these poems to be as good as those she did select, or as appropriate. Poem 504 from this first set compares "Thee" to the image of the man in the moon, her wandering exile "Ishmael." While the trope may be appropriate to her distant lover, the details of the description, as the poem developed, may have seemed too unflattering: "The very Brow—the stooping Eyes—/A-fog. . . ." But there are details in the poems of this first set that closely resemble the interests of the fascicles: poem 400 protests her fidelity, though the "Way" to him is "Interdicted," describes their love as "Beginning with the Day/That Night—begun," and promises that her "Bond" with him will still hold after death.

The four poems of Set 2 are on the same stationery as that used for Fascicle 38. The poems in this set are filled with many alternate readings, and they may not have been considered ready for sending. Also, poem 937 may seem to confess too much that is mentally pathological; Dickinson writes in this poem that she is unable to think consecutive thoughts, that her meanings ravel out like dropped balls of yarn. But once again there are observations relevant to the themes of the fascicles that we would not willingly lose. In poem 939 she dreams of the absent beloved, "and in my Dream—/Do Thee distinguished Grace—/Till jealous Daylight interrupt—/And mar thy perfectness."

Set 3 contains only two poems, on the same stationery as that used in Fascicle 39. The first poem, 943, is a meditation on death but with many alternatives in the final stanza still not settled. But 944 is a magnificent scenario imagining married life with her clergyman lover. I have already commented on it in some detail, but here it might be noted that the intimate sexual innuendo of one of its stanzas may have seemed inappropriate for sending, as Dickinson was writing her way out of the relationship in these last fascicles.

Finally, the two leaves of Set 4a contain three poems on the same paper as that used for Fascicle 40. The first poem begins with a definition of the sexual aspect of love: it comes before life and "confirms" life at its entrance (924). Poem 925 confesses that she was "Struck. . . .Maimed. . . .Robbed" by him, but still loves him, will continue to love him until the Resurrection, "Till the infinite Aurora/In the other's eyes." Perhaps these assertions were too strong to be made in the last fascicle. And the third poem, 926, may also have been judged too intense, as Dickinson defines her troubled and struggling "Patience" which is no patience at all.

The remaining sets do not seem to allow even such generalizations as these. The poems of any given set are written on uniform sheets of paper, but no set uses the same kind of paper as any other. And the poems are fairly clean copies, with very few alternative readings marked. These details seem to indicate that Dickinson periodically sat down to copy out a group of recently completed poems for her own record. Considerations of spacing, binding, and selection of a uniform number of poems—considerations which characterize the production of the fascicles—are no longer in evidence. In fact, more than half of the sets consist of a single folded sheet of stationery each, with from one to four poems copied onto it.

Love poems and references to her marriage are quite frequent in Sets 5-8, quite rare in the remaining sets. Many of them have been considered in chapter 3 above. Poems addressed directly to the beloved "Thee" also appear quite frequently in the earlier sets, much more rarely in the later ones. Thoughts of the isolated self in confrontation with nature come to be the main subjects of these later poems.

Set 6 stands out among the sets. Franklin arranges it into three subsets because of three slightly different papers used. Set 6a contains seventeen poems on four sheets; Set 6b contains thirty-seven poems on nine sheets; and Set 6c contains twenty-two poems on six sheets. As such, these three subsets most closely approximate the condition of the fascicles, as far as their physical size is concerned, except for binding. All of the poems are dated by handwriting at between 1864 and 1866, indicating perhaps an intermediate stage between the fascicles and the sets. They signal a change in Dickinson's work style, but not the reasons for it—unless the closing off of the affair recorded in the last phase of the fascicles was reason enough.

The quality of the poetry does not diminish. In the experience that generated the fascicles, Dickinson had found her subjects and themes as well as her personal style. These continue in the sets, though chastened and sobered; the poems in the sets are characterized almost uniformly by a sustained note of sadness. The latest theme of the fascicles, that of a solitary achievement of the self, a lone and stoic completeness, is one of the most pervasive themes in the sets.

The Fascicle Lists

The poems in the little manuscript booklets which Emily Dickinson herself arranged are here presented for the convenience of the reader. It has already been mentioned that these collections were broken up by Dickinson's first editors shortly after her death. Ralph W. Franklin, whose work is hereby acknowledged, restored these fascicles to their original state and published the facsimiles in 1981. The numbering of the fascicles is Franklin's, to show their chronological ordering as accurately as possible; this numbering supersedes, and is considerably different from, that given by Mabel Loomis Todd and her husband when the poems were first being edited. Within the fascicles the numbers given to the poems are those of Thomas H. Johnson, from his three-volume variorum edition of 1955.

Fascicle 1

18	The Gentian weaves her fringes—
6	Frequently the woods are pink—
19	A sepal, petal, and a thorn
20	Distrustful of the Gentian—
21	We lose—because we win—
22	All these my banners be.
23	I had a guinea golden—
24	There is a morn by men unseen—
323	As if I asked a common alms—
25	She slept beneath a tree—
7	The feet of people walking home
26	It's all I have to bring today—
27	Morns like these—we parted—
28	So has a Daisy vanished
29	If those I loved were lost
30	Adrift! A little boat adrift!
31	Summer for thee, grant I may be
32	When Roses cease to bloom, Sir,
33	*Oh* if remembering were forgetting—
4	On this wondrous sea
34	Garlands for Queens, may be—
35	Nobody knows this little Rose—

Fascicle 2

8	There is a word
9	Through lane it lay—thro' bramble—
15	The Guest is gold and crimson—
36	I counted till they danced so

37	Before the ice is in the pools —
38	By such and such an offering
39	It did not surprise me—
40	When I count the seeds
147	Bless God, he went as soldiers,
56	If I should cease to bring a Rose
14	One Sister have I in the house—
1730	"Lethe" in my flower,
57	To venerate the simple days
1729	I've got an arrow here.
41	I robbed the Woods—
42	A Day! Help! Help! Another Day!
43	Could live—*did* live—
44	If she had been the Mistletoe
10	My wheel is in the dark!
45	There's something quieter than sleep
46	I keep my pledge.
47	Heart! We will forget him!
48	Once more, my now bewildered Dove
17	Baffled for just a day or two—

Fascicle 3

58	Delayed till she had ceased to know—
89	Some things that fly there be—
90	Within my reach!
91	So bashful when I spied her!

149 She went as quiet as the Dew
105 To hang our head—ostensibly—
106 The Daisy follows soft the Sun—
60 Like her the Saints retire,
61 Papa above!
107 'Twas such a little—little boat
62 "Sown in dishonor"!
150 She died—*this* was the way
      she died.
63 If pain for peace prepares
108 Surgeons must be very careful
64 Some Rainbow—coming from the
      Fair!
109 By a flower—By a letter—
65 I cant tell you—but you feel it—

Fascicle 8

165 A *Wounded* Deer—leaps highest—
152 The Sun kept stooping—stooping—
      low!
166 I met a King this afternoon!
167 To learn the Transport by the
      Pain—
168 If the foolish, call them *"flowers"*—
169 In Ebon Box, when years have
      flown
70 Portraits are to daily faces
171 Wait till the Majesty of Death
172 'Tis so much joy! 'Tis so much joy!
173 A fuzzy fellow, without feet,
174 At last, to be identified!
175 I have never seen 'Volcanoes'—
153 Dust is the only Secret—
176 I'm the little "Heart's Ease"!
177 Ah, Necromancy Sweet!
154 Except to Heaven, she is nought.
170 Pictures are to daily faces
178 I cautious, scanned my little life—
179 If I could bribe them by a Rose
180 As if some little Arctic flower

Fascicle 9

186 What shall I do—it whimpers so—
187 How many times these low feet
      staggered—
188 Make me a picture of the sun—
269 Bound—a trouble—
215 What is—"Paradise"—
155 The Murmur of a Bee
156 You love me—you are sure—
162 My River runs to Thee—

189 It's such a little thing to weep—
190 He was weak, and I was
      strong—then—
191 The Skies cant keep their secret!
192 Poor little Heart!
193 I shall know why—when Time is
      over—
194 On this long storm the Rainbow
      rose—
157 Musicians wrestle everywhere—
195 For this—accepted Breath—
196 We dont cry—Tim and I,
158 Dying! Dying in the night!
197 Morning—is the place for Dew—
198 An awful Tempest mashed the air—
199 I'm "wife"—I've finished that—
200 I stole them from a Bee—
201 Two swimmers wrestled on the
      spar—
202 My Eye is fuller than my vase—
203 He forgot—and I—remembered—
204 A Slash of Blue! A sweep of Gray!
205 I should not dare to leave my
      friend,
206 The Flower must not blame the
      Bee—
324 Some—keep the Sabbath—going to
      church—

Fascicle 10

230 We—Bee and I—live by the
      quaffing—
231 God permits industrious Angels—
232 The *Sun—just touched* the Morning—
233 The Lamp burns sure—within—
163 Tho' my destiny be Fustian—
207 Tho' I get home how late—how
      late—
208 The Rose did caper on her cheek—
209 With thee, in the Desert—
185 Faith is a fine invention
210 The thought beneath so slight a
      film—
318 I'll tell you how the Sun rose—
159 A little Bread—a crust—a crumb—
160 Just lost, when I was saved!
211 Come slowly—Eden!
212 Least Rivers—docile to some sea.
270 *One Life* of so much Consequence!
234 You're right—"the way *is* narrow"—
216 Safe in their Alabaster Chambers—

235   The Court is far away—
236   If *He dissolve*—then—there is
          nothing—more—
237   I think just how my shape will rise—
224   I've nothing else—to bring, You
          know—

Fascicle 11

283   A Mien to move a Queen—
284   The Drop, that wrestles in the Sea—
285   The Robin's my Criterion for Tune—
243   I've known a Heaven, like a Tent—
223   I came to buy a smile—today—
287   A Clock stopped—
288   I'm Nobody! Who are you?
245   I held a Jewel in my fingers—
244   It is easy to work when the soul is
          at play—
286   That after Horror—that 'twas *us*—
240   Ah, Moon—and Star!
317   Just so—Christ—raps—
246   Forever at His side to walk—
221   It cant be "Summer"!
247   What would I give to see his face?
1737   Rearrange a "Wife's" affection!
248   Why—do they shut Me out of
          Heaven?
249   Wild Nights—Wild Nights!
250   I shall keep singing!
251   Over the fence—

Fascicle 12

214   I taste a liquor never brewed—
161   A feather from the Whippowil—
181   I lost a World—the other day!
182   If I should'nt be alive
183   I've heard an Organ talk,
          sometimes—
184   A transport one cannot contain
185   "Faith" is a fine invention
293   I got so I could hear his name—
263   A single Screw of Flesh
264   A Weight with Needles on the
          pounds—
217   Father—I bring thee—not Myself—
265   Where Ships of Purple—gently toss—
266   This—is the land—the Sunset
          washes—
294   The Doomed—regard the Sunrise
225   Jesus! thy Crucifix
267   Did we disobey Him?

295   Unto like Story—Trouble has enticed
          me—
296   One Year ago—jots what?
297   It's like the Light—
298   Alone, I cannot be—
273   He put the Belt around my life—
274   The only Ghost I ever saw
275   Doubt Me! My Dim Companion!
276   Many a phrase has the English
          language—
321   Of all the Sounds despatched
          abroad—
514   Her smile was shaped like other
          smiles—
353   A happy lip—breaks sudden—

Fascicle 13

289   I know some lonely Houses off the
          Road
252   I can wade Grief—
253   You see I cannot see—your lifetime—
254   "Hope" is the thing with feathers—
255   To die—takes just a little while—
256   If I'm lost—now—
257   Delight is as the flight—
219   She sweeps with many-colored
          Brooms—
290   Of Bronze—and Blaze—
258   There's a certain Slant of light,
228   Blazing in Gold—and
259   Good Night! Which put the Candle
          out?
260   Read—Sweet—how others—strove—
261   Put up my lute!
322   There came a Day—at Summer's
          full—
262   The lonesome for they know not
          What—
291   How the old Mountains drip with
          Sunset
325   Of Tribulation, these are They,
292   If your Nerve, deny you—

Fascicle 14

319   The maddest dream—recedes—
          unrealized—
277   What if I say I shall not wait!
240   Ah, Moon—and Star!
278   A Shady friend—for Torrid days—
271   A solemn thing—it was—I said—
272   I breathed enough to take the Trick—

238 Kill your Balm—and it's Odors bless
 you—
239 "Heaven"—is what I cannot reach!
7 The feet of people walking home
582 Inconceivably solemn!
422 More Life—went out—when He went
423 The Months have ends—the Years—a
 knot—
424 Removed from Accident of Loss
299 Your Riches—taught me—Poverty.
583 A Toad, can die of Light—
332 There are two Ripenings—
584 It ceased to hurt me, though so slow
310 Give little Anguish,
Missing? (poems unknown)

Fascicle 15

410 The first Day's Night had come—
411 The Color of the Grave is Green—
414 'Twas like a Maelstrom, with a
 notch,
580 I gave myself to Him—
415 Sunset at Night—is natural—
419 We grow accustomed to the Dark—
420 You'll know it—as you know 'tis
 Noon—
421 A Charm invests a face
577 If I may have it, when it's dead,
412 I read my sentence—steadily—
416 A Murmur in the Trees—to note—
417 It is dead—Find it—
418 Not in this World to see his face—
581 I found the words to every thought
413 I never felt at Home—Below—
578 The Body grows without—
579 I had been hungry, all the Years—

Fascicle 16

327 Before I got my eye put out—
607 Of nearness to her sundered Things
279 Tie the Strings to my Life, My Lord,
241 I like a look of Agony,
280 I felt a Funeral, in my Brain,
281 'Tis so appalling—it exhilirates—
282 How noteless Men, and Pleiads,
 stand,
242 When we stand on the tops of
 Things—
445 'Twas just this time, last year, I died.
608 Afraid! Of whom am I afraid?
446 He showed me Hights I never saw—

Fascicle 17

348 I dreaded that first Robin, so,
505 I would not paint—a picture—
506 He touched me, so I live to know
349 I had the Glory—that will do—
507 She sights a Bird—she chuckles—
350 They leave us with the Infinite.
508 I'm ceded—I've stopped being
 Their's—
509 If anybody's friend be dead
510 It was not Death, for I stood up,
511 If you were coming in the Fall,
351 I felt my life with both my hands
352 Perhaps I asked too large—
328 A Bird, came down the Walk—
512 The Soul has Bandaged moments—
513 Like Flowers, that heard the news
 of Dews,

Fascicle 18

495 It's thoughts—and just One Heart—
337 I know a place where Summer
 strives
496 As far from pity, as complaint—
338 I know that He exists.
497 He strained my faith—
339 I tend my flowers for thee—
498 I envy Seas, whereon He rides—
499 Those fair—fictitious People—
500 Within my Garden, rides a Bird
340 Is Bliss then, such Abyss,
341 After great pain, a formal feeling
 comes—
501 This World is not Conclusion.
342 It will be Summer—eventually.
343 My Reward for Being, was This.
344 'Twas the old—road—through pain—
502 At least—to pray—is left—is left—
503 Better—than Music! For I—who
 heard it—

Fascicle 19

333 The Grass so little has to do,
334 All the letters I can write
326 I cannot dance upon my Toes—
425 Good Morning—Midnight—
585 I like to see it lap the Miles—
426 It dont sound so terrible—quite—as it
 did—
427 I'll clutch—and clutch—
428 Taking up the fair Ideal,

316 The Wind did'nt come from the
    Orchard—today—
716 The Day undressed—Herself—
717 The Beggar Lad—dies early—
769 One and One—are One—
770 I lived on Dread—

Fascicle 24

311 It sifts from Leaden Sieves—
595 Like Mighty Foot Lights—burned the
    Red
1712 A Pit—but Heaven over it—
1710 A curious Cloud surprised the Sky,
602 Of Brussels—it was not—
603 He found my Being—set it up—
604 Unto my Books—so good to turn—
605 The Spider holds a Silver Ball
598 Three times—we
    parted—Breath—and I—
599 There is a pain—so utter—
600 It troubled me as once I was—
601 A still—Volcano—Life—
596 When I was small, a Woman died—
441 This is my letter to the World
442 God made a little Gentian—
343 My Reward for Being—was This—
597 It always felt to me—a wrong
443 I tie my Hat—I crease my Shawl—
606 The Trees like Tassels—hit—and
    swung—
444 It feels a shame to be Alive—

Fascicle 25

371 A precious—mouldering
    pleasure—'tis—
532 I tried to think a lonelier Thing
533 Two Butterflies went out at Noon—
304 The Day came slow—till Five
    o'clock—
1053 It was a quiet way—
372 I know lives, I could miss
373 I'm saying every day
305 The difference between Despair
374 I went to Heaven—
375 The Angle of a Landscape—
683 The Soul unto itself
534 We see—Comparatively—
376 Of Course—I prayed—
529 I'm sorry for the Dead—Today—
530 You cannot put a Fire out—
531 We dream—it is good we are
    dreaming—

1727 If ever the lid gets off my head
1739 Some say good night—at night—
535 She's happy, with a new Content—
536 The Heart asks Pleasure—first—

Fascicle 26

628 They called me to the Window, for
669 No Romance sold unto
465 I heard a Fly buzz—when I died—
674 The Soul that hath a Guest,
629 I watched the Moon around the
    House
1181 When I hoped—I feared—
630 The Lightning playeth—all the
    while—
631 Ourselves were wed one
    summer—dear—
466 'Tis little I—could care for Pearls—
632 The Brain—is wider than the Sky—
467 We do not play on Graves—
312 Her—last Poems—
633 When Bells stop
    ringing—Church—begins
468 The Manner of it's Death
469 The Red—Blaze—is the Morning—
634 You'll know Her—by Her Foot—
470 I am alive—I guess—
1067 Except the smaller size—
635 I think the longest Hour of all
329 So glad we are—a stranger'd deem
471 A Night—there lay the Days
    between—

Fascicle 27

389 There's been a Death, in the
    Opposite House,
554 The Black Berry—wears a Thorn in
    his side—
307 The One that could repeat the
    Summer Day—
561 I measure every Grief I meet
562 Conjecturing a Climate
396 There is a Languor of the Life
397 When Diamonds are a Legend,
398 I had not minded—Walls—
399 A House upon the Hight—
390 It's Coming—the postponeless
    Creature—
308 I send Two Sunsets—
391 A Visitor in Marl—
392 Through the Dark Sod—as
    Education—

380 There is a flower that Bees prefer–
381 A Secret told–
382 For Death–or rather
383 Exhiliration–is within–
545 'Tis One by One–the Father
counts–
546 To fill a Gap
547 I've seen a Dying Eye
384 No Rack can torture me–
548 Death is potential to that Man
385 Smiling back from Coronation
549 That I did always love

Fascicle 32

455 Triumph–may be of several kinds–
617 Dont put up my Thread & Needle–
456 So well that I can live without–
618 At leisure is the Soul
457 Sweet–safe–Houses–
619 Glee–The great storm is over–
620 It makes no difference abroad–
621 I asked no other thing–
622 To know just how He
suffered–would be dear–
623 It was too late for Man–
624 Forever–is composed of Nows–
625 'Twas a long Parting–but the time
626 Only God–detect the Sorrow–
458 Like Eyes that looked on Wastes–
459 A Tooth upon Our Peace
460 I know where Wells grow–
627 The Tint I cannot take–is best–
461 A Wife–at Daybreak–I shall be–
462 Why make it doubt–it hurts it so–
463 I live with Him–I see His face–
464 The power to be true to You,

Fascicle 33

636 The Way I read a Letter's–this–
637 The Child's faith is new–
472 Except the Heaven had come so
near–
638 To my small Hearth His fire came–
639 My Portion is Defeat–today–
473 I am ashamed–I hide–
640 I cannot live with You–
641 Size circumscribes–it has no room
474 They put Us far apart–
642 Me from Myself–to banish–
475 Doom is the House without the
Door–
313 I should have been too glad, I see–

476 I meant to have but modest needs–
643 I could suffice for Him, I knew–
644 You left me–Sire–two Legacies–
477 No Man can compass a Despair–

Fascicle 34

645 Bereavement in their death to feel
646 I think To Live–may be a Bliss
647 A little Road–not made of Man–
649 Her Sweet turn to leave the
Homestead
650 Pain–has an Element of Blank–
651 So much Summer
648 Promise This–When You be Dying–
478 I had no time to Hate–
754 My Life had stood–a Loaded Gun–
710 The Sunrise runs for Both–
755 No Bobolink–reverse His Singing
756 One Blessing had I than the rest
690 Victory comes late–
757 The Mountains–grow unnoticed–
758 These–saw Visions–
711 Strong Draughts of Their Refreshing
Minds
993 We miss Her–not because We see–
675 Essential Oils–are wrung–

Fascicle 35

692 The Sun kept setting–setting– still
693 Shells from the Coast mistaking–
694 The Heaven vests for Each
733 The Spirit is the Conscious Ear.
734 If He were living–dare I ask–
695 As if the Sea should part
668 "Nature" is what We see–
735 Upon Concluded Lives
736 Have any like Myself
680 Each Life Converges to some
Centre–
696 Their Hight in Heaven comforts
not–
697 I could bring You Jewels–had I a
mind to–
698 Life–is what we make it–
699 The Judge is like the Owl–
1142 The Props assist the House–
700 You've seen Balloons set–Hav'nt
You?
689 The Zeros taught Us–Phosphorus–
701 A Thought went up my mind
today–
673 The Love a Life can show Below

Notes

Introduction

1. Jean Piaget, *Structuralism*, trans. and ed. Chaninah Maschler (New York: Basic Books, 1970), 14.

2. Ruth Miller, *The Poetry of Emily Dickinson* (Middletown, Conn.: Wesleyan University Press, 1968), 249.

3. Martha O'Keefe, "Primal Thought," *Dickinson Studies* 35 (1979): 8–11.

4. R.W. Franklin, ed., *The Manuscript Books of Emily Dickinson* (Cambridge: Belknap Press of Harvard University Press, 1981), 2 vols.

5. Miller, *Poetry of Emily Dickinson*, 248.

6. R.W. Franklin, "The Emily Dickinson Fascicles," *Studies in Bibliography* 36 (1983): 17.

7. David Porter, "The Crucial Experience in Emily Dickinson's Poetry," *ESQ: A Journal of the American Renaissance* 20 (1974): 280.

Chapter One

1. Frank Kermode, *The Genesis of Secrecy: On the Interpretation of Narrative* (Cambridge, Mass.: Harvard University Press, 1979), 5.

2. Poems in the fascicles in which "You" or "We" (in any of their various forms) seem to exclude the general reader are the following: 4, 31, 32, 35, 54, 85, 92, 102, 106, 124, 162, 180, 181, 186, 190, 200, 202, 203, 209, 211, 212, 215, 223, 224, 234, 235, 237, 238, 246, 247, 249, 253, 256, 259, 260, 267, 273, 274, 275, 276, 277, 279, 284, 286, 288, 293, 296, 299, 317, 322, 325, 336, 339, 343, 350, 355, 366, 368, 376, 388, 394, 402, 415, 429, 433, 434, 438, 440, 447, 449, 453, 456, 458, 461, 462, 464, 470, 474, 480, 487, 495, 511, 523, 532, 537, 549, 550, 568, 577, 587, 589, 611, 616, 640, 644, 646, 648, 659, 671, 682, 689, 693, 697, 704, 715, 725, 728, 729, 730, 738, 740, 748, 754, 765, 775, 786, 788, 800, 903, 909, 961, 965, 966, 1053, 1737.

3. Confining our attention to the fascicle poems exclusively, we find "Sir" or "Sire" in poems 32, 106, 124, 181, 196, 223, 256, 296, 366, 461, 480, 644, 725, 729; "Signor" in 250 and 429; "Sweet" in 260, 482, 523, 541, 549, 644, 659, 704, 961, 966; "Master" in 96, 336, 415, 461, 462, and 754; "Sovreign" in 85, 235, and 247; "Lover" in 512, 537, and 577; "King" in 103 and 235; "Dear" in 434, 462, 631, and 648; "Lord" in 279, 339, and 438; and "Beloved" in 246, 751, and 971.

4. Jay Leyda, *The Years and Hours of Emily Dickinson* (New Haven: Yale University Press, 1960), 1: xxi.

5. Millicent Todd Bingham, *Emily Dickinson's Home: Letters of Edward Dickinson and His Family* (New York: Harper, 1955), 375.

6. Thomas H. Johnson, ed., *The Letters of Emily Dickinson*, (Cambridge, Mass.: Belknap Press of Harvard University Press, 1958), 2: 333.

7. S.P. Rosenbaum, *A Concordance to the Poems of Emily Dickinson* (Ithaca: Cornell University Press, 1964), 169–72.

8. R.W. Franklin, *The Editing of Emily Dickinson: A Reconsideration* (Madison: University of Wisconsin Press, 1967), 46–47.

9. Clark Griffith, *The Long Shadow: Emily Dickinson's Tragic Poetry* (Princeton: Princeton University Press, 1964), 166.

10. One of her earliest readers, William Dean Howells, called this voice Dickinson's "almost hysterical shriek," in "Editor's Study," *Harper's Monthly* 82 (1891): 318–21; Sharon Cameron refers more sympathetically to the poems as "loaded with energy that is . . . close to explosive," in *Lyric Time: Emily Dickinson and the Limits of Genre* (Baltimore: Johns Hopkins University Press, 1979), 87.

11. See Thomas H. Johnson, ed., (Cambridge: Belknap Press of Harvard University Press, 1955), 1: 180.

12. Griffith, *Long Shadows*, 78, 150, 154, 162.

13. William R. Sherwood, *Circumference and Circumstance: Stages in the Mind and Art of Emily Dickinson* (New York: Columbia University Press, 1968), 84, 85, 138–39; Miller, *Poetry of Emily Dickinson*, 111ff, 138; Inder Nath Kher, *The Landscape of Absence: Emily Dickinson's Poetry* (New Haven: Yale University Press, 1974), 140, 147.

14. John Crowe Ransom, "Emily Dickinson: A Poet Restored," *Perspectives USA* (Spring 1956); reprinted in *Emily Dickinson: A Collection of Critical Essays*, ed. Richard B. Sewall (Englewood Cliffs, N.J.: Prentice-Hall, 1963), 93, 97.

15. Nancy F. Cott, *The Bonds of Womanhood: "Woman's Sphere" in New England, 1780–1835* (New Haven: Yale University Press, 1977); Barbara J. Berg, *The Remembered Gate: Origins of American Feminism: The Woman and the City, 1800–1860* (New York: Oxford University Press, 1978).

16. Nathaniel Hawthorne, *The Scarlet Letter*, Centenary Edition (Columbus: Ohio State University Press, 1962), 80; subsequent quotations are from this edition.

17. Leyda, *Years and Hours*, 1: 283, 291.

18 Vivian R. Pollak, "Thirst and Starvation in Emily Dickinson's Poetry," *American Literature* 51 (March 1979): 33–49.

19. I follow the list of "suicide" poems suggested by John Cody in *After Great Pain: The Inner Life of Emily Dickinson* (Cambridge: Belknap Press of Harvard University Press, 1971), 297; Cody's list includes those poems that others have also suggested as suicidal.

20. Richard B. Sewall, *The Life of Emily Dickinson* (New York: Farrar, Straus and Giroux, 1974), 2: 606. Cody, *After Great Pain*, 24, 30, 291ff, 328ff.

21. Cody, *After Great Pain*, 426.

22. John Evangelist Walsh lists numerous parallels to Mrs. Browning's *Aurora Leigh* in the poems of Emily Dickinson; see his *The Hidden Life of Emily Dickinson: A Biography* (New York: Simon and Schuster, 1971). Ellen Moers sanely rebuts Walsh's contention that Dickinson "plagiarised" Browning, and discusses the parallels with great insight in *Literary Women: The Great Writers* (New York: Doubleday, 1977).

23. Yvor Winters, "Emily Dickinson and the Limits of Judgment," in his *In Defense of Reason* (Denver: Alan Swallow, 1937), 286–89; Richard Chase, *Emily Dickinson* (New York: William Sloane, 1951), 122; R.P. Blackmur, "Emily Dickinson's Notation," *Kenyon Review* 18 (Spring 1956); reprinted in *Emily Dickinson: A Collection of Critical Essays*, ed. Richard B. Sewall (Englewood Cliffs, N.J.: Prentice-Hall, 1963), 82.

24. Eleanor Wilner, "The Poetics of Emily Dickinson," *ELH* 38 (March 1971): 126, 136, 138, 147.

25. Roland Hagenbüchle, "Precision and Indeterminacy in the Poetry of Emily Dickinson," *ESQ: A Journal of the American Renaissance* 20 (1st Quarter 1974): 33-56.

26. Robert Weisbuch, *Emily Dickinson's Poetry* (Chicago: University of Chicago Press, 1975), 23–33 passim, 48.

27. Cameron, *Lyric Time*, 206–8. See also the interview with Cameron in *Johns Hopkins Journal* 13 (Fall 1979): 3.

28. See W. Daniel Wilson, "Readers in Texts," *PMLA* 96.5 (October 1981): 849.

Chapter Two

1. Foreword to Violette Leduc, *La Bâtarde*, trans. Derek Coltman (New York: Farrar, Straus and Giroux, 1965), vi.

2. Thomas H. Johnson, ed., *The Letters of Emily Dickinson* (Cambridge: Belknap Press of Harvard University Press, 1958), 2:333, letter 187.

3. Ibid., 389, letter 246.

4. Ibid., 453, letter 318.

5. Sandra M. Gilbert and Susan Gubar, *The Madwoman in the Attic: The Woman Writer and the Nineteenth Century Literary Imagination* (New Haven: Yale University Press, 1979), 601.

6. George Frisbie Whicher, *This Was a Poet: A Critical Biography of Emily Dickinson* (New York: Charles Scribner's Sons, 1938), 101.

7. Leyda, *Years and Hours*, 2: 112.

8. David T. Porter, *The Art of Emily Dickinson's Early Poetry* (Cambridge: Harvard University Press, 1966), 85.

9. Porter, "Crucial Experience," 280–90; reprinted in Porter, *Dickinson: The Modern Idiom* (Cambridge: Harvard University Press, 1981), 9–24.

10. The text of this poem is R.W. Franklin's correction of Johnson, from a recently discovered manuscript; see *American Literature* 50 (March 1978): 112–13.

11. Leyda, *Years and Hours*, 1: xxi.

12. Johnson, *Letters*, 2: 374, letter 233. The parentheses indicate Dickinson's alternative reading.

13. Bingham, *Emily Dickinson's Home*, 421.

14. Leyda, *Years and Hours*, 1: 352.

15. Ibid., 371–72.

16. Ibid., 274.

17. Johnson, *Letters*, 2: 383–84, Letter 243.

18. Ibid., 389, Letter 246.

19. Ibid., 334, letter 198.

20. Ibid., 391, Letter 248.

21. Albert Gelpi, "Emily Dickinson and the Deerslayer: The Dilemma of the Woman Poet in America," in *Shakespeare's Sisters: Feminist Essays on Woman Poets*, ed. Sandra M. Gilbert and Susan Gubar (Bloomington: Indiana University Press, 1979), 124.

22. Cameron, *Lyric Time*, 67.

23. Johnson, *Letters*, 2: 391, letter 248.

Chapter Three

1. Madame de Staël, *Corinne; or Italy*, trans. and with an introduction by Isabel Hill (New York: A.L. Burt, n.d.), x.

2. Sewall, *Life of Emily Dickinson*, 1: xi; Porter, *Dickinson: The Modern Idiom*, 1.

3. Walsh, *Hidden Life*; Moers, *Literary Women*.

4. Henry David Thoreau, *A Week on the Concord and Merrimack Rivers*, ed. Carl F. Hovde *et al.* (Princeton: Princeton University Press, 1980), 269–70.

5. *The Lyman Letters: New Light on Emily Dickinson and Her Family*, ed. Richard B. Sewall (Amherst: University of Massachusetts Press, 1965), 21.

6. Northdrop Frye, "Emily Dickinson," in *Fables of Identity: Studies in Poetic Mythology*

(New York: Harcourt Brace and World, 1963), 198; Sherwood, *Circumference and Circumstance*, 69; Whicher, *This Was a Poet*, 79.

7. E.M.W. Tillyard, *Milton* (New York: Dial Press, 1930), 1.

8. Richard Ellman, *Golden Codgers: Biographical Speculations* (New York: Oxford University Press, 1973); James E. Miller, *T.S. Eliot's Personal Wasteland* (University Park: Pennsylvania State University Press, 1977), x.

9. Robert Weisbuch, *Emily Dickinson's Poetry* (Chicago: University of Chicago Press, 1975), 183; see also Sherwood, *Circumference and Circumstance*, 71, for a similar assertion.

10. Johnson, *Letters*, 2: 412, Letter 268.

11. Brita Lindberg-Seyersted, *The Voice of the Poet: Aspects of Style in the Poetry of Emily Dickinson* (Uppsala, Sweden: Acta Universitatis Upsaliensis, 1968), 33–35.

12. Gilbert and Gubar, *Madwoman in the Attic*, 583.

13. See, for example, Chester P. Sadowy, "Dickinson's 'He touched me, so I live to know,' " *Explicator* 37 (Fall 1978): 4–5.

14. Winters, *In Defense of Reason*, 288; Donald E. Thackery, *Emily Dickinson's Approach to Poetry* (Lincoln: University of Nebraska Press, 1954), 29.

15. Charles Anderson, *Emily Dickinson's Poetry: Stairway of Surprise* (New York: Holt, 1960), 180–87; Louise Bogan, "A Mystical Poet," in *Emily Dickinson: Three Views* (Amherst: Amherst College Press, 1960); Olive Rabe, "Emily Dickinson as Mystic," *Colorado Quarterly* 14 (Winter 1966): 280-88; Michael Dressman, "The Empress of Calvary: Mystical Marriage in the Poems of Emily Dickinson," *South Atlantic Bulletin* 42 (January 1977): 39–43.

16. Theodora Ward, *The Capsule of the Mind: Chapters in the Life of Emily Dickinson* (Cambridge: Belknap Press of Harvard University Press, 1961), 74; Sherwood, *Circumference and Circumstance*, 84, 138–39.

17. Miller, *Poetry of Emily Dickinson*, 4, 80.

18. Ibid., 80–81.

19. Rabe, "Emily Dickinson as Mystic," 280–88.

20. Rebecca Patterson, *The Riddle of Emily Dickinson* (Boston: Houghton Mifflin, 1951); *Emily Dickinson's Imagery*, ed. Margaret H. Freeman (Amherst: University of Massachusetts Press, 1979), 223.

21. Carroll Smith-Rosenberg, "The Female World of Love and Ritual: Relations between Women in 19th Century America," *Signs: A Journal of Women in Culture and Society*, 1, no. 1 (1975): 1–29.

22. Lillian Faderman, "Emily Dickinson's Letters to Sue Gilbert, "*Massachusetts Review* 43 (1977): 197–225; idem; "Emily Dickinson's Homoerotic Poetry," *Higginson Journal* 18 (1977): 19–27; Adrienne Rich, "Vesuvius at Home: The Power of Emily Dickinson," in her *On Lies, Secrets, and Silence* (New York: W.W. Norton, 1979), 157; the author cited is Toni McNaron, from an unpublished essay.

23. George S. Merriam, *Life and Times of Samuel Bowles* (New York: Century, 1885); *The Dictionary of American Biography*, ed. Allen Johnson (New York: Scribner's, 1929), 2:514-18.

24. Johnson, *Letters*, 2:574, letter 489.

25. Other supporters for the cause of Bowles as Dickinson's lover are Jean McClure Mudge, *Emily Dickinson and the Image of Home* (Amherst: University of Massachusetts Press, 1975); David Higgins, *Portrait of Emily Dickinson: The Poet and her Prose* (New Brunswick, N. J.: Rutgers University Press, 1967); and Winfield Townley Scott, "Emily Dickinson and Samuel Bowles," *Fresco: The University of Detroit Tri-Quarterly* 10 (Summer 1960): 3-13.

26. Rebecca Patterson and Myra Himelhock, "The Dating of Emily Dickinson's Letters to the Bowles Family, 1858-1862," *Emily Dickinson Bulletin* 20 (1972): 1-28.

27. *Emily Dickinson's Letters to Dr. and Mrs. Josiah Gilbert Holland*, ed. Theodora Van Wagenen Ward (Cambridge: Harvard University Press, 1951), 106.

28. Leyda, *Years and Hours*, 1:1xxvii.

29. Martha Winburn England, "Emily Dickinson and Isaac Watts: Puritan Hymnodists," *Bulletin of the New York Public Library* 69, no. 2 (February 1965): 104-5.

30. *Encyclopaedia of the Presbyterian Church in the United States of America*, ed. Alfred Nevin (Philadelphia: Presbyterian Encyclopaedia Publishing Co. 1884), 978.

31. Leyda, *Years and Hours*, 2:142.

32. Mary Elizabeth Barbot, in "Emily Dickinson Parallels," *New England Quarterly* 14 (1941): 689-96, found striking parallels between Wadsworth's sermons and nine of Dickinson's poems; Sewall *(Life of Emily Dickinson*, 2:455) discusses two of these and adds three more.

33. Vivian R. Pollak, "The Last Years of Emily Dickinson's 'Dearest Earthly Friend,' " *Dickinson Studies*, no. 34 (1978): 13-16.

34. See Anna Mary Wells, "Emily Dickinson Forgeries," *Dickinson Studies* 34 (1978): 12-15.

35. Johnson, *Letters*, 2:617 (letter 562); 3:663-64 (letter 645); 727-29 (letter 750); and 753-54 (letter 790).

36. Leyda, *Years and Hours*, 2:217; *Encyclopaedia of the Presbyterian Church* (1884), 978.

37. These last four lines of the poem, missing for many years, were recorded and published by R.W. Franklin in "Three Additional Dickinson Manuscripts," *American Literature* 50 (March 1978): 113.

38. Johnson, *Letters*, 2:382-83, letter 242.

39. Carl N. Degler, *At Odds: Women and the Family in American from the Revolution to the Present* (New York: Oxford University Press, 1980), 227-48.

40. Sewall, *Life of Emily Dickinson*, 1:188-89.

41. Leyda, *Years and Hours*, 2:38.

42. R.W. Franklin, *The Editing of Emily Dickinson: A Reconsideration* (Madison: University of Wisconsin Press, 1967), 40-46.

43. In his edition of *The Manuscript Books of Emily Dickinson*, 1:703-4, R.W. Franklin conjectures that this line, "Seed—Summer—Tomb," may have been created by Mabel Loomis Todd. Her copyist, Harriet Graves, did not include it on her typescript of the poem and Todd inserted it later. Since the two handwritten versions of this poem have disappeared, this adds to the mystery. One should note that if Todd did create an entire line for one of Dickinson's poems, this was quite extraordinary, quite contrary to her usual practice. Secondly, it hardly seems likely that Todd would have selected these three words, for which nothing else in the poem supplies any natural preparation or setting, unless this is another instance in which Todd shows herself more familiar with the secrets of Austin's family than she would later admit in print.

44. Martha Dickinson Bianchi, *The Life and Letters of Emily Dickinson* (Boston: Houghton Mifflin, 1924), 46-47.

45. Millicent Todd Bingham, *Ancestors' Brocades: The Literary Debut of Emily Dickinson* (New York: Harper and Brothers, 1945), 97, 320-22, 383.

46. Millicent Todd Bingham, *Emily Dickinson: A Revelation* (New York: Harper and Brothers, 1954), 4-9.

47. Suzanne Juhasz, *Naked and Fiery Forms: Modern American Poetry of Women, A New Tradition* (New York: Octagon Books, 1976), 10.

48. Gilbert and Gubar, *Madwoman in the Attic*, 601, 607.

Conclusion

1. Karl Keller, *The Only Kangaroo among the Beauty: Emily Dickinson and America* (Baltimore: Johns Hopkins University Press, 1979).

2. Johnson, *Letters*, 2:392, letter 248A.

3. Ibid., 404, letter 216, dated 25 April 1862.

General Index

Index of Poems
by First Line

Terminal punctuation is omitted.

Index of Poems
by Number

Poem numbers are those assigned by Thomas H. Johnson in his edition of *The Poems of Emily Dickinson* (1955).